Believe in miracles
2 Cor. 5:7
Jenny Peterson

She Walked
by *Faith*
Not by Sight

Jenny Peterson

She Walked By Faith Not By Sight

Library of Congress Control Number: 2014917495

ISBN: 978-0-9906485-0-5

First Edition

www.shewalkedbyfaith.com

Printed in the United States by Morris Publishing®
3212 East Highway 30
Kearney, NE 68847
1-800-650-7888

DEDICATION

To my husband Ron, without your journaling for ninety-six days, sometimes hourly, this book could have never been written. Your commitment to not only this but to our marriage and family is just amazing. For all you have done and all you have been over the years, I thank you.

All my love,
Jenny

ACKNOWLEDGEMENTS

To my sister Vicki, who gave a part of her own eye to help me see again, I love you and I thank you.

To my sister Cathy, as we walk in faith together and grow closer as sisters and friends, for all that and so much more I thank you and I love you.

For all the rest of my family, friends and neighbors, for all you've done, I thank you.

To all the doctors, who over the years cared for me with understanding and empathy, I thank you.

To each of you, who encouraged me to write a book, I know God put you in my path to get me started on this adventure and I thank you.

Jenny Peterson
2014

April 29, 1976

    Good Friday had come and gone. My husband, Ron, and I and our two children were out in the garden. Chad was five and Heather was two. It was past my family's traditional time of planting peas and potatoes. We had never paid much attention to the biblical side of Good Friday. It meant a day off from school and getting together with family for a feast on Easter Sunday. Ron was brought up going to church and learning all about God and what religious holidays meant, but I was not, and I had no motivation to sit for an hour each week keeping the little ones quiet during a sermon that I didn't understand. It was just easier to stay home.

    I had had a sore throat for about a week already, but didn't feel I could take a day off from my baby-sitting service to go to the doctor. Ron was a school teacher so money was always tight. I didn't make much but I felt every little bit helped. We finished planting the garden and I had an appointment to get my hair cut at 5:30 that evening. After cleaning the garden dirt off, I suddenly felt so very tired. My throat felt like it was on fire and I could barely swallow. It was already after five o'clock, and the doctor's office was closed.

1

I said to Ron, "I think I need to go to the doctor."

"Now?" he asked. "We will have to pay for an ER visit."

"Yes, I know, but I need to go now. I can't put this off any longer."

Ron took me to the emergency room of our local hospital. Chad and Heather stayed with a neighbor. On our way, we stopped by my beautician's shop and cancelled my appointment. I just didn't feel well enough to get a haircut. I was so tired I could barely stay awake. I felt exhausted.

Dr. Bell, our family physician, was out of town, so that evening in the ER I was seen by the on-call physician. He asked if I was allergic to any medication. I assured him that I wasn't. All I wanted was something to make me feel better. A throat culture was done and I was given a shot of Bicillin, which is an injection of double strength Penicillin. I was also given sample pills of a different medication to take in the ER. More pills were given to me to take when I went to bed that night. I was not kept for more than twenty minutes to check for a reaction before being sent home. I never learned the results of that throat culture. I didn't know what the sample pills were that I took at the hospital or at home.

When we arrived back home, Ron got the kids from the neighbors and came home to fix supper. I just wanted to go to bed. But first, I got myself a glass of water.

Ron reminded me, "You're supposed to take those pills when you go to bed."

"I'm going to bed now," I said.

I took the pills and went right to sleep. Ron came to bed after watching the news and getting the kids settled in for the night. I was restless, tossing and turning through the night. Our bedroom felt very warm. I got up, but felt off balance, unable to navigate very well down the hallway to the bathroom. I bumped into a door casing and brushed along the wall. For some reason I seemed to be having trouble walking. I walked into the bathroom and turned on the light. It was so bright that my eyes hurt, and yet everything seemed out of focus. I looked into the mirror. The mirror seemed fogged over as if someone had just showered. I leaned closer to the mirror, and through blurred vision I could see a big red patch on my cheek. I put my hand up to my cheek thinking to rub the spot off. There was a stinging sensation and fluid ran down my face. The skin hanging from my cheek told me it was a blister that had broken.

I'm thinking, "What's wrong? Why can't I see my face clearly? Why do I have this blister?" I was scared, shaking, not sure what to do. "Should I wake Ron or wait until morning?" My thoughts would not settle on one thing.

Ron noticed I was not in bed and came looking for me. When he saw my face, he was shocked. "We need to go back to the hospital," he said to me.

"What about the kids?" I asked.

"We'll have the neighbor come over to stay with them."

"What time is it?" I asked.

"It's 5:15 in the morning," Ron said.

"Do you think we should wait a little while? It's so early."

"We have no other choice. You need to go to the hospital again," Ron told me.

I was in no state of mind to decide anything, so I simply agreed with what Ron was saying. He called the next door neighbor to stay with Chad and Heather while we went back to the hospital. After being examined by the on-call doctor again, I was admitted. Two nurses were walking me down the hallway to a room, one on either side of me.

One of them asked, "Are you okay?"

"I think so," I said.

Then suddenly I began to fall. Just before hitting the floor, each nurse braced an arm under mine and caught me. I woke up in a hospital bed with an IV in my arm.

A nurse asked, "How are you feeling?"

I struggled to speak. "My throat hurts."

3

She gave me a spray for my throat. I kept spitting something out. I could feel the skin in my mouth and throat hanging loose in places.

I asked, "What is this?" pointing to the IV.

The nurse replied, "IV antibiotics."

Later that day I began to have a reaction to the IV antibiotic Keflex that had been started that morning. I broke out with small blisters on my neck, face and arms.

Ron asked the doctor, "What is wrong with Jenny?"

"It seems she is having a reaction to both last night's antibiotic and the IV we started today. The strep test isn't back yet so we haven't ruled that out either. She isn't getting better."

Overnight, my condition had worsened. Ron called our parents, Frank and Mary Martz and Ellsworth and Ida Peterson, who lived in and around Centerville, South Dakota.

"Jenny is in the hospital," he told them. "Her skin is blistering. She is sick, very sick. She's not awake right now, but I think you should come."

The drive from Centerville to DeSmet would take about two hours. Meanwhile, some of our friends came to the hospital but I wasn't even aware of their presence. While Ron waited for our parents to arrive, I was oblivious to anything that was going on. And while the fight for life raced on, I slept.

Three hours after Ron called our parents, they arrived in DeSmet. Mom and Dad came directly to the hospital.

Ron met them at the hospital door, "I'm so glad you're here."

By the look on his face, they knew I was not doing well. Ron brought them down to my room. As soon as Mom saw me, she started to cry. Dad even fought back tears. What Ron had told them did not prepare them for what they saw. The huge water blister under my chin was the size of a baseball. The raw spots on my face where blisters had already broken looked fiery red. Ron was torn between staying with me and being home with the kids. Now, with

4

his parents staying with Chad and Heather at our home, he was at ease about them. Once again, overnight, my condition worsened.

The doctor told Ron, "I feel we have done everything we can for Jenny. I think she needs to be transferred out by ambulance to a larger hospital." Ron agreed.

Our parents and Ron planned how to proceed. Mom and Dad would follow the ambulance to Sioux Falls, and Ron's parents would take the kids to his sister and brother-in-law's, Priscilla and Dick Landsman, who lived near Centerville. Ron would ride with me and the doctor in the ambulance. Ron's brother Buddy, who lived in Sioux Falls with his wife Claire, had been called about my transfer and met the ambulance at the hospital. I looked over the edge of the stretcher as it was pulled from the ambulance and saw Buddy's face through still blurred vision. As our eyes met, he leaned against the brick wall of the hospital bay. From the shocked look on his face I thought, "Girl, you have got a fight on your hands."

I was admitted to a Sioux Falls hospital. The admitting doctor and staff were scrambling. No one was exactly sure what was wrong with me. They decided to put me in the Intensive Care Unit until a team of doctors including Dr. Lynn DeMarco from Internal Medicine and Dr. Eugene Hoxtell of Dermatology could assess the situation. They immediately put me in isolation while they decided on a diagnosis. The gardening had confused things even more. The doctors wondered whether or not I had been exposed to something in the garden and was having an allergic reaction to it. The considerations were wide ranged, from a change in hair products to a gardening fertilizer and even staph infection or a drug reaction.

Dr. Hoxtell and Dr. DeMarco came to Ron.

Dr. Hoxtell spoke first. "What your wife has is the worst version of Stevens-Johnson called Toxic Epidermal Necrolysis, wherein the skin blisters and sheds. The difference between Stevens-Johnson and TEN is that TEN has a deeper burn and not a very good prognosis for survival."

Then Dr. DeMarco spoke, "TEN is a disease caused by staph infection or a drug-induced reaction. We have ruled out a staph infection and have a diagnosis of a drug-induced reaction from Bicillin complicated by a secondary reaction from IV Keflex. What Jenny has is very rare, and very few doctors have even seen a case such as this due to the involvement of the entire body. We checked with the Burn Center in Minnesota but they are not willing to accept her as a patient due to the risk of infection to Jenny and their other patients. We want you to know that we will do our best to help her but it doesn't look very good."

Ron was speechless. He could barely take in the fact that I was sick much less believe that I could die.

The doctors, who had been studying up on my condition, spoke to Ron. "We have discovered six other cases like this in the United States wherein the patients have had involvement of 100% of their skin," said Dr. Hoxtell.

"None of the prior cases survived, so you must prepare yourself for the worst," added Dr. DeMarco.

Ron could not accept what they were telling him. "She has to get better." Then he put his face in his hands and wept.

I didn't remember much of those first days but Ron kept a journal. His journal not only helped to inform people who came into the waiting room about my condition but also gave him something to do to stay sane during this very trying time. Ron was faithful to daily and even hourly updates in his journal. I was kept under sedation for most of the time. Anyone entering my room was required to put on a sterile gown, gloves and mask. Ron would gown up and come into my room to help care for me by feeding me, encouraging me, and yes, even praying with me. While Ron stayed close by my side, relatives took care of our children.

From Ron's journal:
PRAY
April 30, 1976 (Day 1)
On April 30, 1976, at 5:30 a.m. Jenny was transferred by ambulance from DeSmet to Sioux Falls Hospital. The doctor from DeSmet and I rode with her in the ambulance. She was in and out of consciousness during the trip. At times Jenny responds to my voice. The flashing lights and sirens waken her as we enter the city.
Diagnosis: _Toxic Epidermal Necrolysis_ *"Scalded Skin Syndrome"*
Dr. DeMarco says the treatment will be like for second-degree burns. Jenny will lose most of her skin. They will administer Demerol for pain relief, Valium for relaxation. Not very encouraged. Said he doesn't know how she can take it. Her vital signs seem to be okay, but her temperature is bouncing around. She is young and strong and that is on her side however. Time will tell.
Morning Prayer service: Pastor Helgeson from Sioux Falls Lutheran Church
Afternoon Prayer service: Pastor Grorud from Centerville Lutheran Church

On the circular bed, I was to be turned every few hours to let my blistered skin get air and to change the dressings. A circle bed was two metal tracks standing up on edge, like two hula-hoops about two feet apart hooked together with a board in the middle. The metal hoops were about seven to eight feet tall. The board in the middle was the bed. When a patient was on the bed and had to be turned from back to stomach or vice versa, the nurses would strap another bed board over the top of the patient and to the bottom bed board, sandwiching the patient in the middle of the two boards. A switch was then flipped, and the bed would slowly turn the patient head over heels, front to back or back to front, as needed.

Dr. Hoxtell tried everything he could think of to help keep moisture on my blister-covered body. He decided to use cloth diapers for packing moisture on my skin. The purchasing department searched and found sixty dozen cloth diapers to serve as wet packs. The diapers were soaked in a saline solution and placed flat on my body. As they dried, they would stick to me. So after turning me on the circle bed, the nurses had to pull the wet packs off my raw body. I was given Demerol, usually 25 mg before the process began and 25 mg afterwards. Sometimes it didn't seem to dull any of the pain. It just knocked me out so I could get away from it for awhile.

I was not tall enough to brace my feet on the end of the bed. The first time I was turned, the top board was strapped on and the switch was flipped. As the bed started to turn, I could feel my body starting to slide to the bottom of the bed between the sheets, but my blistered skin stayed with the wet packs at the top.

"Stop, stop! Oh God, help me," I cried, as tears ran down my face.

I was shaking from the pain. I don't remember screaming but the pain was excruciating. Demerol was quickly administered. To prevent this from happening again a wooden box was placed at the bottom of the bed to brace my feet against while I was being turned. It prevented another body slide but my heels became very sore from constantly pushing at the box.

From Ron's journal:
PRAY
May 1, 1976 (Day 2)
8:30 a.m. Saw Jenny ½ hour
Dr. DeMarco not very encouraged. He said he was a pessimist anyway. Jenny-blisters on face, neck, and upper part of body and back. Losing skin on face. She said she is tired of fighting. I think it is mostly from being so tired and being flipped and being dressed every hour. Jenny talked to Chad and Heather on phone. Heather bashful. Didn't talk. I slept most of day.

6:00 p.m. Saw Jenny for 1 hour. She wanted everyone not to worry. Wanted no one to get sick worrying about her. Said prayer then left.

I missed my babies. At only five, Chad had just started school and was excited about everything. Heather, my little Heather, was only two. She hadn't been away from me before now, so this had to be very scary for her. I so wanted to hold them in my arms again, cuddle with them, and just love them. Neither child could truly understand what had happened or why I was not with them anymore. It broke my heart.

Ron's sisters and brother, my sisters and brothers, and yes, even friends, took turns staying overnight at the hospital with him. Most of the time, there were five people staying all night. They slept in the cold lobby. At times, the "campers" moved into the closet to sleep where it was warmer. They tried to keep a neat camp.

From Ron's journal:
PRAY
May 2, 1976 (Day 3)
7:30 a.m. Dr. Hoxtell and Dr. DeMarco are here on rounds. Dr. DeMarco was still not very encouraging. Jenny is hungry but doesn't want a drink of water. Many came to window to talk to Jenny. Her spirits were down, but that has to be expected. Bud and I attended Catholic Mass. Jenny cried some when she saw people at door.
12:30 p.m. Rev. Helgeson led everyone in prayer service. Chad and Heather are up to see 'Mommy'. Jenny is in better spirits because she can see the kids.
5:00 Rev. Johnson led prayer service.
Six people stayed in the cold lobby tonight.

I knew everyone was out in the lobby and I wanted to be there too. I loved being around people, especially family. Ron's brother, Buddy, came to the hospital and stayed with him often. We all needed the 'Higher Power' to be in control. Only God could help us all survive this disease. Never in a million years would I have thought I would be separated from my kids like this. My spirits were high today because I could talk to them.

"Ron," I said.

"What, what do you want to say?" Ron asked.

"I miss the kids. It was so good to talk to them today. Can we have them come up again soon?"

Ron replied quietly, "We will have someone bring them up again soon. I promise."

Each night before Ron left my ICU room, we prayed together. I was not good at praying, so Ron prayed for both of us.

From Ron's journal:
PRAY
May 3, 1976 (Day 4)
8:30 a.m. see Jenny for 20 minutes. Dr. Hoxtell was pleased with the progress Jenny is making.

Dr. Hoxtell entered my room. "Let's see now how it looks today." As he removed the wet packs, he looked very closely for any new skin cells on my back, face and arms. "You are making good progress," he said. "Looks good. Things are doing okay."

"When can I get out of ICU?" I asked.

"Well, gee, maybe ten days or so. We'll see how things go," he replied.

I told Ron I wanted him to go to McDonald's and get me a hamburger. I just wanted to get to back to doing the things I would normally do.

Music was always a big part of my family. I had hoped I would be able to listen to music again soon.

Ron said, "We are trying to get a radio into your room, but the doctors are worried about it not being sterile."

"Put the radio inside a surgical glove," Buddy suggested. "Wouldn't that keep it sterile?"

Everyone was wracking their brains to help. Ron had not left the hospital in four days, and no one could persuade him to go.

"Come out to our house and change the oil in your hair," Buddy teased.

Reluctantly, Ron agreed. "Okay. I'll leave just long enough to shower and change clothes."

Ron had just returned from Buddy and Claire's when his sister, Eldonna called for a progress report.

Dr. Meyers, the ophthalmologist, had come to examine my eyes. He assured us, "This is not going to affect the eyes."

We were all so relieved. At least this was some good news.

Many people were calling and expressing their concern to Ron. They told him that they were praying for good news. Ron came into my room and read cards, the names of callers, and a note from the pastor in Centerville which read:

Remember Jenny,
There is a reason! Jesus has NOT forgotten you. Some day you will understand. Stay close to Him and He will stay close to you. What more do any of us need? We are keeping on praying for you. –Pastor Grorud

"I hope he is right about Jesus being close to me," I thought. I needed help.

I wanted a Citizens Band radio in my room so I could talk to all who were in the lobby. CB's were a huge way to communicate in the 1970's. I still wanted to be able to keep in touch with friends and family, but realistically, I wasn't able to operate a CB. Heck, I couldn't even lift my arms to eat.

My aunts and uncles drove in from Iowa and Nebraska and flew in from Indiana to visit with Ron and our families and to give their support and check on my progress.

11

From Ron's journal:
(Day 4 cont.)
1:30 p.m. Went in to see Jenny (45 min.) Many came to talk to Jenny through the window in the ICU. Jenny wanted 7Up but couldn't drink it. Took a couple of sips of water instead. Nurses said in 2 or 3 days they may stop flipping her. Has radio in room now. Would like to "rip nurse's throats out" for rubbing skin too hard. Days seem like they are going faster. More friends and family called, sent love and prayers. Whenever someone from our families or friends were in Sioux Falls they stop and visit to see how we are all doing. Jenny wanted me to call her on the phone so I wouldn't have to gown up. She talked to me, Dad Martz, Mom Peterson, Mom Martz, and her sisters, Cathy and Vicki.

This was a very emotional conversation with Cathy. As sisters, we never really got along. Words were said that could not be taken back. Now that I was fighting for my life, we both realized the anger, petty arguments and trouble between us was nothing compared to losing a sister.

From Ron's journal:
(Day 4 cont.)
Many blisters on hands, fingers, arms, and legs. Throat is feeling better, and tongue is too. Skin is peeling off back, neck and face. Dr. Hoxtell's report was encouraging. Skin will start to grow back soon.
7:30 p.m. Went into see Jenny (15 min.) The nurses had cut Jenny's ring off. Said prayer.

Our friends and neighbors from DeSmet looked in on me.

Ron spoke, "Look who's here," and I opened my eyes wide.

12

After they had all seen me, they took Ron to McDonald's to eat. I talked to Mom and Dad and asked them to send Ron in when they left.

Ron assured me, "Everyone is getting their rest and food." We prayed and then Ron left.

From Ron's journal:
PRAY
May 4, 1976 (Day 5)
8:00 a.m. Went to see Jenny (15 min.)
Asked about her youngest brother, Royce. Jenny took 60cc chocolate malt (1/4 cup). This is a good sign. Still has blisters on fingers and hands. Most have broken on upper arms and body. Biopsies are taken every day to see if any infection is setting in. Blood is tested by Dr. Hoxtell to make sure there is enough nutrients in IV. The suction tube has been taken out of Jenny's mouth today. Eldonna called and said she, Ronnie and sister, Marlys would be up to spend the night.

Dr. Hoxtell told Ron, "She is talking more today. That's a good sign."

Chad and Heather were brought up to the hospital. Chad wanted to ride in the elevator. He told Ron, "I miss my Mom."

I was still able to see pictures of them that Ron brought into my room but it was not the same as being together as a family. Ron said, "Your eyes are open and that is good. Your face is looking better. Everyone is praying for you to get well."

I answered, "I have faith in God."

From Ron's journal:
(Day 5 cont.)
'Today is the first day of the rest of your life'. Got cards from teachers and wrestlers.
Windy outside.

'Learn from Yesterday...Live for Today...Hope for Tomorrow'. Day by Day.
8:30 p.m. Jenny took some spoons of malt.
Will talk to Dr. DeMarco soon.
8:45 p.m. Saw Jenny (1/2 hour).

Even as sick as I was, I asked Ron to send a card to my girlfriend for a baby gift explaining why I was late with the card. Ron had to leave my room to take a call from a co-worker. The call was to let us know that everyone in DeSmet sent best wishes and was praying for me. When Ron hung up, he gowned up again and came back in to see me. "I am sweating like a stuck hog," I said.

The nurse said to Ron, "This is the first time she hasn't been cold. She hasn't had a shot of Demerol since 4:30 p.m."

I worried aloud, "I hope I will be able to walk again."

The nurse said, "This has nothing to do with your walking."

Ron asked me, "What do you want for Mother's Day?"

I replied, "I would like to sit up."

I'm not sure Ron could accomplish this gift for me, but I knew if he could convince the doctors, I would be sitting up on Mother's Day. I started to wonder if things were going to be the same. Ron prayed and left my room.

Friends and family were still staying overnight at the hospital. Ron had not given up his bedside vigil of me, and the ones who loved us both didn't want to leave him to hold it alone. Five family members spent the night in the hospital waiting room.

From Ron's journal:
PRAY
May 5, 1976 (Day 6)
Stayed all night in the camper. Ronnie and Eldonna took Jenny's sister, Pam and I for breakfast at McKennan Café. Looked in on Jenny at 8:15. Did not go in. Resting good. Nurses said she had a good night. Jenny was getting drops

in her eyes. Drank some malt. Talked to Dr. Hoxtell this morning. Said by weekend we should see some change in skin on face.

A patient in ICU was being transferred to Rochester today. God be with them.

9:45 a.m. Went in to see Jenny (1/2 hour). Saw her from shoulders down. Has large blisters on palms of hands and starting now on her feet. Dr. DeMarco says we're still hanging in there. Bodily functions are not doing much and we are slightly concerned. Will watch this closely and give it time to recover. Disease is not just affecting the skin, it is throughout internal system also. Will see what the next week brings.

3:20 p.m. (45 min.) I told her the three Pastors were here to express concern. Family members remain constantly at the hospital. Their visits often overlap. When one person came to the hospital the people who had been with me for a while go home. Visits from Pastor Helgeson, Pastor Johnson, and Pastor Grorud are comforting to everyone. Quote from Jenny: "The nurses will know it the hard way if I have a bowel movement," Says she enjoys having Pastor Johnson come in and pray with her. Jenny was cold last night and wondered why I didn't sneak past the nurses and cuddle beside her. Says she misses the kids.

Turned on radio and found that it needs new batteries. Read Jenny a list of people that sent cards and visited today. Jenny does the praying for us tonight before I leave her ICU room. Dick and I are going to McDonald's to eat. I bring back chocolate and strawberry malts for Jenny. She only takes one sip of strawberry, doesn't want anymore, three visitors tonight.

10:00 p.m. Went to Jenny's ICU room to say goodnight. I tell her that Russel Means had been shot. Jenny says, "That's too bad. I really don't want anyone to have to be in pain."

11:00 p.m. Looked in on Jenny through window, went out to the camper to sleep.

From Ron's journal:
PRAY
May 6, 1976 (Day 7)
Cold in the camper last night, just like outside, 25 degrees.
9:00 a.m. checked on how Jenny's night went. Wasn't her
best night. Restless and in a lot of pain at midnight and
two a.m. Nurses reported Jenny was resting better at four
and six a.m. She is very tired but not in much pain, just
had a shot of Demerol. Starting to lose some of the
fingernails. She isn't complaining of them hurting. Went to
Buddy's to change clothes. Jenny resting pretty good. Lips
look kind of swollen.
10:50 a.m. She didn't talk very much this visit. Very tired,
was given more pain reliever. Needs lots of sleep. Dr.
DeMarco was in. Said she is still hanging in there. Next
couple of days will be a lot of pain.

Ron was not encouraged by this news. The doctors took photos of my blister-ravaged body for a medical journal. One fingernail had fallen off. The skin on my face, neck, chin and side was hanging from blisters. When the doctor from DeSmet arrived in Sioux Falls, he came into my room to check on my progress. He advised me to never take penicillin again and to throw away my new hairspray.

From Ron's journal:
(Day 7 cont.)
2:15 p.m., went in to see Jenny, very talkative, flying pretty
high on drugs. She talked through the door to Mom and
Dad, Ellsworth and Ida, Marlys, Priscilla, Buddy and
Claire, and their son, Joe.
5:15 p.m. Looked at Jenny's hands, losing some
fingernails. Talked with people through the door. Jenny's
sister, Vicki, is also here. Jenny is just not interested in any
food or drink. Wondered why Noble hasn't been up to see
her. Talking about her black nightie and asked about the
kids.

16

*7:30p.m. Went in to see Jenny (1/2 hour) She wants me to
tell her friends from DeSmet and all the family that were
here tonight 'hi and thanks for coming.' She was talking
about the little nurse with the accent from Boston that
when she first came to South Dakota that they thought they
were going to come by covered wagon.*

I was beginning to realize that my whole life may
change once I got out of here. I really would like to visit
here every time we come to Sioux Falls and more visits to
DeSmet Hospital. Knowing everyone who has taken time
to come and visit and share prayers with Ron and the
family, I can see how much it means to those whose family
members are ill.

"We need to remember how much it means to us, Ron,
and be better at visiting others who are having a tough
time."

Ron replied, "Okay Jenny, we will."

We even discussed teaching Sunday school and better
church attendance.

From Ron's journal:
(Day 7 cont.)
*10:30 p.m. Went in to see Jenny. She's in a lot of pain (left
hand). She says she wants to go home. Dr. Hoxtell said he
would take another blood sample tomorrow. Nurse said
she couldn't get wet packs off Jenny's face so it is causing
her a lot of pain. Dr. Hoxtell can see skin growing back on
both shoulders and one arm. Dr. Hoxtell suggests pouring
warm water over the packs to loosen them before removing
them. He doesn't want to tear off any new skin cells that
may be growing on Jenny's face. Prayed and then left.
Jenny is crying due to so much pain. The nurse brought in
another dose of Demerol.*

From Ron's journal:
PRAY
May 7, 1976 (Day 8)

17

One week today since we brought Jenny in ambulance.
10:00 a.m. Nurse takes Jenny's face pack off while I am in
there. Jenny said she is tired of all this. The blood work
results are in, the doctors decide to use only the Derm
Packs on the open wounds.
Long days, long nights.

Priscilla woke up early and walked down to check on me. I heard someone at my ICU room door, opened one eye and said, "Hi."

"Good morning," said Priscilla. "How are you this morning?"

"I'm okay. Dr. Hoxtell is coming in a little while to draw blood. We will know more then."

Ron came down to my room. I was kind of down in the dumps. I only got a little sleep last night because I was in a lot of pain. I opened my eyes and looked at Ron. I didn't have too many wet packs left on my body. I will be turned at 11:00 a.m. regardless of having fewer packs. I could still feel my fingernails floating around.

Ron said, "You have all white new skin under one eye."

"That's good," I said. "But Ron, I'm tired of all of this."

"I know, just hang in there. You're getting better." Ron left my room. When he returned two hours later, the fingernails on my right hand were gone. I wanted another shot of Demerol.

"Ron, my feet are sore from pushing on this box," I said.

Dick and Priscilla brought Chad and Heather up to see me. Chad loved to operate the elevators and give Heather rides up and down on them. I hadn't seen the kids for so long and I missed them desperately. I felt like I was missing out on their lives.

Ron took the kids to Burger King to eat. When he returned to my room, he asked, "How was your day?"

I said, "I was just listening to *Match Game* and *Search for Tomorrow* but I can't really see the TV very well. I wanted to go to Burger King with you too," I cried to Ron.

18

"I know," Ron quietly replied. "And you will soon. Just rest and get better."

"I miss the kids. Will they remember me when I get out?"

In a voice also filled with concern, Ron said, "Of course they will."

"Ron, if you take the kids to Captain 11, I could see them on TV."

Captain 11 was a local popular after school show where parents would bring their children to celebrate birthdays by letting them flip their favorite colored switch and watch cartoons. I thought if the kids were on television, I might be able to watch them playing. "Maybe on Monday," Ron said. By Monday, I probably would have forgotten about it.

At 6:30 p.m., Ron looked in on me. My face was very red.

When Dr. Hoxtell came in, he said, "Your vital signs are good today. I am going to try something new to apply on the bad areas. This will then form a crust and fall off when the new skin forms." Then, to Ron, he said, "Things look good. I didn't think she would make it this far. I heard there is a similar case in Sioux Valley."

Ron and I were left alone. We didn't talk very much. I kind of smiled when Ron told me that Noble, his brother-in-law, was outside the door to say 'hi'.

Ron asked me, "Do you want me to tell anyone anything?"

"They're turning me every four hours instead of every two."

We prayed the 23rd Psalm together before Ron left. Ron was really the one reciting it because I didn't know it. "I need to learn more of these verses from the Bible," I told Ron.

"We can do that when you get out of here."

May 8, 1976 (Day 9)

At 7:30 a.m. Ron came into my ICU room just as the nurses were getting ready to turn me, so he didn't stay. By 9:15, he came back and stayed for forty minutes. I told him, "I had a bad night."

Ron observed, "Your lips are starting to bleed. The nurses have orders to turn you again at 10:30 or 11:00, so back to every two hours."

"I can't wait to get out of ICU and go back home again. Ron, please say 'hi' to everyone for me. Please give the kids a kiss for me."

At 11:45, Dr. Hoxtell spoke to Ron after taking blood samples again. He said, "The blood sample this morning shows that Jenny is losing a lot of protein. I'm going to replace it with plasma."

At lunch time, Ron visited with both Dr. DeMarco and Dr. Hoxtell. "There is not very much new skin coming back yet," they told him. "We are still using the Owens packs, which are doing a good job, but Jenny needs more protein. I don't want the level to get below 4, and right now it's 4.6. We may have to check the IV and put in a bigger one. It's encouraging to know that her throat is better and she is not spitting as much. We are coating her lips with Eucerin cream. She is now resting on her back pretty well. I think by Tuesday we should be able to see new skin growth." Ron hoped this was true.

I drank a little over half a cup of malt after lunch. Ron thought this was good. I said to him, "Can you pull the curtain so people won't gawk at me? I can hear them at the door talking about my blisters." Ron complied with my wishes. We watched TV for a while, a baseball game and *Issues and Answers.*

Ron turned the TV off and turned the radio on. "The nurses will be back in about half an hour to turn you again," he said.

"Okay, but my legs and ankles hurt from the sheet tucked under my feet. Can you pull it out a little?"

20

Ron pulled the sheet loose from under my feet and it helped.

"Thanks honey," I said.

It was too warm in my room for people to put on gowns, masks, and gloves, so many of them just talked to me through the door. Ron always took the time to gown up so he could come into my room. At 5:40 p.m. Ron gave me some sips of pop. I decided maybe next time I would try 7-Up since the Coke kind of stung my mouth.

My mom and dad were at the window. Dad tapped on the window with his finger to let me know they were there. This was how I always knew my parents were at my ICU door—by the tapping noise. They would stand in the hallway and we would visit a little through the door because neither of them could stand the heat in my room.

"I think I am feeling better tonight than I have felt since being admitted," I told them. "I think I'm going to be okay. Don't worry and I will see you tomorrow?"

Dad responded with, "That's good, by golly. We'll see you tomorrow after I get this dugout finished."

After my parents left the ICU, they went to the lobby to say their good-byes to everyone. Then Dick came to my door. He didn't stay long. I was kind of tired, since I had just had another shot of Demerol as the pain was getting worse. My temperature was starting to go up, and was now 102 degrees. I was in a lot of pain.

Dick went back to the waiting room where my parents were still saying their last farewells to people. He said to them, "She isn't looking too good. Maybe you should stick around a little bit." Mom and Dad decided to stay awhile.

Shortly after they left my ICU room, I turned to the nurse who had been sitting by my bedside that day and I said, "I think I'm dying."

She reminded me, "You just told your parents you were feeling better. There are over seventy family and friends in the waiting room praying for you. You're going to be okay."

21

I said, "I know, but this feeling has come over me, and I'm dying now." And with that, I did. A code blue was called, and all those in the waiting room who heard it just knew in their hearts it was for me.

I didn't hear the code blue called or notice the doctors and nurses working on my body. I was in the upper corner of my ICU room looking down on the scene. Something was very different. There was a pure white Light that surrounded me. It was peaceful, loving, and gentle. As I looked down to my right, I could see into the nurse's station. There was the nurse who had been sitting with me. She was crying, and another nurse was comforting her. As I looked down to my left, I saw a young woman lying on a hospital bed. Doctors and nurses surrounded her. They were scraping through blisters on her arms and then I realized it was me. I couldn't figure out why I was not feeling any pain from the doctors breaking through the blisters on my arms. Then, it was as if this pure white Light was cradling me in His arms, and I thought of God. I thought, "Why is God holding me in His arms? I don't know God."

And with that very thought, I was back on the hospital bed. My spirit had returned to my body with broken blisters on my arms and the pain that comes from those broken blisters was back also.

Dr. DeMarco said to Ron, "You know the body can only take so much. I am very discouraged. We have learned that Jenny is the seventh person to be diagnosed with TEN and I want you to know, none of the others survived."

Ron was shocked and left speechless.

Dad heard the conversation between Ron and Dr. DeMarco as he stood at the window of the hospital overlooking the lights of the city, "She's in God's hands. Now all we can do is pray," he said.

My mom was crying hysterically because she thought she had just lost her young daughter to this disease.

Nine people stayed overnight that night. Everyone slept in the lobby. I did not get to sit up on Mother's Day. Instead, I got to meet God face to face.

Sunday, May 9, 1976 (Day 10) Mother's Day

During the night, my IV stopped working. I started itching and my pain was at a level ten. A technician was called up to ICU to start a new IV so I could be given medications since I had not had them for a few hours. The technician worked for an hour and a half trying to find a vein that would take an IV. He called for another technician to help him, and together they worked diligently to try to get an IV in place but with no success. I was in extreme pain, itching from head to toe, and I felt like a pin cushion. Finally, the two of them agreed to stop poking me and wait for a surgeon to start the IV. It would probably be morning before this happened. I was in great distress.

I asked God for help. "Please God, help me. I need You." I told one nurse, "If I could get out of this bed, I would jump out of the window."

She said, "Let me call down to the ER and see if a surgeon is in house." She came back into my room. "A surgeon is on his way up." It was 4:00 a.m.

I said, "Thank You, God, thank You."

This was the first time I actually felt in my heart that God had heard and answered my prayer. The surgeon put an IV in a vein in my neck resulting in blessed relief from the itching and pain so I could rest.

It was 5:00 in the morning. Ron found me to be better but still in a lot of pain. We prayed and as he left my room I told him, "I will see you later."

At 7:00 a.m. Ron came back.

I asked, "Can I have my hair washed?"

Doctor's orders were to leave me on my back until they decided to turn me. The nurses were trying to change the sheet under me. They asked me, "Can you lift your butt up off the bed so we can slide the old sheet out and a fresh one under you?"

I braced my arms and elbows under me enough to raise my butt off the bed. I was dumbfounded. Panting from exertion I said, "I can't. Oh my God, I can't even lift my own body up off a bed. Just how weak am I?"

The nurse saw that this was upsetting to me and said, "It's okay. We can just turn you, change the sheet, and turn you to your back again. You're doing fine and your temperature is back down to 99.6 degrees."

Later, I told Ron, "I didn't mean to scare everyone last night. I know I just about died twice, and I was with God."

Ron, with thankfulness in his voice, said, "Yes, but you didn't die. You are still with me. You are really something, my Jenny. You know what happened to you, and yet you worry about scaring others. You are always thinking about others. I love you."

I said, "I love you too."

Ron came in again at 2:00 in the afternoon. I was feeling better. He told me all that were here. He said, "The kids sent Mother's Day cards that they made themselves."

I was so moved that I couldn't speak. I missed them so much. The doctors came to take blood. I asked Ron, "Will you buy Mother's Day cards for our Moms?"

Mom and Dad came later that evening to see for themselves that I was okay. They felt better after our visit. Dad said, "How are you doing today?"

"I'm okay, Dad," I answered, "but I just want to go home."

Then he said, "We can fix a bedroom downstairs for you and..."

"No, Dad, I mean go to my home."

"Oh," said Dad. "Yeah, well, you will one of these days."

I was sorry to hurt his feelings, but I needed to be clear about going to our home, Ron's and mine.

Ron came in again later. I was talking and crying a lot today, quite emotional. I was talking about going home. "Ron, can you cancel all my baby-sitting people?"

He said, "Yes, I will."

After ten days, I was sure they had already found places to take their kids. Time didn't mean much to me. I just couldn't get a handle on it.

Buddy and Claire were so generous to open their home up to anyone who wanted to stay. All of our parents went out to their home and stayed the night.

Ron sent a note to the school in DeSmet, where he taught and coached, to be read at the Athletic Banquet in our absence:

For May 10, 1976 Banquet
To: All the special athletes of DeSmet High School.
From: Jenny and Ron Peterson

Battles are won and lost every day on the field, on the court, on the mat, on the track and off. At this time, Jenny is fighting the battle of life. When in the contest and the going gets tough, we can never give up. We have to be proud, we have to be strong, and we have to have faith in God. You as DeSmet athletes are strong and proud. You have proved that. You have fought to the finish—win or lose. But if you do get beat and still have that faith in the Lord, you will never lose.
We thank you as athletes, cheerleaders, fellow coaches, and all that are associated with athletics and all of the great people of DeSmet for prayers, concerns, cards, visits, and many calls. God be with everyone here at this banquet tonight.
Remember these 2 things:
1) Winners never quit and quitters never win!
2) Today is the first day of the rest of your life.

Ron was a great teacher and was respected by not only the students and faculty, but also by the community in which we lived.

Over the next few days and weeks, I tried to talk to people about what had happened to me. They didn't have to tell me that I died—I already knew that. They didn't

25

need to tell me that God had held me in His arms—I knew that too. But the thing I didn't know was what God wanted me to do now. Then one of the Catholic Sisters came into my ICU room, and I asked her. "What does God want me to do now?" I had these wild thoughts that I needed to move to a third world country and live in a little grass hut to serve God.

She told me, "You go home and take care of your family, and God will use you right where you live."

I was amazed. God could use an ordinary person like me who is just living an ordinary life for His service? I wondered how?

Ron was losing weight during my hospital stay. This was no surprise to any of our family members. He had lost twelve pounds in the first twelve days. He spent his days coming in and out of my room, feeding me, praying with me, and updating me on what our two kids were doing. I missed them so much. I was becoming more aware of what was going on around me. Another patient in the ICU died during the night, and I didn't understand why I lived. I only knew one thing for sure, and that was God had held me in His arms and saved my life to do something with it. I hoped I would not disappoint Him.

My food was changed from liquids to cooked cereals. Ron still fed me. I thought even a plain hotdog would taste delicious. The pastors continued to stop and visit and pray with us. God heard each and every whispered prayer, I just knew it. The doctors talked about some of my internal organs being affected, particularly my liver, but they thought it would improve on its own. I talked about going home to DeSmet. I was just trusting that my eyes were going to be okay because the ophthalmologist said so.

I had lots of visitors. Sometimes as many as ten people from DeSmet came down at one time. My Dad's sister, Aunt Pete, from Indiana flew in to visit. She brought me a pretty peignoir set to help me want to shed my hospital gown and get better. I was exhausted for the next few days after so many people were at my door. After this happened a couple of times, visitors were limited to two at a time for five minutes at a time. Parents, brothers and sisters, were allowed, and of course Ron, but my own little darlings were not allowed down to see me for awhile. I missed them so.

My blood was being drawn and tested at least every two days. Bacteria in my blood did not concern the doctors too much because there was no bacterium on my skin. I was still being turned every two hours to give air to open areas on my skin. I got depressed and complained and then realized what a blessing it was just to be alive. Sometimes it was hard not to be depressed. After all, I had been in the hospital now for two whole weeks.

Dr. Hoxtell came in to look for new skin cells. Before, he was afraid to touch it since he thought it might come off. When he touched the new skin today, it held. He was concerned about infection. Dr. Pietry said I would not lose my hair and my fingernails would grow back. They were just guessing, as only God truly knew what the future held for us.

I was given canned milk and other high caloric foods. Dr. Hoxtell was worried about infection on my arms and legs from being exposed. The dead skin from under my arms was removed and sprayed with Betadine. It hurt for a little bit but knowing the kids would be coming tomorrow made me smile.

From Ron's journal:
PRAY
May 13-15, 1976 (Days 14-16)
8:30 a.m. talked with Dr. Hoxtell. Said things look good, not seeing any new skin this morning. Vital signs are good. No new skin is slowing the healing process and exposes Jenny to possible infections.
9:15 a.m. Voice sounds better and she is holding her head up. She says she is feeling pretty good right now. She wants a TV on a stand so she can see it while on her stomach. I told her that Chad and Heather will be here

27

today. She can't wait. Aunt Pete took Bud and I to breakfast.

11:45 a.m. Finally got another TV in her room. The doctor from DeSmet is here also. He rode down on his motorcycle just to see how she is doing. Jenny says she is feeling real good today. Is going to watch her soap opera at 12:30. Wants to see the kids while on her back.

2:00 p.m. Talked to Dr. Hoxtell. Said when skin grows it doesn't know where it grows. May grow fingers together, but this can always be fixed. For now we will wrap each finger to see if that prevents the skin from webbing them together. Just so it doesn't grow under eyelid to the eyeball.

Ron was silent from this news. Each day there seemed to be a new problem to absorb. Also, today the IV was plugged, but one of the nurses got it running again. Chad and Heather got to come see me. Heather didn't say much. Chad talked some. I felt sorry for them to have to see me like this. After the kids left my room, Ron came back in.

I told him, "I can't believe I died the other night."

I started crying. I was kind of down in the dumps from just the thought of dying. Also, little Heather not saying too much left me saddened. Where was the bubbly, laughing little daughter we had? "Ron please kiss and hug the kids for me."

An eye doctor came in. He said, "Your eyes will be okay. You need to just get through this and not worry about your eyes."

I called the nurse. "Can I get a shot so I can rest?" Ron had fed me one-fourth of a bowl of vanilla pudding when I said to him. "Ron, the spoon is so big. Let me try to use a straw to suck the pudding up." I also took a few sips of milk. I wondered aloud, "Why was I the one to have this disease. I'm only twenty-three years old."

Ron said, "With the good report from the doctors today, you have to keep your chin up. I think I will go out for a while now."

"Turn the TV and lights off," I said.

Ron slept for an hour and a half. This was exhausting for him too. At 6:30 that evening Ron brought the kids down to my ICU window. He held Chad and Heather up to the window so they could say bye-bye to me. They were leaving without me once again. Ron said good-bye to the kids and came in to visit about the day with me. "How are you now?" he asked.

"I'm okay," I said. "I just ate supper and am going to watch *The Waltons.* Do you want to watch it with me?" We always watched *The Waltons* as a family, and at least I could have one member with me as I watched it tonight.

The nurse came into my room and noticed the floor was wet and thought my IV must have come out or broken. I was lying on my stomach, so they were going to have to turn me to get the IV put back in.

Ron said, "I'll leave now so you can work on getting the IV going."

By 10:15 p.m. Ron had spoken to Dr. Hoxtell. He told Ron, "I am going to give Jenny Valium instead of Demerol. She has been sleeping well, and we don't want to give her any more Demerol than we have to. I saw another case history of this disease where it took longer than we thought to grow the skin back. All of Jenny's vital signs are good, so we are not worried about that aspect of her condition. We are worried, however, about getting infection in the open areas on her arms and feet. Her protein level is down, but not that much. It is really encouraging to see her take food by mouth since some patients that have had either Stevens-Johnson or TEN develop digestive lesions across internal organs such as the esophagus, stomach, and intestines."

After speaking with Dr. Hoxtell, Ron came into my room.

"I slept well this afternoon. I think I want something so I can sleep tonight," I told him.

He said. "Bud and I are going to DeSmet tomorrow. We grilled hot dogs and had a cookout this afternoon." We said our nightly prayer, and Ron left just as the nurses came in to turn me onto my stomach.

The doctor came in and told me, "Well, we are not seeing any new skin growing on your body."

"What does that mean?" I asked.

"That means that it will probably be another two weeks in ICU."

"Oh no," I cried. "I can't imagine that I will have to stay a whole month in the hospital. I just want to go home."

It's very depressing to me when Ron goes to DeSmet and I am unable to go home with him. The Catholic Sisters making their rounds tried to cheer me up after such news. When I became depressed about delays or lack of progress or setbacks, I just wanted to sleep away the nightmare I was living. God help me.

Dr. Hoxtell was speaking to the nurse. "Because an infection is beginning on the patient's face, we are ordering an application of wet packs to clean it up and possibly help with the infection. So let's get her face packed and see if that helps over the next couple of days."

The nurses put heavy, wet towels used as wet packs on my face. They were wrapped around my nose and mouth, leaving the barest of breathing holes. Once when I moved my head, the wet pack slipped over my nose making it difficult to breathe. I tried to turn my head the other way, and the other side slipped over what breathing space I had left. Now I panicked. I tried to shake off the wet rolled-up towel, but it slipped down over my mouth, preventing me from breathing air easily. I reached out for the old desk bell the nurses had put on my bed tray, but in my haste I only succeeded in knocking it off onto the floor. I thought the noise would get someone's attention, but it didn't, as I continued to struggle for breath and move my head around. I finally got a breathing space whipped in the wet material. This was scary and frustrating at the same time, knowing that I couldn't even reach up and pull a wet cloth off my face so I could breathe. I was not thrilled giving up this much control of my life. It was not what I had planned, and I didn't like it at all.

Anything that was too cold or too hot or too acidic hurt my mouth. Juices and pop were hard to drink.

Dr. Hoxtell came into my room. "We are going to try to take the old skin off your hands today. You need to tell me if it hurts at all."

"Okay," I responded.

"There is more new skin growing now, but it is mostly on your back. I am going to have the nurses put wet packs on your hands now to get more of the dead skin loosened. We can remove it more easily then. I didn't think any skin would grow back four days ago when I saw you. We actually had planned to do skin grafting, but today new skin is growing all over. This is great news, golly, this is great news!" he exclaimed. I guess I should have been happy about this, too. "I want you to try to eat more," he continued. "I see on your chart that you eat only about half a bowl of cereal and half of the Jell-O. You need to eat more to get stronger and get out of here."

I didn't know that I had to eat my way out of the hospital. "I think I can do that," I replied, "if it means getting out of here. But before I can begin to eat more, my mouth has to heal. The tissue inside my mouth has blisters and is still shedding, so I am spitting skin into a cup all the time. Now my mouth is too sore to eat anything other than bland and soft foods. But I will do my best to eat more."

I was making huge strides now and was able to start moving my hands and feet all by myself. I didn't realize I was unable to move on my own. I had just been sleeping my way back to life again.

The nurses were putting cream on my lips, cheeks, and nose. Ron and I always said a prayer before he went to the waiting room for the night.

May 16, 1976 (Day 17)

I didn't even know what was happening. I just wanted to sleep. My eyes had a lot of drainage coming from them.

The doctors did a culture on the drainage. I was not sure how much I had been seeing up to this point. I had some sight at least, but not much.

The nurses kept spraying Betadine on my body to prevent infection. They were turning me on the circle bed every two hours to give air to the open raw areas of my body. Some days, new skin would show up and some days not so much. I just wanted Ron to take me home. I had a lot of questions like, "Am I going to be the same Jenny?" I seemed to be tired all the time, but with the nurses putting wet packs on my face every hour all night long, I was not getting much sleep.

Dr. Hoxtell said, "You are going to lose a lot of weight and be weak, but the physical therapy people are good in getting patients back on their feet. We are not going to worry about rehab yet."

Ron told me, "Chad and Heather are coming up tomorrow."

I couldn't wait to see them again. I wanted to talk to them, at least on the phone.

From Ron's journal:
PRAY
May 17, 1976 (Day 18)
8:15 a.m. Went in to feed Jenny breakfast (1/2 hour). Dr. Hoxtell was in there too. He wants to wet pack the face all day to clean the dead skin off. Skin on outer parts of eyes is growing together and she can't see very well. She ate a bowl of oatmeal, some sips of orange juice. Said the juice was hard to swallow. Chad and Heather may just have to talk on the phone today as Mommy can't see them with the packs on her face. She didn't want any Sustacal. I'm going to Buddy's to get cleaned up and bring Marlys back. Jenny's moving her head and hands around. One hand was wet packed and the other wasn't. The wet packed hand looks better than the other.
1:10 p.m. Jenny said she feels real comfortable on her stomach but wants to be turned so she can eat. She talked

to Chad, Heather, Mom & Dad, Pam and my niece, Julie on the phone. She said when she's on her back and can get her eyes focused she wanted to see the kids. I'm going back in when she's turned to feed her dinner.

2:05 p.m. (20 min) Jenny is on her back so I fed her dinner. Her eyes are kind of mattered shut. She ate a full bowl of soup, some sips of apple juice, and about 50cc of chocolate malt with Sustacal. This is good amount for her to eat. Said she felt like she had a sore throat but after she ate she didn't. She is listening to Archie Bunker Show and Match Game. Wants to go to sleep now. Give Chad and Heather a big hug and kiss for her. She can't see them because of her eyes. Going to go have dinner.

4:00 p.m. Devotions with Pastor Helgeson.

5:30 p.m. Went over to café and got Jenny some homemade ice cream for dessert. Going to go in and feed her after nurse comes back from supper. Jenny has wet packs all over her face to loosen up dead skin and scabs and to get rid of infection.

5:45 p.m. Fed Jenny supper (1 Hour). Really in good spirits. She ate bowl of cream of celery soup, about 60cc of Sustacal, some ice cream she didn't like (1/2 bowl), and some whole milk (1/2 carton). She was really glad to talk to the kids today. Told her Chad got some new shoes at Lewis. Dr. Hoxtell came in when I was in there, after Jenny ate. He said her face is really looking good and getting cleaned up pretty good except under her nose. More islands of skin coming on face, forehead, neck, sides, and arms. She still has one blister on top of her left hand. Lost some fingernails on left hand. This was the only hand I saw. He looked at her feet and said this is the way they are supposed to be. Said she is getting more skin all the time. The skin looks like little white blisters, and this will all grow together. The people who have volunteered to donate skin if Jenny needs skin grafting may not be needed. Amazing that friends and family would put their own skin to help restore Jenny. More skin growing around eyes and growing shut. He said this can be fixed later, and this kind of got her down, worrying about not seeing again. The ophthalmologist is coming in again to see her. Jenny asked him so many questions he said he thought he was getting the first degree or 3rd degree (whatever). She was just going to be turned to her stomach. They are going to spray some more Betadine on her underarms. This might hurt again just like yesterday. They did it wrong yesterday. They were supposed to spray the packs instead of her skin. Yesterday, they sprayed right on the body and weren't supposed to. He said by the end of the week that she may be standing up in the bed on the box and may stand awhile when they turn her.

7:45 p.m. Went to Hot Fish Shop with Ronnie and Eldonna for supper. (Fish and chips).

9:00 p.m. Talked to Dr. DeMarco. First time he had been in and seen Jenny for a week. He said, "She's making progress and doing good. She will make medical history. No other patient in the nation has lost 100% of their skin and survived. She's one in a hundred million."

9:45 p.m. Talked to Jenny through the door. She said to tell Marlys if the Sustacal is supposed to help grow the skin that she's going to pour it over her head. Real good spirits. Going to turn her at 10:00.

11:00 p.m. Went in to say good-night. She said they gave her 50cc of Demerol so she could sleep on her stomach, but it didn't help her, so she doesn't want anymore. Her face is all covered with gauze to dry skin up under her nose. We said prayer and then I left.

May 18, 1976 (Day 19)

I had been lying flat, either on my back or my stomach for almost three weeks now. The doctor thought it was time for me to be held half way through the turning process in a semi-upright position until I got used to standing again. The first few times I was stopped at about half way between lying and standing I felt the blood rush from my head and I passed out. The nurses would lay me flat again and then I would come to. The next time they left me in the half-way position and again I passed out. This happened several times until the nurses slowly started getting me upright by stopping the circle bed at an angle halfway between lying and standing. As my body got used to a more elevated position, they increased it until I could tolerate being upright for several minutes. I tried marching on my box and singing marching songs just to strengthen my legs and the length of time I could be upright. The nurses maybe thought I had lost my mind but it passed the time and I was celebrating no longer being in a prone position. Hurray and praise the Lord!

Grapefruit juice was sent on my tray and was too strong for my mouth, so Ron drank it. Dr. Hoxtell again saw skin that had grown just overnight, the nurse was combing my hair for me and combed about half of my hair out. So much for me not losing my hair. My sister Vicki, who was a beautician, was nervous about cutting my hair in an ICU while wearing a mask. Not her usual hair cutting attire, but she did a good job. I felt I looked like a goon, the one on *Popeye,* but with my hair cut to within an inch of my scalp. Just what the doctor ordered. With my hair this short, my scalp would heal faster.

An eye doctor came in to look at my eyes. He flipped my bed so I was face up and jerked my eyes open. I didn't know what was going on, but it hurt. I was hoping he didn't rip any of the new skin off or damage my eyes.

From Ron's journal:
PRAY
May 19, 1976 (Day 20)
8:50 a.m. Went in to feed Jenny breakfast. She's really down again. She kept asking "why me?" She said she's not improving, just at a stand-still. I told her Dr. Hoxtell said there was more new skin on her face. She knew this but it doesn't help. Dr. Hoxtell and Dr. Reynolds were talking about putting in another IV on the other side of Jenny's chest, but she doesn't know about this. They were also going to soak the old Owens packs off and put on new ones. Jenny was worried that this would not only hurt but take off the new skin. Jenny's temperature was up last night from her hair being wet. It's back to normal now. She said she doesn't know if she can take anymore of this. The doctors are going to have her start Physical Therapy. They will have her start moving her fingers to get strength in them. If her skin starts cracking the therapist will have to stop. I got Jenny to promise to try to be in better spirits next time I come in to visit.

11:00 a.m. Jenny wants to get out of here. She is really down. Her spirits bounce up and down. The IV is not working well, the nurse irrigated it but it didn't change the flow rate. Anesthesiology will put a new IV into her arm but Jenny doesn't know this yet. All Jenny says to me is "Take me home." I only wish I could.

May 20, 1976 (Day 21)

The physical therapist came into my ICU room and said, "We are going to start therapy on your hands. I want you to try to touch your little finger to your thumb."

I thought, "Is she crazy to ask me to do such a simple thing? What kind of therapist is this?" Then I tried to do it and I could not get them to come together. The skin was so tight on my hand that it didn't allow my fingers to touch. The nurse watched my skin very closely as I attempted to move my fingers closer together.

"If there is any cracking of the skin or blood oozing from the skin we will have to stop the PT," she informed me.

I couldn't get my fingers to touch but I had plenty of time to practice this even without a therapist present. When I got bored with just lying on my bed I worked hard to get my fingers to touch each other.

One night a visiting doctor came in with Dr. Hoxtell. As I was lying on my stomach, the wet packs were pulled down to examine the groups of skin cells that were growing between my shoulder blades. The removal of the wet packs caused me to lose what little body heat I had generated and it irritated me.

Dr. Hoxtell said, "She's filling out quite nicely don't you think?"

To which I replied, "It's about time. I'm twenty-three years old."

The wet packs were pulled up and the doctors left my room without another word. I apologized the next morning for my comment.

Dr. Hoxtell said, "That's okay, it shows spunk and spirit."

Oh yeah, I probably had an overabundance of that.

May 21-26, 1976 (Days 22-27)

For the next week I was encouraged to eat more, drink more and try to keep my spirits up. I was continually worrying about my eyes since I was not seeing much but I was excited about seeing Chad and Heather or at least talking to them. Ron, grandpa and grandma and Chad were going to DeSmet during this week for Chad's last day of school which included a picnic and field day. That would be fun for them to get back home. I only wished I could go too. Therapists continued to work with strengthening my hands but when the skin would start to crack and bleed, they would stop. My IV quit working again and I told them I could wait until morning to have it put back in. This may be my last one, so they said. I could only pray it was so.

I was making progress but it didn't seem to be fast enough for me. I continued getting Demerol and Valium so I could sleep in between turnings and cleaning up some of the dead skin every hour. My blood count was low for an unknown reason so I needed transfusions. I was standing up straighter in the circle bed now. They were planning to get me up standing on the floor next week. The doctors came in on their daily rounds, morning and evening, with their entourage of interns.

Dr. Hoxtell and Dr. DeMarco told me, "In another ten days to two weeks things will be better. Your skin will be filled in and the IV's will be out as long as you can continue to eat and drink enough fluids. We will move you off the circle bed as soon as your skin is good enough to withstand the pressure of weight on it without being turned to give it a rest and air."

I so looked forward to that day but each time another week went by, something else would occur medically to delay my healing thus delaying my getting out of ICU.

May 27, 1976 (Day 28)

Ron came in this morning. He said, "Good morning, how was your night?"

I told him I was getting another unit of blood this morning.

Dr. Hoxtell came in at 8:30a.m. He said "Your skin is really coming on now. The islands on your trunk that were dime-sized are now quarter-sized and it won't be long before they've grown together. Your temperature is bouncing around (99-100) but I'm not too worried about it."

The physical therapist was in my room now working with my hands. I was on my stomach so breakfast had to wait for me to be flipped to my back. It was hard to swallow while lying on my stomach.

Ron came in later that morning to feed me breakfast. Priscilla came too. I ate pretty well. Ron pulled a piece of loose skin out of my mouth. There were no new skin clusters on my neck. I had a good visit with Priscilla. We talked about the Saturday night I died and the nurse flipping me by herself. I complained about my legs hurting.

The doctors told Ron, "Jenny is getting better and out of the danger zone but still needs to be in ICU. The nurses are pretty busy in ICU and they can only be in with her now when they turn her so if any of you want to go in and keep her company just so she doesn't get lonely that would be fine. However, if she's sleeping don't go in and wake her. It's a good thing she has started complaining since it shows she's getting better. Jenny doesn't need the constant nursing she has been getting. The nurses are going to start working the TV and light from outside her door tonight."

Ron looked nervous.

"She's going to be okay. Don't worry," they told him,

"We will be here if something happens."

Ron came in at 5:30 p.m. to feed me supper. "You ate real good and you are in pretty good spirits too."

"I have a little pain in my heels and legs," I said.

Sister Jan told Ron to bring the paper in and read it to me. I was starting to have a lot of pain. The doctors wrote a new order for pain pills and Ron gave them to me.

I asked Ron, "Will you come back in when Dr. Hoxtell comes? I don't want to take too much Demerol. I think the doctors are trying to cut down on it anyway so that is a good idea."

"I will come back in when Dr. Hoxtell comes," Ron promised.

Sister Jan and Dr. DeMarco spoke to Ron. "She was real hot from the pills we gave her for pain. We gave her some Demerol. Her temperature was 100 but there is no need to worry about that. This is only the second time she's had Demerol today. She says she doesn't want to get hooked on it."

Dr. DeMarco said. "I assured her that she won't." He said, "There's not another one like your wife in the records. We won't withdraw her all at once from the Demerol."

I was so thrilled that Heather came down to talk to me through the door. I so enjoyed that. During therapy I was able to touch my finger to my nose with my left hand but not my right hand. I was making progress each day. I felt pretty good now. I was listening to a basketball game.

Ron asked Dr. DeMarco, "Will Jenny be out of isolation when all of her skin comes back?"

Dr. DeMarco said, "Probably before that."

Ron came in to say goodnight. I had to show him that I could touch my finger to my nose, bend my legs and touch my thumb to all of my fingers. I could even fold my hands when we prayed.

Ron told me, "Don't overdue your tricks and don't itch with your fingers."

Buddy came to my door and we had a good visit. Ron and I prayed together before he left to go out to Buddy and Claire's.

I had been standing up for ten minutes now. Wow! Even if I was still strapped to the circle bed while standing, at least I was vertical. After a month of lying flat, I could actually stand up. What a feeling! Progress was not as fast as I wanted however. I was still not feeding myself or doing much of anything on my own. Imagine this, I was twenty-three years old and my best trick was being able to touch my thumb to all of my fingers and bend my arms and legs. It seemed silly but just being able to move thrilled me. Yes, it was progress, but I needed to get out of ICU.

Each day Ron received cards and donations of both money and snacks. People were very generous. God was blessing us with all of the visitors for Ron and those who took care of Chad and Heather while I was trying to get well and back home.

I would get 'down in the dumps' fairly easily. Just being told I would be in ICU for two more weeks would depress me. The doctor informed me that, only when more skin fills in and I could sit in a chair and get up by myself, would I get into a regular hospital bed. UGH!!

The nurses were starting to clean up the dead skin and debris from around my eyes three times a day now.

They asked me, "Can you open your eyes for me?"

My answer was, "It doesn't matter if I can or not. All I can see is white now."

I had pain but wasn't sure myself if the pain was just from moving or from another source. I wanted to sleep away the nightmare of being blind. Spending this time away from my kids was not what I had planned. I was not able to even get up and go to the bathroom on my own. I was not sure how I was ever going to be the same independent person I was before.

May 30, 1976 (Day 31)

After thirty-one days in the hospital, I once again had pseudomonas on the trunk of my body.

The doctor said, "We cleared this up overnight last time. We are going to use double isolation to protect not only you from infection and diseases but also the ones visiting and the other patients in the ward in case you have a bacteria." He told Ron, "There is oozing on Jenny's back in between the skin clusters and it looks like what was on her forehead a while back. We are going to treat it with wet packs."

The gowns people used to visit me were taken off inside my ICU room and bagged there to keep others safe. The pseudomonas may have been why my temperature was going up and down. Ron was staying on the couch in the lobby again. I felt bad about this.

I had had all I wanted of the care I was getting. I was depressed and tired from being turned every two hours. The nurses spent every other hour cleaning up some of the bad areas on my body so I really only had an hour at a time that I could rest.

The Catholic Sisters and nurses told Ron, "We are leaving it up to you to get Jenny to eat instead of sleep."

41

He was exhausted from this routine by now but he didn't give up on me. He stood strong and tough and believed I would get better and he would be able to take our little family home again someday. He just didn't know when that day would come.

My protein and blood counts were coming up on their own and that was a good sign. My temperature jumped around depending on what was being done for me. Due to all of the above symptoms my standing up was going to be postponed until some of those areas were cleaned up. Each day the nurse asked Ron to get me to eat more since eating more was just as important as the sleep I so desperately wanted.

One day Ron said to me, "You're talking goofy." He spoke to the nurse about what medications I had been given.

She said, "We gave her a sleeping pill and Demerol at the same time. That may have caused her to talk that way." Some would say I have always talked that way but not my Ron.

I was thrilled to be able to talk to Chad and Heather again. They were the reason I was trying to get better, to be able to go home and spend time with them. I hoped I wasn't being too optimistic.

Ron asked me, "Are you hungry?"

I said out of the blue, "What flowers are blooming outside today?"

Later Ron came in and seemed to think I was better. At least I was making sense anyway. I was actually being given regular food now instead of ground or pureed.

Ron said to me, "Wow, you ate quite a bit."

I responded, "I don't think it tastes all that good but they said I had to eat to get better and get out of here."

I hadn't gotten much rest during the past twenty-four hours so the doctor's orders were, "Do not to disturb Jenny after having eaten a good meal and new Owens packs have been placed. She needs her rest also."

I just ate whatever Ron put on the spoon, drank the protein drinks and prayed to get better.

"I have a lot of pain in my feet and legs," I told Ron. The skin continued to grow and clump together and now I had graduated from being turned every two hours to three hour turnings. We were making progress in little baby steps, but it was progress. I thought I was doing better until Ron said, "I think I'll stay in the lobby tonight."

"Why, what's going on?" I asked.

"Nothing, you're getting better. I just feel I want to stay tonight." So he did.

The nurse said to Ron, "I wonder if Jenny needs all the Demerol she is asking for. We are trying to give her enemas and pain killers at the same time. The problem is the pain killers can cause constipation. Jenny may have some scar tissue growing across the inside of the intestines causing some of the pain. We can't be sure however. She hasn't had a bowel movement for over a month so it is bound to be difficult for her and cause her pain. We are going to assist her in having a BM and hopefully, together, we get some results."

This subject was humiliating and embarrassing but just plain necessary. The doctors did not want me to have a BM before, but now when I began eating food and was still not having any, they became concerned. The nurse told Ron and me that she was going to "help me." With me on my stomach, she proceeded to put a gloved finger inside my rectum and try to pull pieces of dried poop out.

She asked, "Can you push?"

I did try to push her finger out of me with no results. One nurse thought if they turned me to my back on the circle bed and cut a hole in the mattress that I would have better pushing ability. Well when I felt this cutting beneath me I grew worried.

"What if you cut through the mattress into me?" I asked nervously.

"Hopefully we won't do that," one nurse said.

"I hope you don't either."

43

After working on cutting through the mattress for over an hour, the nurses finally gave up. I probably paid for that mattress and many other things I didn't realize at the time.

"Whatever it takes to get me well and out of this ICU, I am willing to endure," I told Ron.

Even though I was making progress, problems were still cropping up and I was still unable to be moved from ICU. The routine was getting old and I suspected not just for me.

June 2, 1976 (Day 34)

Dr. Hoxtell talked to Ron this morning. He said, "Jenny needs to have a bowel movement. I think she will be more comfortable after that. She also still has some pseudomonas growing but not on the areas that we cleaned up. She has new skin on about seventy percent of her body, big blotches of skin on her back, and her hands are all covered with skin up to her elbows. She has skin from her feet to her knees and all over her face. There is some skin on her upper legs too. She has something growing on the blood cultures so we are going to change her medication today and see if that helps get rid of it."

I finally had a real good BM before breakfast. We celebrated every small victory at this point. I ate as much as I could for breakfast but not really much at all. I was more tired than hungry. The therapist came in while Ron was in my room and he watched me do my 'tricks' for her. When she left, she promised to return the next day.

"Next you're going to make facial expressions to stretch the new skin on your face," she informed me.

I said to Ron, "I'm very tired."

He praised me for my progress, "Well, you had a great workout. You lifted your arms up five times and out to the side five times. You touched all your fingers to your thumb, rotated your wrists, made fists of your hands, spread your fingers and waved with your wrists. You did a great job! You also bent your elbows to your shoulders and bent your knees. That's a lot, I'll leave and let you rest

44

now. Will you eat a good dinner since you didn't eat much breakfast?"

I agreed.

Ron also told me before he left, "I can see a lot of new skin growing on your neck too." As Ron left, I dropped into an exhausted sleep.

Ron returned to feed me dinner. My temperature was 101.4. I was in a lot of pain mostly in the rectum area. They gave me a laxative that would take about twenty-four hours to work. I ate as much as I could which consisted of half a Swedish meatball, a small potato, all the bananas and whipped cream, all of my fruit cocktail, half a carton of milk, five bites of green beans and a glass of water. My mind was made up, I was getting out of here and if eating was what it took then I would eat.

I told Ron, "If I have to stay in here two more weeks I think I'll go crazy."

Ron said, "If you can have another good BM the pain might not be quite as bad."

I could ring the light on by myself now. I didn't finish all of my therapy because it made me nauseous. The nurse thought it was probably from the medications. I rested well in the afternoon on my stomach until Ron came in to feed me supper.

I had been listening to TV. Supper arrived and I ate as much as I could. I was still having problems with BM's. I didn't like to show that I was in pain when anyone was at the door.

Ron noted, "This is the first time today we've really talked." Ron left my room and would come back later.

Dr. Hoxtell told me, "The skin looks better than it did earlier today. There is more new skin all the time. The blood cultures came out good. Your temperature is down. Your pulse is good. With all the epidermis you have now, it won't be long before you can regulate your own body temperature. I may have to check on the new medications to see if that is making you nauseous." Dr. Hoxtell said to Ron, "We're back to where we were before the weekend and then some. She's on her stomach now and resting so that is good."

Ron, with relief in his voice and tears in his eyes said, "That's good."

Ron came in to say good-night. We had been talking for a while when I asked him, "When did you start smoking?"

Ron asked, "How did you know I was smoking?"

"I smell it," I said. End of conversation. We prayed and then Ron left for Buddy and Claire's. The nurses were having trouble with my IV clogging up again but they got it irrigated clear. Thank God.

For as long as I had been in the hospital, the doctors seemed surprised by how good I looked. They said this because number one, I had an infection of some kind in my blood, number two, I couldn't poop without severe pain and number three, I didn't have all my skin back yet. The doctor was ordering my IV removed but I still had to have six to seven shots a day. Tomorrow the catheter would come out. They were thinking one of these two lines may be causing the infection. My blood count was down to 8.3 and if it dropped much lower I may need a new IV and blood transfusion. Not sure when this roller-coaster would end.

June 4-5, 1976 (Days 36-37)

This was our thirty-sixth day since being admitted. I was eating more too because Ron told me I had to since I didn't have an IV anymore. I was now getting Demerol in tablet form. I was still being turned on the circle bed, however.

Dr. DeMarco said, "The bug in your blood is resistant to Gentamicin. It isn't a bad bug just the same one that has been there. It is sensitive to penicillin but we don't want to use that." Dr. DeMarco called Mayo Clinic and had them re-culture the blood. He said, "By Monday a new antibiotic will be here from New York that might work but I don't think it will because it is in the 'mycin' family and the bug is not sensitive to Gentamicin. If it doesn't work, I think

46

you can fight this off by yourself as your resistance is getting better. If you would have had this bug when you were real sick it would have been bad."

When I realized that I had now been in the hospital for five weeks Ron said to me, "Your expression tells me you would have rolled your eyes had they been open."

I was still complaining of pain in my legs, heels and underarm areas. My temperature was 99.8 so something was still "bugging" me. I said to the physical therapist, "I want to be out of the hospital by the fifteenth of June, my little Heather's birthday. That gives me two weeks from today to get out of here."

The nurse quietly said, "I hope it happens for you."

I could bend my right leg all the way back but not the left. I could touch one arm to my head when stretched out. I was still kind of raw under my arms and still having stomach cramps. I opened my eyes wide and I could see the TV clearly.

Ron said, "Good, this is the first time you have had your eyes open for about two weeks."

I was starting to itch all over so Ron helped me scratch. I was still having trouble with BM's or the lack thereof. The doctor said, "It's a good thing you're tough."

I asked, "Why is that?"

"Well," he said, "due to the constipation, the possibility of getting an infection in your intestine is greater."

At this point I was not sure being tough was such a good deal. The doctor was encouraging lots of fluids, lots of food and rest.

He spoke encouragingly, "Most of your skin should be grown back by the weekend, just a few scattered areas left to fill in."

I hoped this was true but I had my doubts since I had heard this before and it seemed like something always happened to postpone my improvement.

June 6-9, 1976 (Days 38-41)

Dr. Hoxtell ordered the Owens packs to be changed every hour, so once again, I was tired. Ron continued to attend church and mass as he was able. We continued to pray every day and our children were still in the care of family members while Ron stayed at the hospital with me. My blood count was back up and new skin was growing like crazy, Ron encouraged me to eat better.

Dr. DeMarco told Ron, "I think Jenny is going to make it. She is a tough gal."

I didn't agree. I was not sure how in this world I was going to deal with any of what was coming my way. I thought I would just stay in a drugged state and let the world pass me by. But then there was my family. I desperately wanted to just go home and take care of my kids again.

I was itching from new skin growing all over. I was given Valium, Demerol and an itching pill. The doctors talked about moving me to their regular isolation room in ICU.

Dr. Hoxtell told Ron, "I would like to put Jenny in a big tank of saline water during physical therapy but we may have to wait on that."

I was getting better. I needed to get better. Chad and Heather came up to see me and I tried to open my eyes as wide as I could to see them also. Heather just looked at me a lot.

I asked them, "What do you want for your birthdays?"

Chad said, "I want Sesame Street for my birthday."

Heather only whispered, "M&M's." I wanted to hold them in my arms so badly. I was determined to get better so I could do that very thing.

Great Day! I was moved to a regular isolation room in ICU. The maintenance people were fogging my room with my coat and suitcase in it.

Dr. Hoxtell and Dr. DeMarco visited with Ron, "We are very pleased with her progress and we feel all her skin should be grown back in about ten days."

When Ron told me this I said, "I've heard that before." There were too many extenuating circumstances to give an accurate estimate of when I would have all my skin back. One of the major road blocks was infection which impedes skin growth. Whenever it happened would be too slow for me.

June 10, 1976 (Day 42, 6 weeks)

Dr. Hoxtell and Dr. Dennis D. Knutson, Dermatology talked to Ron. "We are going to take out the Foley catheter today to prevent more infection in Jenny's blood. If we have to, we can always put it back in. We haven't taken any blood cultures since she's had the IV out but we are going to try and get a culture today." To me they said, "Your breakfast is here but we have more to discuss with you. Do you mind waiting?"

I answered, "No." Food was not my main interest now.

Dr. Hoxtell continued, "I would like to do three blood tests today. In all there are twelve tests and it's cheaper to do all twelve so we will order it that way. I am leaving for Rapid City and an American Medical Association convention but I will be back in a week. I want to see more improvement when I return, okay?"

I didn't answer but I sincerely hoped so.

Day after day Ron continued to come to my room to feed me at meal times. One day I told him, "I didn't sleep good last night because I was so cold. The heat doesn't seem to work in this room. I had five blankets on last night and I was still cold. I just want to sleep in this morning. I want the heat fixed too."

The nurses drew blood again this morning. My temperature was up in the night to 101 but was back to normal when Ron came in. He told me, "Dr. Hoxtell said you were the main topic at the AMA convention last week."

I didn't care. I only wanted to leave this hospital. Before Ron left, the nurse came in to regulate the heat and bring another blanket. He said, "I may not be back for dinner."

The nurse said, "I can feed her if you aren't here."

I was now on my stomach. The area on my back had some infection and was being left exposed to the air. The bacteria cannot live in the open air. The area measured about four by twelve inches. I was in quite a bit of pain again.

I rested until Ron came in to feed me dinner. I was in good spirits. My catheter was taken out that morning. I ate a whole ham and lettuce sandwich, three-fourths of a brownie, Jell-O salad with bananas, half a small sack of potato chips, a glass of lemonade and two cartons of milk, one white and one chocolate. I got to stand up a little until I felt dizzy. Ron was in my room when I started to feel dizzy and I complained of a headache. The nurse took my blood pressure and temperature. My temp was 100, my pulse was fast and my blood pressure was OK.

I said, "I hope I am not having a setback."

I asked Ron to get a carpet sample for our basement floor the next day and bring it back so I could see it. We prayed and Ron left so I could rest. The nurse stayed with me.

June 11-14, 1976 (Days 43-46)

I took three steps forward and two steps back. The catheter had to be replaced since I couldn't urinate. I was still being turned on the circle bed although not as frequently. It was 102 outside and I was freezing in my room so they were trying to get the heat regulated. I was trying to eat as much as I could but wasn't really consuming much. If I drank pop even within an hour of my meal, I was too full to eat. I wanted my eyes opened before Heather's third birthday on the fifteenth of June. The doctors thought things were going well. One percentage of skin on my stomach was left to grow back, just dime-sized spots.

Dr. Hoxtell expressed, "It's neat that your entire body grew a whole new layer of skin. Your eyelids may have to be cut open since eyelashes are growing and I'm not sure now if your fingernails will grow back. Time will tell."

Some of the nurses were due for a much deserved vacation. A nurse named Maxine was transferred to ICU from another floor. I immediately noticed the difference of how seriously the regular ICU nurses took my situation compared to Maxine's care of me. She was not following procedure or protocol for my situation of gowning to come into my isolation room. She did not wear a mask or gloves to take my temperature. She used the same blankets when changing my bed. I was disgusted with this nurse putting me and others in the ICU in jeopardy just because she didn't want to follow protocol.

Ron told Maxine, "The therapist is coming in to do therapy with Jenny so she should not be turned to her stomach until therapy is done."

Ron returned with the therapist to my room within five minutes and said, "She's been turned to her stomach. Can you still do her therapy?"

The therapist replied, "Could you do Jenny's therapy tonight when she is on her back again?"

Ron said, "What do I do?"

"Just the same stretching things she's been doing?"

Ron and the therapist were both frustrated with this nurse. The therapist had more patients than me to help so Ron did my therapy after I had been turned to my back again. I was not able to move my right arm as well as my left so of course I worried about it and then I remembered God. I thought, "Should I bother Him with this?" 'Bring everything to Him in prayer' was something I remembered, but from where, I didn't know, but I prayed.

I was very concerned about this nurse and her non-compliance of my care. Sister Jan came in to visit. I was upset as she could tell.

She said to me, "Is something bothering you?"

51

I answered, "Yes, but I don't want to get anyone in trouble. Still, I don't think I can let this continue."

"Would you like to tell me about it?" she asked.

"Yes."

I talked to her about Maxine and my concerns not only for me but for the other patients in ICU. Sister Jan left my room after finishing her vital check. Nurse Maxine was never on my case again. I'm not sure what happened to her.

I still had pseudomonas on my back so the Owens packs were removed and Betadine sprayed on the infected areas. It did hurt some. A culture was taken from the catheter area and it too grew something. Not sure what though.

Dr. DeMarco thought my stomach area looked good. There were still some open areas on my legs. Ron and I were both tired. It had been forty-six days since my admission and I asked, "Could I give Ron a good-night kiss?"

Dr. DeMarco replied, "If Ron can keep himself under control." I got a kiss.

The next day was my little Heather's third birthday. I was not going to be out of ICU let alone out of the hospital for her birthday. I hated that I was missing all the important events in my kid's lives.

From Ron's journal:
PRAY
June 15, 1976 (Day 47)Heather's 3rd birthday
8:10 a.m. Talked to Dr. Knutson. He said all vital signs are good. Hemoglobin is up to 10.1. If all other cultures come back OK, they may take her off antibiotics (Gentamicin and Erythromycin)

Maintenance had just brought an electric heater into my room. They couldn't regulate the hospital's heating and cooling system to heat my room and cool the rest of the building. My breakfast came but I was still on my stomach. Even though the nurse told Ron, "We're just

52

ready to turn her," he came back forty minutes later to find my breakfast still sitting there and I had not been turned yet. The nurses changed my packs and I was finally turned, then it was lunch time.

I told Ron, "I was shaking in the night because I was so cold and they didn't have any more blankets."

I was kind of depressed this morning. I wanted to spend the whole day with Heather but that wasn't going to happen.

"Ron, I want her to have a good time for her birthday so you make sure she does, okay?"

"I will," Ron promised. "I am taking the kids to Shakey's Pizza for Heather's party."

I started crying and said, "The doctors can't give me a date when I might be out of the hospital. They wet pack, then put on Owens packs, then dry pack then spray Betadine and then start all over again. They just never quit. I'm tired of it all."

They were wet packing my neck again because the skin would grow faster when there was moisture added.

Ron said, "I'll leave and let you get some sleep and I'll come back after the nurses turn you." Ron fed me my breakfast. I was eating pretty well now.

I said, "Is there not a 'quiet zone' sign outside the hospital? I think I will go crazy if they don't stop soon."

Ron told me they were breaking up the steps outside with an air hammer. He turned the TV up loud so the noise outside wouldn't bother me as much. Ron left when the therapist came. Later he brought Chad and Heather in to talk to 'Mommy'.

I asked, "How old are you now Heather?" Through blurred vision I saw her hold up three tiny little fingers.

Chad said, "We're going to Shakey's to get our birthday treats."

The kids talked most of the time. Chad more than Heather about what they had been doing and where they were staying. They left after about fifteen minutes.

I told Heather, "Happy Birthday, honey."

Ron stayed to help me with dinner. I couldn't choke down one bite. Tears were filling my very being. I was sick at heart because I was not able to attend my own daughter's birthday party. Ron left and took Chad, Heather and Kathy, Priscilla's second daughter, and Marlys to Shakey's. Buddy and Claire's son and daughter, Jon and Jill were there too. The kids got a free pizza, drink, balloon and hat. Shakey's played the birthday song for them too.

Ron said, "This is not the way a three-year-old should have a birthday. Without her 'Mommy' I mean. Heather needs her Mommy now. She is only three!"

Ron was back that evening to feed me supper. He told me what he did with the kids in the afternoon and assured me that they had a good time.

I said, "I had a good talk with Pastor Johnson. I told him about the time I was sitting up in the corner of the ceiling watching the doctors and nurses working on my body."

I ate some of what was on my dinner tray but not much. Ron left and said he would be back again in a while. Around 9:00 p.m. Ron came to say good-night to me. The nurses were ready to turn me when one of them flushed the stool and water ran all over the floor. Maintenance was called but the two nurses mopped and scrubbed the floor before maintenance got there.

I joked, "Could I have my old room back again?"

I was in real good spirits. Ron and I prayed and before he left to go out to Buddy and Claire's he said to me, "I'll bring you some birthday cake tomorrow."

"Okay, that will be good," I replied.

The doctors were once again pleased with the areas of my body that had been wet packed. The nurses were still spraying Betadine on raw open areas. The sterilizer had broken down so gowns were in short supply and Chad and Ron were unable to come in to visit with me. Chad talked to me through the door. I was eating sporadically, some days half of what was sent, some days a couple of bites and sometimes nothing but pop or a malt. Ron spent some time with the kids and that was good. He took Chad to goofy golf, swimming and tried to be Daddy and nurse all at the same time. Superman! My prayer was, "God bless Ron and those caring for my little ones." I missed taking care of them myself but I knew they were in good hands.

The circle bed was being held at a seventy degree angle now and I wanted to be able to stand on the floor in a few days without passing out. My temperature was down all day. My trunk skin was doing well but my legs were slower to fill in. Our home town of DeSmet was starting benefits to help with the expenses of my long hospital stay and being away from home. There was something growing on my legs but not on my trunk. More testing was done.

Dr. Hoxtell spoke, "We want you to stand more and try to stand on one foot at a time too. We want to put you in the whirlpool once all your skin is back to get the rest of the dead skin off your body. We are also talking about moving you to another room in ICU since the toilet in this room had a problem and the smell is bad."

I asked, "This is my third room in ICU. Will my next one be on the regular floor?"

Dr. Hoxtell said, "I want the eye doctor to come and see you. Your corneas are swollen so I want Dr. Meyers to come in and see what he thinks. Try to stand up straight in the bed when it is vertical half way through the turning process until you don't feel lightheaded anymore. Do you think you can do that?"

"I can do it," I replied.

I stood marching in place and then would get lightheaded. The nurses returned the bed to a flat position to let me recover then we repeated the process.

Ron was helping me with my tomato soup when, after spilling several drops on my bedding, I suggested, "Maybe I could use a straw to sip it up." The soup was lukewarm on the top where Ron was spooning it from but boiling hot in the bottom where the straw was resting. After taking my first draw on the straw I sat straight up in bed. The hot soup caused the new skin in my mouth to peel out like the lining of a chicken gizzard when you cleaned it.

Ron said, "I didn't know you could sit up on your own. Are you okay? I am so sorry."

This was the first time I had eaten good in days and now I had to quit due to my mouth being raw again.

I assured Ron, "I will be okay."

After I sat straight up in bed from the hot soup it occurred to me I could move on my own. I wanted to see how long I could sit upright without assistance. I made it one and half minutes, not much but I would practice, a huge accomplishment.

The doctors were now concerned about the condition of my eyes. I could count fingers close in front of my face but my eyes were mattery most of the time. The eye doctor definitely needed to come in to check this out. I was discouraged. It seemed like life was passing me by and everything the doctors told me didn't happen or the date was pushed back by some unforeseen event. Sometimes what they told me would happen, but that wasn't the good news I was waiting for. The doctors told me not to worry about my eyes, that they would not be affected, but they were. I didn't want to live blind. I didn't even want to go on living. It was too hard. It would be so much easier just to melt back into my Demerol haze and let life and Ron and our kids go on without me. I wasn't seeing God anywhere at this point. I wasn't sure being in the presence of God even helped. One thing I did know, I had been in God's presence and He saved my life for some reason. I just wasn't sure what that reason was but I couldn't shake that feeling.

Dr. Meyers came in to exam my eyes. He told us, "Something has grown over the cornea of your eyes. The left may be more affected than the right. I am not sure if you will be able to see or not." With that he left my room.

Ron and I were both devastated. Fear overtook me and I felt like I was becoming more and more of a burden to Ron with each day. Now, being fifty days in the hospital, Ron and I were starting to do two things at a time. Ron fed me while I would do physical therapy. I needed to be busy to keep my mind off what was happening.

I asked Ron, "What will you do if I am blind?"

He said, "We don't need to talk about it. We will be okay."

"I don't want to be blind and add another thing for you to do. What can I do if I am blind?" I was crying by now.

"We'll figure this out. This news is a blow to all of us. It'll be okay."

Ron left but came back later to see me, "You're in good spirits."

"I wonder why that is Ron? What keeps me rallying each time a doctor gives us bad news?" Ron didn't have an answer.

Dr. Hoxtell was also there to check on my progress. He said, "I am encouraged with the amount of skin that has grown back, but there is a different kind of skin growing on your legs. It is not as smooth as the rest of the regrowth. I would like to get your eyes opened too. Also, if there are any changes to be made in your medications, we will plan it so if you begin to have any problems, the entire lab would be on staff. So, Monday will usually be the day when a medication will be stopped or a new one started or any change in your scheduled procedures or medications." Dr. Hoxtell watched me stand and walk in place for five minutes. My feet got tired before I became light-headed. I was upset and being upset made me work even harder. "We may be putting you in the Hubbard tank next week to remove some of the dead skin. We'll see how things go before deciding that," He stated. "Your vitals are okay today so we will go from there."

The nurses were picking off old Owens packs and dead skin as they turned me now. I picked off the dead skin on my fingers out of boredom. I called the blood work people "bloodsuckers" since they drew my blood so often. Our families and friends were still visiting regularly. I wanted them all to get back to a normal life. Eventually, I wanted that for us too, I hoped anyway.

June 21, 1976 (Day 53)

I asked for Demerol for each pain, earache, leg ache, and heel pain…every little ache. My temperature was up every night but the doctor thought that was normal for most people. I thought if I had my guitar I could at least entertain myself for a little while each day. Ron cleaned it up and brought it in. I couldn't play. My fingers were too weak and of course no longer calloused. It was discouraging.

Ron called a girl in New Ulm, Minnesota since he had heard she had gone through a similar disease. She and her mother came to visit me. The mother said, "You will be just fine. I kept my daughter on the couch with dry sheets and sponged her off and her blisters got better and it didn't affect her eyes at all."

I know they were trying to be encouraging but I said, "I don't believe you. If you had the same thing as me, how did you not have all the infections and not have to have sterile packs and gown in and out? How can you say you had the same disease as I do and you didn't even enter a hospital? I'm still in the hospital, still trying to grow skin back and can't even get my eyes open after almost two months. It doesn't sound like the same disease to me!"

They pretty much left after that. I wanted desperately to get back to normal just like this girl but I didn't see that happening. I was scared. In my heart I knew life had changed for me forever and not only for me but for Ron, Chad, Heather, my family, Ron's family and for everyone around us. I was praying to God to help me deal with this. Whenever a patient who had been very, very sick in the ICU with me came back to visit after they had recovered, it depressed me. I just wanted to get out of there too. I opened my eyes and all I could see was gray light. I started to not believe anything the doctors were telling me. I had a list of things they were wrong about like it wouldn't affect

58

my eyes and I wouldn't lose my fingernails. Both of these things had already happened and it was terrifying me. What else had they assured me about that wasn't correct?

June 22, 1976 (Day 54)
One good thing was that the kids were getting wonderful care. They were brought to Sioux Falls and Ron was going and doing things with them. At least he tried to keep their visits fun despite the fact that they came to the hospital to see their mommy. Chad gave Heather rides up and down in the elevator. The play room at the hospital had cameras in it so our family could see what they were doing from the ICU waiting room. I couldn't stop talking about the fact that I was going to remain blind. Ron encouraged me as did the nurses. They all reminded me that I could see the red, green and yellow of the derm packs. Also, I could see more when the lights were on.

Dr. Hoxtell said, "Maybe you could get a pass to go out of the hospital for your son, Chad's birthday in eight days. However, you would be in a wheelchair."

I thought, "I won't be able to see anything." I said, "That wouldn't be much fun. I don't want to go out that way. It would just be more work for Ron. I'll just stay here."

When Chad came in my room to visit, he was excited from the fun day. He told me about swimming, what he and Heather did for her birthday and his planned birthday coming up. He described what they had been doing the past few days.

I said, "That sounds like a lot of fun." I was so saddened that I had missed out on their lives for two months. I reminded them both, "We are going home to DeSmet when I get out of the hospital."

Chad thought that would be okay. He gave me a kiss and left my room. I'm beyond sad.

Everyone was doing whatever they could to get me to eat. No matter what my request was, I got it. One nurse's husband even made me popcorn at their home and brought it out to the hospital for me. I was getting wonderful care but I just wanted to go home. Ron and I continued praying. The nurses were still turning me on the circle bed.

Dr. Hoxtell told me, "Another week to ten days and maybe you will be out of ICU. Dr. Meyers won't fix your eyes for two weeks. This set back is due to the skin on your sides not growing as fast as I would like."

"Maybe it wasn't going to grow back," was my thought. This depressed me since I had heard it all before. Each time Dr. Hoxtell saw me he told us it would be longer before I got out. From morning to night things had changed from two weeks to a month.

"God help me," was what I was now praying.

My blood was still being drawn a couple of times a day. I was still being encouraged to eat more than two bites of this and a sip of that. My right knee was awfully swollen but therapy was going well.

I told Ron, "Sleep later in the mornings and don't feel you need to be at the hospital so much. Don't worry about me."

I needed to start doing more on my own since I was going to be blind. Feeding myself was going to be the first hurdle. The bedding was still being double bagged from my room. The skin on my back was almost all filled in but on my sides there was a little more to come yet.

Dr. Hoxtell said, "There is ten to twelve percent of your skin left to grow back so that is good. You will be in ICU for about two more weeks." He asked Ron, "Have her arms ever been thin?"

Ron said, "No, but they are now."

I apologized to the doctors and nurses when I would get upset because I couldn't get out of the ICU, but they all reassured me that they understood my frustration.

I was now eating fifteen hundred calories a day and could barely get that down. Dr. Hoxtell wanted me to increase that to three thousand calories daily. Yikes! How in the world?

"Ron," I murmured, "My eyes are burning whether they are open or shut. Can someone do something about them?"

He said, "I will check on it."

June 23, 1976 (Day 55)

The Gentamicin shots would be stopped pretty soon. My skin was almost all grown back now after fifty-five days in the hospital. I could now turn over on my side by myself so I was becoming a little more mobile.

"Dr. Meyers, the ophthalmologist, is coming in the morning to look at your eyes again," Ron told me.

"Good," was my only reply. My head was starting to itch and the Vistaril wasn't helping much.

Ron said, "I'll be here to talk to the eye doctor in the morning."

"Okay," I replied.

Dr. Meyers came in and examined my eyes. He said, "Like before, your right eye looks okay. The left eye may have some vision problems. Due to the 106 temperature you had, and all you have been through, the blood vessels in the eyes grew over the corneas. I think your left eye may be real poor but might be surprisingly good too." Dr. Meyers turned and spoke to Ron, "I can do a minor surgery to open the corners of her eyes when she gets out of the hospital. That may give her a little more sight." He then left my room.

I told Ron, "In other words he doesn't know any more than I do. I'm going to stay blind and he just doesn't want to say so. Man, I can't believe people, especially professionals who don't just give me straight talk. At least then there is no false hope. If I know what I have to deal with I can cry, get mad, get over it and move on." Needless to say I was down in the dumps again.

Ron's nephew, Joe Peterson, Buddy and Claire's oldest son, brought his guitar to the hospital. He and Chad were singing together. That brought my spirits up a little for the day. Joe later made a tape of songs so I could listen to them whenever I wanted. The doctors were still unsure

61

when I would get out of the hospital because each day something new came along to slow down the healing process. What no one had told me was that I was the first patient to survive TEN and the doctors just didn't know how to treat me. I was only getting one Demerol shot a day now so slowly they were tapering me off. Wonderful!

June 24, 1976 (Day 56)

The kids came to visit and told me all they had been doing. I felt left out but didn't want them to know that. I wanted them to enjoy their summer and time with family.

Dr. Hoxtell said, "I think in another ten days you will be out of ICU."

I thought, "So what else is new? I've heard this before and it doesn't happen. I am not going to plan on it and then I won't be disappointed when it doesn't happen."

Almost all of the Owens packs were picked off now. The Gentamicin shots might be stopped by Monday. I had heard that before too. I cried at times when the kids came in to see me but I didn't want them to think I was sad to see them so I held my emotions in check until they left.

One afternoon Ron was out at Buddy and Claire's, I called their house and asked Ron to bring me KFC chicken. They were all surprised that I was able to use a phone.

I said, "I've been hungry for chicken for a while."

Ron eagerly agreed to bring me some when he came. He brought me two pieces of chicken and two ribs.

He said, "I'll put it right in front of you and you can pick it up with your fingers to eat."

I reached out and touched the piece of chicken. I grasped the piece with my fingers and couldn't raise it to my mouth. The piece of chicken was too heavy for me to lift. Now I knew why I wasn't out of ICU yet. It was a huge chicken thigh but it was still a wake up call to me. I used to carry five gallon pails of water and ground feed to the chickens at home when I was a kid and now I couldn't even lift a piece of chicken. The work was far from over

62

for me to get back to 'normal'. I was shocked but knew I had to work harder than ever to get my strength back.

June 28, 1976 (Day 60)

Monday was finally here and no more shots after today. I wanted to celebrate. Then Dr. Hoxtell saw my blood work. He wrote orders to not stop the Gentamicin shots yet. The nurses didn't tell me why. When Ron came into my room I grabbed him frantically.

I said, "Take me home. I need to go home."

I was depressed. I didn't want any more of the turning every two hours, picking off the Owens packs, shots, or being told I would be out of ICU in ten more days just to remain longer and longer.

Ron said, "We will as soon as the doctors say you can go."

This was really out of my hands, and I didn't like it. I had lost two toenails and my temperature was 100. Doctors that hadn't seen me in ten days or so thought I looked great.

"Compared to what?" I wanted to know.

The only part of my body that was being wet packed now was my right shoulder. My legs were being dry packed, but no other part was being packed at all. I could sit up in bed, so the doctors could see the skin on my back. The order was given that once again I should try to stand more each day, up to five minutes at a time at first. I was getting stronger. One day, as I stretched my arms above my head while lying in bed, I felt a bar hanging there. I reached up to the bar and did two pull-ups. They were not perfect in form, but I did raise my back and shoulders off the bed.

Later Ron came in to help me eat.

I said, "See the bar above my head? I can pull myself up on it."

He reported this to Dr. Hoxtell, who ordered physical therapy to get two three-pound sandbags for me to lift with my legs and arms. He also ordered a stop on the Gentamicin shots. I took liquid Erythromycin instead.

Dr. Hoxtell told me, "When you can stand without getting dizzy, we will get a chair for you to sit in."

"Not a wheelchair," I said.

"No, a regular, comfortable chair. It might be mid-week before we can do that. Work hard at being able to stand and sit and we'll see how it goes."

I was thrilled. Maybe by the end of the week I would be sitting in a chair. A real chair!

"After that," he continued, "we will see if we can get you in the Hubbard tank on Thursday to help clean up some of the areas. You need to report to the nurses any spots that hurt so they can spray Betadine on them and wet pack them so you don't get infection on your skin again."

I agreed to do this.

Dr. Hoxtell tried to give me incentive to do better by telling me, "The sooner you get all your skin back, the sooner we will have the ophthalmologist open your eyes."

I wanted this so badly. I was willing to work harder than I ever had to get my eyes open so I could see again.

Dr. DeMarco reported, "I hear you are giving Dr. Hoxtell a bad time about not answering all of your questions directly and beating around the bush with answers that are really not answers."

"I just need the truth," I said.

Dr. DeMarco said, "You must be getting better since it sounds like you are full of piss and vinegar. Pardon the expression."

The entire staff was upbeat and thrilled to see that I had improved to this point. I was reeling from excitement that night.

From Ron's journal:
PRAY
June 29, 1976 (Day 61) Chad's 6th birthday
7:30 a.m. Dr. Hoxtell was here, missed him.

11:30 a.m. Went in to see Jenny. Couldn't get in any sooner because no gowns. Stayed about 20 minutes. I told her we're going to Happy Chef Café to get the kids their free meals. The nurse will feed Jenny dinner. By the time we get back, there will be enough gowns for the kids to go in.

12:00 p.m. Went to Happy Chef. Chad and Heather both ate all their meal and enjoyed little birthday cakes. Jenny had some goulash, but not much. She didn't feel like eating.

2:30 p.m. Chad, Heather and I went in to see Jenny with a nurse. The nurse made two cakes (one for Chad and one for Heather). Jenny sang 'Happy Birthday' to Chad. Sounded real good. Chad and Heather each had fudge bars and orange pop in Mommy's room. We took pictures in there too. Jenny said, "We have to remember it like it is." We left and went down to the cafeteria so we could all have cake. We left a piece for Jenny in her room. We went out to the car and the kids opened their presents in the back end of the station wagon. Chad, Grandpa and I went to the driving range and hit golf balls. Chad hit them 50-75 yards. He had a good day.

5:30 p.m. Went in to feed Jenny supper. She ate while on her stomach. She said she was tired from all the therapy and she's tired of the circle bed. Dr. Hoxtell came in while I was there. She just finished eating. He asked what kind of therapy she had today. Sitting and standing Jenny told him. They will put a chair in her room to sit in tomorrow or Thursday. Hubbard Tank on Thursday too at 10:00 a.m. at about 100-101 degrees. She asked him if she could have another bed. He said he would think about it tonight and let her know in the morning. It sounds pretty good that she might get one. He asked questions about how they would turn her, change the sheets, etc. The nurse said they could sit Jenny in the chair while they changed the bedding. This would be a regular hospital bed that she could sit up in and bend her back. The only spot Dr. Hoxtell was concerned about is on her back with the other bed. He said

65

he would think about it, but this too sounds pretty good. We left so the nurse could turn her to her back. I told her I will be back later. She was still tired from the whole day. 9:00 p.m. Went in to say good-night. She ate ¾ piece of birthday cake, popcorn and two glasses of Coke.

June 30, 1976 (Day 62)
12:30 p.m. dinner came. Jenny opened her eyes and tried to see what she had to eat. She fed herself most of the meal of Swedish meatballs, potatoes, string beans, and fresh fruit salad. I fed her the last of the meal because she said her eyes got tired. She stopped eating and said she hadn't seen me for a long time, so she looked up into my face and touched her fingers to my cheek and started crying. She said, "I was concentrating so hard on seeing what I was eating I forgot I had my eyes open and hadn't even looked into your eyes yet. I just need to look at your face again for a minute, even if it is a little burry." I left to go eat when the physical therapist came in. She had physical therapy twice today.

Ron came down to ICU and found my brother, Rick, visiting me without a gown.

"I have been taken out of isolation," I said. "Surprise! The nurses only gown up now when they are going to change my packs. I'm getting off the circle bed too. Hallelujah!"

I was having a lot of pain in my legs, and the nurse got me something for it. I was wheeled out of my room on the circle bed and a regular hospital bed with electric controls was moved into my room. With the help of nurses, I walked into the room and got into bed. This was proof that I was getting better. I was hungry, so that was a good sign too. I ran not only the bed controls but also the TV by myself. Wow, what an accomplishment! I went from not being able to touch my thumb to my other fingers to running controls on a hospital bed and TV. Amazing!

From Ron's journal:
PRAY
July 1, 1976 (Day 63)
8:00 a.m. Getting brakes fixed at Sears.
9:30 a.m. Came up to see Jenny. She's sleeping. They just got her turned to her back. Temp. 100.4 degrees. Already eaten breakfast. They are going to take Jenny to the Hubbard Tank at 10:30 a.m. after they sterilize it. The nurse made Jenny a cake with a circle bed on it to celebrate her getting into a regular hospital bed.
In the Hubbard Tank for half an hour, three physical therapists washed dead skin and some Owens packs off. She should be pretty tired for the rest of the day. There were two whirlpools on in the Hubbard tank. She laid on her back and side. Got water in one ear, and it hurt pretty bad. I was in there the whole time. She's going to get these every day at 10:00 a.m. They transferred Jenny from her bed to another bed with a waterproof stretcher on it. They then lowered the stretcher with Jenny on it into the water by way of electronic hoist.
The Hubbard Tank held 400 gallons of water, or 1,514 liters. The tank itself was made of stainless steal and was sanitized before filled with sterile saline.
10:45 a.m. Back to her room. She opened her eyes on the way back from therapy to her room. Ate pretty good dinner. She is sleeping most of the afternoon. Went to get the car from Sears and brought Jenny a submarine sandwich with barbecue chips for supper. The nurse put a sign on Jenny's room door for visitors - two at a time and for two to five minutes only.
We both ate submarine sandwiches in Jenny's room for supper. She is still tired from therapy. We have to be <u>strict</u> about how long people stay in here. The nurses said they would have to start clamping down on visitors.
Three nurses came in to help Jenny sit on the edge of her bed while the bedding was being changed. She is very tired from therapy and the whirlpool.

I became less inhibited with things around me. I would go down for a whirlpool treatment and when the therapists or nurses brought me back to my room, even before the door closed, I would start taking off my gown. I thought, "So many doctors and nurses have already seen my 'everything', it doesn't bother me anymore to undress in front of them." I had forgotten that even though I couldn't see hospital visitors, they could still see me.

I was eating better and sleeping better. I had a scarf for my bald head and tennis shoes to wear without having them sterilized. This was progress.

Dr. Hoxtell told me, "Maybe next week we can move you to another room out of ICU. Not out of the hospital yet though. I will talk to Dr. DeMarco."

I thought they were in cahoots together to prevent me from getting out. After all they had done to get me well, I hoped that they understood I just wanted to go home to DeSmet.

July 3, 1976 (Day 65)

By the time Ron got to the hospital, I had already been put in the Hubbard Tank. Ron helped for a while.

"She will maybe be moved out of ICU the first of next week," Dr. Hoxtell told him. "She slept pretty well last night."

I ate a good lunch and at 1:00 p.m. Chad and Heather came in to see me and talk to me. I got up and walked around the bed with a nurse's help. I sat in a chair for a while and picked up Heather.

Ron said, "You are pretty strong to lift her."

"She ain't heavy, she's my little Heather," I said.

I got on a scale and weighed 100 pounds. I had always wanted to lose weight, but really, not like this. Ron was taking the kids to *Peter Pan* at the K-Cinema later that afternoon. Ron brought Chad and Heather back to see me again after the movie. While they were in my room, a nurse came to give me supper. I was sitting up in a chair, feeding myself. I felt it would scare the two little ones even more if I were being fed. Ron took the kids to Country Kitchen for their supper and then out to Buddy and Claire's to make popcorn to bring to 'Mommy'. The kids and Ron came back at 7:30 in the evening. I ate two bowls of popcorn and drank half a can of pop. It was so good to be able to just share popcorn with my little family again. Ron left with the kids at 8:30 p.m., but I wanted to hold Heather again before they went. I lifted her up onto my legs, and after saying good-bye and telling her I loved her, she slid down to the floor. I had instant pain in my thighs and the blood started seeping through my gown. None of us knew my skin was going to be so fragile. I tried not to let Chad and Heather see the blood. It wasn't really much, but we needed to change my gown after they left. This was my child that I hadn't gotten to hold for a few months now. It was worth every drop of blood to have her little body next to me again.

The kids were being brought up to the hospital to see me more now. Each time they left, I missed them more and more. I was eating better, drinking better, walking around my hospital bed a couple of times a day, and sitting up in a chair for twenty minutes at a time. I was not getting to the chair under my own power, however. The nurses were helping me move from one place to another. Improvement? Yes, but not that much. Still, I was better than I was sixty-six days ago when I wasn't expected to live. So again I asked myself, "Was I really better? Compared to what?"

July 5, 1976 (Day 67)

Ron was still living between trying to do things with the kids and trying to be with me at the hospital. I could see why he had lost weight, but I was not sure how much. I would be moving out of ICU the next day. Dr. Hoxtell was going to talk to Dr. Meyers first about my eyes.

He said to Ron, "Maybe they will fix her eyes first and then move her out of ICU."

69

I ate everything on my tray for dinner, the first time since being admitted to the hospital. Ron felt it was going to be glad times and sad times with my moving out of ICU. I knew he had gotten used to the nurses there in the unit, but progress sometimes brought sadness with it. I started to get little blisters on my arms and legs. I freaked out, thinking the disease was starting all over again. The nurses called Dr. Hoxtell, and he said he had seen them before and that they were probably clogged sweat glands. He said he would look at them on his next rounds. He didn't seem very concerned about them.

Then the doctors started the sandwich-after-supper routine. The doctors wanted me to consume as many calories as possible in a 24-hour period. I ate supper at 5:30 p.m. and by 6:30 p.m. a sandwich showed up in my room. Most of the time I couldn't eat it because I wasn't hungry and the little white blisters were now forming in my mouth. If my younger brothers were visiting me, I just told them to eat it since there was no way I could, and they did.

July 6-9, 1976 (Days 68-71)

After sixty-seven days in ICU I was moved to the first floor. This meant new nurses and a new routine. I was still going to the whirlpool for therapy. The doctors were talking to Dr. Meyers about fixing my eyes.

I asked, "Will they put me out to cut open my eyelids?"

Dr. DeMarco answered jokingly, "Yes, they will hit you over the head." Our patient/doctor relationship was a little different from your everyday one. We and these doctors had survived something they had never seen before and probably would not see again.

They gave me a cane to walk with now. Dick and Priscilla sent flowers to my new room. I got to use a bathroom for the first time in over two months. The song *Celebrate! Celebrate!* came to mind but I was not dancing to any music yet.

70

The ICU nurses came down to see me when they got a chance. I was told the catheter would be removed soon. One more step forward and hopefully, I would continue improving. Walking was something I needed to do with two nurses assisting me. My muscles were barely strong enough to keep me upright but I was working hard to get home. Not only were my muscles weakened or practically nonexistent, but I needed to trust the nurses when they said there were no steps in front of me to fall down, just the straight flat hallway.

"Are you sure there are no steps?" As I felt the floor in front of me with my foot outstretched, the nurses assured me over and over that they would not let me fall and that there were no steps. Trust is something very hard to do when you can't see and someone is asking you to take steps out on a walkway. Eventually, I walked along and learned to trust, all a part of God's plan. First trust in God, then in others.

What the doctors told me about removing the catheter proved to be mostly hopeful thinking. When the actual doctor in charge of that situation came in, he had a whole different plan. The catheter would stay in until I could get up by myself to use the bathroom. My sheets were being changed every three hours now.

Dr. Meyer hadn't decided what to do about my eyes.

I thought, "They don't want to tell me I'm going to stay this way. Blind." I wished they would just tell me so I could get over the grief and deal with it. At the same time I wanted to believe that my eyes could be fixed. Dr. DeMarco introduced me to other doctors as his "most famous patient". I never wanted that distinction. I started to have muscle spasms due to prolonged immobility. The x-rays of my back were negative, however, so it was nothing serious.

From Ron's journal:
PRAY
July 10, 1976 (Day 72)
10:10 a.m. Jenny was already at the whirlpool.
I brought her a radio. I see they found her brown scarf they said was 'lost'. She slept good except for when they changed sheets last night. Spent half an hour in the whirlpool this morning. Dinner will be here about 12:00 or 12:30 p.m.
Jenny ate chili and cheese and crackers for dinner. Dr. Meyers hasn't been here this week yet. He better come next week (first part) so she can see what she's doing. I went to the Mall this afternoon.
5:30 p.m. Jenny ate supper. Said she wants to get out of here. She's kind of depressed, but gets over it easy. She has some itching and asks for something to help that. She said she wants to walk tonight to get stronger. Went to the refrigerator by nurse's station and then sat in her chair for half an hour. Dr. Hoxtell hasn't been in yet tonight. Jenny is tired.

July 11, 1976 (Day 73)

Ron got to the hospital at about 9:30 a.m. The nurse reported to him, "Jenny had a pretty good night except for itching. She didn't order breakfast yesterday, but they sent up a tray anyway. She didn't want any of it."

Ron helped me plan the menu for the next day, but I didn't order breakfast again. I was just not a breakfast person. The nurses were going to sit me up in a chair while they changed my sheets. Dr. Hoxtell wasn't here last night, but would be here today.

When he came in and looked at my skin, I asked him, "Can you try to get Dr. Meyers here tomorrow to look at my eyes?"

Dinner came, but I didn't feel like eating.

Dr. Hoxtell said, "You should eat something later today at least. I will be back tomorrow and check on your appetite."

Ron went out to watch Joe's baseball game. He was back at the hospital by 3:00 p.m.

The nurse told Ron, "Jenny didn't eat anything. She did walk in the hall until she got dizzy and said she had to go back to bed. We would like her to be up more than she is."

Ron said, "I will try to convince her to do that."

At 6:00 p.m. I ate a supper of roast beef, gravy, hash browns, corn, ice cream, and milk while sitting in a chair. I actually sat there for about forty-five minutes. Then a nurse came in and took me for a walk. We walked down to the refrigerator at the nurse's station and back, then I went to bed.

The nurse told Ron, "She's getting better at walking each day."

"Good," said Ron, "I hope Dr. Meyers comes tomorrow to look at her eyes."

Later that evening we ordered a small pepperoni pizza from Pizza Hut. I had hoped it wouldn't be cold when it arrived in an hour and it wasn't. Ron and I had pizza and pop together. It was a simple meal and nice to have Ron sharing it with me. The nurse was going to change my bed, so Ron said goodnight and left.

From Ron's journal:
PRAY
July 12-13, 1976 (Days 74-75)
10:00 a.m. Jenny was just going to whirlpool. She got back at 10:45 a.m. In pool for 25 minutes until she got cold. Dr. Hoxtell was in and looked at the sides of her legs. He said everything is filling in good. He and Dr. DeMarco said it won't be long until Jenny is out of here. Dr. Meyers will have to get her eyes open first and she has to get a little more steady on her feet.
12:20 p.m. Dinner came. They sent two sandwiches. Jenny ate one and I ate the other. She didn't want anything else. She took 1 bite of cake and drank a carton of milk. I ate the rest of her dinner. I stayed here all day, may go golfing tomorrow.

5:30 p.m. Supper came. Jenny ate pretty good. The nurse was going to give Jenny some water, poured from her glass to Jenny's glass and Jenny moved the glass. The nurse poured a whole glass of water on Jenny. The bedding had to be changed. Jenny walked down the hallway but not quite as far as the refrigerator as she got dizzy.

8:30 p.m. Said good-night then left and went to Joe's baseball game.

I was still getting dizzy at times when I walked, so I tried to eat as much as I could, but I got full so quickly. Ron came and went as often as he could and still kept a relationship going for himself and the kids. Thank God for those who were taking care of Chad and Heather while we couldn't.

I was walking better using a four-legged cane. I still slept a lot after activity. I was able to start feeding myself, which was quite an accomplishment to learn to eat without seeing where my food was located. The catheter was bothering me, and we found out that there was an infection causing me pain. Claire brought popcorn out and baked Ron a peach pie. The catheter was changed so that helped. Everyone was trying to get the eye doctor to come and look at my eyes again. Ron was threatening to go out to Dr. Meyers' office to talk to him.

July 15, 1976 (Day 77)

I was in the whirlpool almost daily. I was sitting in a wheelchair when Ron and Chad came.

I told Ron, "Last night they moved everyone out into the hall when the tornado warning siren went off."

Ron helped me plan my menu for the next day. It was so good to hear Chad's little voice.

"Dad and I are going to the zoo this afternoon," he told me.

"That sounds like so much fun." I thought this was a good idea and wished in my heart I could go too.

Ron finally got a hold of Dr. Meyers about my eyes. He said, "I'm on vacation."

So Ron talked to Dr. DeMarco. I got the feeling that Dr. Meyers didn't want to have anything to do with my eyes.

I said to Ron, "If he doesn't want to come out to look at me, he should just say so. Then we will quit calling him."

I walked all the way around the nurse's station while Chad, Ron, Joe, and Jon went to the zoo. I lost another toenail, my big one.

I said to Ron, "I'm going to keep bugging the doctors about getting my eyes fixed, and when they get tired of me calling, maybe they will do something for me."

The dinner trays came up, and the nurse had an extra tray, so Ron ate that one. I would get cold from drinking milk or any cold foods.

I told the nurses, "If Dr. DeMarco or Dr. Hoxtell come in, I want to see them so they can get Dr. Meyers to come in and at least look at my eyes."

Dr. DeMarco came in and reported, "Dr. Meyers will be by tomorrow. We got a hold of him at home, and he said he would be here."

I walked around the 'block' after supper. The block was the section of rooms inside the hospital.

I saw Ron and said, "You have red and blue on. That's not much better than red and yellow."

Dr. DeMarco asked me, "Can you see me?" Turning my head from side to side, trying to catch a glimpse of him, I replied, "No, but I can see light where the door is."

"Would it have been better four or five weeks ago to try and pry her eyes open?" Ron asked.

Dr. DeMarco said, "No, she probably would have gotten a corneal infection."

I said, "I can't see anything with my left eye, not even light."

"Let's pray, and I will leave so you can rest," said Ron.

75

July 16, 1976 (Day 78)

Ron called me from Elmwood Golf course. He, Buddy and Joe had gone golfing. I reported to Ron that I had French toast, juice, Rice Krispies, and milk for breakfast and that I had gone to the whirlpool for ten minutes.

Ron got to the hospital at 1:00 p.m. just as I was going down to therapy to walk so he came along. I walked three different times with rest in between for this session. I did pretty well, only I wished Dr. Meyers would come to open my eyes so I could see better. That was pretty frustrating. I was depressed that he didn't come up here and see me. I had a casserole for dinner. I knew I had to eat to get stronger and leave, so I did the best I could with each meal.

That afternoon, Ron called Dr. DeMarco.

I asked Ron, "What did he say?"

"He said Dr. Meyers will be out of town for another week, and he will get another eye doctor here within twenty-four hours." I asked for a painkiller for my eyes. They were starting to hurt me.

I called Dr. Kepes, ophthalmologist that Dr. Hoxtell said might be able to check my eye condition.

I asked him, "Will you come out to the hospital and evaluate my eyes?"

"I don't want to step on anyone's toes and do something with your eyes until Dr. Hoxtell says so."

I thought, "No one wanted to just flat out tell me what my gut was already letting me know. I was going to be blind. I would have some vision, but it was not going to be as good as I wanted." Mentally I was not dealing with all of these new hurdles life was giving me.

Ron started feeding me supper one evening when Dr. Kepes came in and examined my eyes.

He said, "The corneal membranes are growing together. Left eye is bad, right eye might be okay. I wouldn't dare do anything to her eyes right now. She will be dismissed from the hospital before anything is done to her eyes. Nature is the best healer. It is best if her eyes are closed rather than opened." It didn't take him five minutes. He looked and left.

Ron paused to get his emotions under control. I didn't eat the rest of my supper. I knew I would be blind. I was afraid Ron wouldn't want me anymore if I was blind. Ron tried to convince me otherwise, but it didn't do much good. I wanted to see my kids grow up. Ron told me I couldn't give up on my eyes. I only said that he wouldn't want me anymore, and I wouldn't blame him if he didn't. Then my mind went wild. How was I going to take care of the kids? I was devastated. I always wanted to believe I would not be blind. I could not imagine being able to do anything as a blind person. I wondered what God had planned for me? He knew this stubborn woman would not give up, even though I myself didn't. I didn't even know all that our families did to help Ron during this summer of change. Ron called Buddy and Claire to come and help deal with our disappointing news.

"Ron, I don't expect you to stay with me," I said. "You can find someone else to marry and help raise our kids."

Ron said, "We are not going to talk this way."

"I know, but how am I going to do anything? How could I take care of Chad and Heather, attend their school functions, and enjoy life without sight? Oh God, help me," I cried.

After I calmed down, Ron went over to McKennan Café and brought me back a barbecue and French fries. I drank a Coke too. I walked around the nurse's station after getting up and sitting in a chair so the nurse could change my bedding. I was mad.

"Why didn't anyone tell me this a long time ago? I have had enough," I fumed.

I thought to myself, "I'm getting out of this place."

Ron was leaving for the night. I had to find a way to absorb and deal with this new development. I continued to say I wanted honesty, now I have to live with the truth I didn't want to hear. So I prayed. Although I was devastated, I knew that falling apart was not going to accomplish anything. I believed the doctors were putting off telling me what they all knew, that I was going to be blind. No one could help me with my eyes, either to get them opened again or give me clearer vision. What was I going to do? Get out of the hospital was the first order of business. I was going to work hard in therapy and eat as much as I could to gain weight and strength and get out of there.

The next days were filled with therapy, eating as much as I could, walking, whirlpools, and doctors telling me I could probably go home in a week. Ron was trying to spend more time with the kids. This was great, except I wanted to do that too. I was feeding myself, since I had to learn how sometime. I was getting Demerol for pain yet. I was not sure how real the pain was or whether I was just trying to get away from the reality of blindness. I was continuing to improve in therapy, balancing was hard on my tiptoes. I was always hurting by the time I got back from walking or therapy but I was determined to get out of the hospital and go home. I was not sure how I would do things at home or what I would be able to do. One step at a time.

I did a lot of sleeping in between the therapy. I was allowed outside. It seemed if it was cold outside, I was cold. If it was hot outside, I was hot. Dr. Hoxtell wrote a prescription for an air conditioner for our home in DeSmet to help regulate my temperature. Everything upset me. I didn't understand the reason I was alive if I couldn't see to do anything.

I thought stubbornly, "Okay, if this is how it is, then get used to it, quit whining, and get on with life. Figure it out. There will be a way to do things while not looking. There just has to be."

Then, as I would get tired and the darkness never ended, I once again crawled into my bed and faded away into a Demerol haze.

July 23, 1976 (Day 85)

Ron was at the hospital by 9:30 this morning. I was at the whirlpool.

When I got back, I said, "I am going to change my whirlpool time back to 10:00 a.m. I just can't get awake before then."

Ron brought me a fried roll, and I had some milk for breakfast. He said, "I am going to bring you something back from Burger King for dinner."

Dr. Hoxtell came in early. He didn't say too much.

Dr. Schnore, from urology, came in and told the nurse, "Get a urine specimen to see if this patient has any infection."

Dr. DeMarco was on rounds and I asked him, "When can I go home?"

He said, "Soon. I have to talk to Dr. Hoxtell first. You're doing well. I see you had Demerol last night for pain in your legs before you could go to sleep."

Ron helped me plan a meal menu for the next day. I was going to rest as I usually did after my whirlpool treatment.

Ron brought food from Burger King. We ate dinner, and then my tray from the hospital was delivered. I ate some cake and drank a little coffee. The nurse took a urine sample to see whether there was any infection in my bladder. I went down to therapy and walked the steps to outside. Then we went down and visited the ICU nurses.

All the nurses down there left their patients and came to talk with me. When I got back to my room, I got a shot of Demerol. The therapist gave me a one-legged cane to use when walking at night.

She said to Ron, "You should take Jenny for walks and get her outside this weekend."

So we went for a walk after supper. I ate the sandwich and drank some milk. I walked again to the elevators and back with Ron. I asked for Demerol when I got back to my room. I would go to the whirlpool at ten in the morning again. We prayed and Ron left.

From Ron's journal:
PRAY
July 24, 1976 (Day 86)
10:00a.m. Got to the hospital. Jenny's just ready to go to whirlpool. She's still upset from last night when Dr. Hoxtell wouldn't give her anything for pain. He only ordered 25mg of Demerol when 75mg doesn't even help her pain. She came back from whirlpool pretty upset and was bound and determined to go home. She was getting her blue case and wanted to go. She bent down to pick up her case and just about fell but I caught her.

She didn't use the bed pan last night at all but got up by herself and went to the bathroom. I asked her if she called a nurse. She said she wouldn't call them if she was choking to death. She called Dr. Hoxtell to get a release form to get out of here. He told her to talk to Dr. DeMarco. She doesn't itch too much. I asked her if she went home and had some pain what would she do? She said the same thing she does now. She would just have the pain because she doesn't get anything for it anyway.

Jenny didn't eat very much lunch. I made out her menu. She wouldn't because she said she wouldn't be here tomorrow.

Therapist came to get Jenny but she wouldn't go. She won't take any of her medications either. I asked her if she wanted to walk while the nurse changed her bedding. She said she would so we walked to the elevators and she wanted to get on them so we went up to therapy. She walked outside and did some steps and balancing. She got back to her room (walked all the way back) and her leg hurt her, but she wouldn't take any Demerol. She's in a lot of pain.

Dr. Hoxtell called Jenny. He didn't know anything about the Demerol. Dr. DeMarco must have taken her off it. He said she wasn't ready to go anyway because of thermal regulation of heat. He said he will give us a prescription for the air conditioner so it will be tax deductible. He said they are going to look at her eyes too. Dr. Hoxtell will be

*by tomorrow. This is the worst day I've spent in the
hospital!*

*I left and ate at Taco John's. Jenny ate a little supper, she
said she will be hungry when her sandwich comes.*

*Jenny had an itching pill last night for the first time in four
days.*

July 25-August 2, 1976 (Days 87–95)

It didn't take long before the pain drove me back to taking Demerol. I was walking farther each time Ron took me for a walk. I didn't want only 25mg of Demerol because it didn't seem to help, so I tried not to take any for as long as I could stand the pain. I was told that I would not get out of the hospital until I was more stable. I told Ron that I needed to go for a walk so I could get more stable and get out of there. I didn't know they meant mentally. Dr. Hoxtell said, "I think you will be ready to go home next week." I wondered which "next week" he was talking about. I was nervous since going home was one thing but going home legally blind was quite another. Regardless, I was pushing myself to do more each day. I needed to sleep a lot.

Ronnie Bartlett and Ron went to DeSmet to install the air conditioner so we could go home. The next week was full of walking, therapy, and eating as much and as often as I could.

"Ron," I said, "I can barely stand to swallow another bite, but if this is what it takes for me to get home, I'll do it."

August 3, 1976 (Day 96)

Dr. Knutson came to my room and said, "You can go home, but you have to wait to see Dr. Meyers about your eyes. Also, Dr. Hoxtell wants to see you back in two to three weeks. Dr. DeMarco will see you then, too."

"So, am I free to go home?"

I don't believe him. After all this time they are letting me go home. I am so excited and yet nervous because I still can't see.

I thought, "We can stop by Dr. Meyers' office and get my eyelids open and then go home to DeSmet."

Dr. Knutson smiled and said, "Yes, we are getting your paperwork together now."

I couldn't wait to be home, so everything could get back to normal. Many of the nurses from ICU came to say good-bye to us and wished us luck. It was a moment of gladness and sadness.

By 11:00a.m. we were out, actually out of the hospital. It felt so good to have the sunshine on my face again. We went to Buddy and Claire's where Ron's parents were bringing Chad and Heather. We had lunch then were on our way home by early afternoon.

The trip was uneventful. We talked about what we would do when we got home and the kids were excited to play with toys they hadn't seen for over three months.

We thought we could do this, just until Dr. Meyers opened my eyelids in two weeks so I could see again. Ron was going to start meetings at school by mid-August. He struggled mentally with leaving Heather with me when he and Chad went to school.

We arrived home, Ron unloaded the car and we started to get settled. I was trying to get around the house using light from the windows and furniture to lean on in case I lost my balance. I could walk from the kitchen wall to the hallway wall by myself to get back and forth to the bathroom and bedrooms. I used a cane at times but I couldn't carry anything with a cane in my hand.

We soon found out that life was not going to be easy just because I had accepted Jesus Christ as my Savior and had been held in the arms of God. First of all, I couldn't see clearly. I had some vision, but it was blurry and cloudy, unlike I wanted it to be. I would need to find another way to do housework, cooking, laundry, and bathing the kids. I thought giving baths would be easy. At

82

least they would be confined to a tub where I could get to them quickly without tripping over anything. Well, maybe easy was not a good word. As soon as I tried doing something as simple as changing sheets on our bed, my muscles went into spasms. I had been without Demerol for a couple of days now and I got a back spasm between my shoulder blades. I was so nauseated from the pain that I started to gag. The local doctor was called and came out to the house to give me a shot of Demerol which stopped the spasms.

Two weeks after I got home, I had an appointment with Dr. Meyers. Dick and Priscilla planned to meet us in Sioux Falls and watch the kids while we saw the doctor.

He examined my eyes and told me flat out, "You are going to be blind. There is nothing we can do to fix your eyes. You have scarring on your corneas and there is no fix for that."

I cried out, "But Dr. DeMarco and Dr. Hoxtell said it wouldn't affect my eyes. You said before that it wouldn't affect my eyes."

"We were all wrong. We had never seen anything like this before and just didn't know what was going to happen. Again there is no fix for this." Dr. Meyers left the exam room.

Ron and I were devastated by this news. I fell apart. Ron was not only mad, he was ready to kill the doctor who started this nightmare. Ron helped me out to the car. I could barely walk on my own, I was so distraught. We drove out to Buddy's where Dick and Priscilla met us. I was crying uncontrollably.

"I don't want to be blind. What can I do? What will I do? Oh, God, you have to help me. What will we do now?"

I was scared to death and inconsolable. I lay on a bed upstairs.

Priscilla was beside me but couldn't even find words to console me. She couldn't believe it herself. We all thought my blindness would only be for a short time, until my eyelids could be opened. We were told for ninety-six days that this would not affect my eyes and we believed the doctors.

While I was upstairs with Priscilla, Dick was downstairs trying to calm Ron down. He was fuming mad.

Ron kept saying, "That doctor did this, he needs to die." Ron was no longer scared, he was furious and wanted revenge for what had been done to us.

Dick and Priscilla started to think of other doctors that might help. They knew of an eye doctor in Yankton, S. D. and immediately called him to get a second opinion. We were given an appointment that afternoon with Dr. Tom Willcockson. We drove directly from Sioux Falls to Yankton for this appointment.

Dr. Tom examined my eyes and said, "Nothing of this magnitude has ever entered my practice before. I want to talk to Dr. Farris in New York City about your case and get his opinion and any ideas he might have regarding treatment. He's been a colleague of mine in the past and we will visit and let you know what we decide."

On the way home I thought, "Thank God, I am going to get help. I am going to see again."

Ron drove home in silence.

Dr. Willcockson called a few days later. We would have to travel to New York City for a surgery. Before that happened, we made many trips back and forth to Sioux Falls. Each time I was admitted to the hospital, I was not sure what the diagnosis would be. I was given daily Demerol injections at home, and they were probably trying to cut my doses down.

From the cover of Ron's second journal:
Into hospital April 29, 1976
Out of isolation June 30, 1976
Out of ICU July 6, 1976
Out of hospital August 3, 1976
In hospital August 31, 1976
Out of hospital September 10, 1976
In hospital September. 16, 1976

I was admitted all of these times back into the Sioux Falls hospital where everyone knew me and I had more attention. I was not sure whether there was actually anything wrong with me, but I was kept for six to ten days each time.

Ron said, "I think the doctors are trying to decrease the Demerol or get you off it altogether."

One more thing we weren't to worry about was now a fact, drug addiction. We found out that I was not able to care for Heather at home, or cook, or clean. Food preparation was another hurdle. Peeling potatoes and getting all the skin off and the eyes out was a challenge. Ron would help by doing the finishing work on peeling vegetables and grilling so I didn't have to do a lot. I just wasn't strong enough for a full eight hours of working.

Ron spoke to his mom and dad. My parents were still working, and Ron's parents were partially retired, so they decided they would close up their home and move into ours to take care of us and they did just that. They were angels by coming in and lending a hand, not asking for anything in return. Grandma and Grandpa Peterson cared for our home, Heather, and me during the day. They entertained Chad and Heather after school because most of the time I was too drugged to do it myself. They would watch *The Little Rascals* and *Captain 11* with the kids. After supper, Grandma would sit with a coloring book on her knees, and as she colored one page, Heather, now three and kneeling in front of Grandma's legs, colored the other page. Chad, now six, played rummy with Grandpa. Grandpa loved to play cards, and rummy was a game he taught many of the grandchildren. Once in a while, they beat him too.

Our laundry room was in the basement, so Grandma would put dirty clothes in a pillowcase and throw it down the steps so she wouldn't fall going down carrying a basket. Grandpa went to the grocery store and the gas station just to get out of the house.

Grandma asked me one day, "What can I fix for you that you will eat?"

"A can of corn over a piece of buttered bread," I answered.

"Uff dah, I'm not sure what that is," she said.

Since I needed to gain weight, she listened carefully as I explained. "Butter the bread and put it in a bowl. Drain some of the juice off a can of corn and put enough milk in the pan to cover the corn. Then heat the corn on the stove and pour it over the bread."

I ate the whole can of corn that way, the most I had eaten at one time in months. I had no interest in watching TV or coloring since I couldn't see. Actually, I had no interest in life of any kind. This was no way to raise a family, or even to live for that matter. I was trying to convince myself that I was going to get over the blindness and see again in just a little while. Then at the end of each day, as evening came and I was still blind, I started to "need" a shot of Demerol. A nurse would come from the hospital about two blocks away and give me a shot. This went on for about six weeks after being released from the Sioux Falls hospital.

September 28, 1976

We went on our first trip to New York City for my appointment with Dr. Linsy Farris, ophthalmologist and surgeon, at Presbyterian Medical Center in Harlem. This doctor was going to help restore my sight. I was thrilled and couldn't wait to see Ron and the kids again. Our appointment was in September for a pre-op exam by Dr. Farris.

He said, "We can do a new procedure called a Cordona Keratoprosthesis in your left eye as it seems to have had the most vascular scarring to the cornea." I couldn't see much light through the heavy scarring on the cornea and actually could see more through my right eye. This

86

appointment started a series of eight trips to New York City. I thought after one surgery I would be back to normal. Normal eyes, normal vision, normal life. It wasn't to be. Furthermore, normal was never mentioned by any of the doctors. I heard it only in my heart.

From Ron's journal:
PRAY
October 18-19, 1976
First Surgery left eye, Cordona Implant
Priscilla, Dick, Jenny and I fly to New York City. We flew over the Statue of Liberty and Manhattan and landed at LaGuardia Airport in Queens at 12:15 p.m. We checked into rooms at Holiday Inn. Planes took off and landed every minute over the motel. No one rested very well. Jenny has to be at the hospital on the morning of October 19.

We had started for the hospital when Ron said, "Cars, cars, cars everywhere. We are going over the Triboro Bridge to get to the hospital."

I wasn't interested. I couldn't see anything. The traffic noise was overwhelming. We arrived and Dr. Farris examined me. He said, "You are going to be admitted today and have surgery tomorrow. What we plan to do during this surgery is remove the lens of your left eye and put a Cordona Implant in through the front of your cornea."

"What is the Cordona Implant?" Ron asked.

Dr. Farris explained, "The Cordona Implant consists of a round, plastic apparatus shaped like an old telephone dial with holes around the edge. The middle threads screw the optics into the front part through the cornea. The telescope in a plastic tube, also with threads, flips the picture coming back from the optic nerve and allows the patient to see images upright."

I was nervous, yet I knew I needed to do this to see again. I was praying, asking God to let me see.

87

October 20, 1976

After surgery I came out of the procedure in screaming pain and sick from the anesthesia.

"Please give me something for this pain," I said to the recovery nurse.

"We have given you everything we can here in recovery," she said. "You need to get to your room before you can have any real pain medications."

I said through clenched teeth, "Then get me there."

After surgery, Dr. Farris reported to Ron, "The surgery was a success. She needs to stay in the hospital for five days, after that, home for three months to heal. Then you will need to return for another surgery to remove the covering from her eye."

"Will she see then?" Ron asked.

"There is a good chance the way this surgery went, but time will tell," answered Dr. Farris.

It rained all day. After I had gotten settled into a room, Ron, Dick, and Priscilla went grocery shopping for the apartment they were staying in.

I thought, "Oh, how I wish I could go too, but I won't be able to see anything so what difference does it make?"

I argued with myself, reminding me that life was not the same, wouldn't be the same, so let others enjoy the sights and don't be a burden.

October 21, 1976

Dick, Priscilla and Ron came to check on me. I told them I was fine and to go see the sights. They went to the top of the Empire State Building, down 5th Avenue, and stopped in a Macy's Department store. They went to Madison Square Garden and saw Toots Shores. The bus ride back to the hospital from Harlem was one-and-a-half hours long. After the three of them told me about their day and left for their room, I was lonely.

A noise going down the hallway of the hospital was the wheels on a cart. It stopped outside my room. A volunteer stepped to my door. "I have reading material, would you like anything?" she asked. Then she was silent. As I turned my head towards her voice, she continued, "I have just gotten a player from a patient who was dismissed. The book they were reading may not be interesting to you but would you like to listen to it?"

I hesitated to answer.

"If you don't like it you can always turn it off and I will get it on my next rounds."

"I would like to listen to it," I told her.

The machine was set up and she explained the buttons and their function. I found I enjoyed listening to books. This was how I could deal with blindness. I could escape being blind by reading.

October 22-23, 1976

Once again I encouraged the three sightseers to go and see New York City. I told Ron, Dick, and Priscilla, "Go ahead. No need to stay with me. I'll probably sleep most of the day anyway." They came back each afternoon tired and excited with things to tell me. I was thankful that I didn't go along, all that walking and me not able to see any of it. There was always some little thing to give thanks for.

From Ron's journal:
PRAY
October 24, 1976
Today is a day of rest for us sightseers. Dr. Farris comes in and examines Jenny's eye. "I think you can go home tomorrow," he said. Jenny almost jumps out of bed with the news.

We got flights back home the next day at 2:00 in the afternoon. It was drizzling outside as Dick, Priscilla, and Ron packed their bags. I was thankful to go home. After I was released from the hospital, I told them one reason that I was so thrilled to be out of there. A nurse had come in to take my vitals and check on my pain level. Before leaving my room she said, "Can I get you anything else?"

I was thirsty and asked her, "Could I get a can of pop?"

"What do you need?"

"A can of pop, a soda, something to drink," I repeated.

"What the hell for?" was her response. I tried not to ask her for anything else that wasn't necessary.

"That's why I was really ready to go home."

On the flight home I start thinking, "I thought I was going home with vision but that isn't how it went. Three months of healing, another surgery and then, I will be able to see."

I started to ask a few people, "Do you know what God has planned for me? Do you think He ever let's people see again?"

They answered, "I just don't know."

But mostly, I heard doubt and pity in their voices.

From Ron's journal:
PRAY
January 18–25, 1977
Second surgery on Jenny's left eye to remove covering.
Buddy travels with us to New York.

The surgery to remove the covering was a success and the next day Dr. Farris came in to remove my eye patch. Buddy and Ron stood together at the end of my bed. As the patch was partially removed by Dr. Farris and partially by Ron, I saw bits and pieces of their faces. Ron handed me a newspaper and I read, *Jimmy Carter Inaugurated.* I looked to the end of my bed and Buddy stood there with tears in his eyes. Ron was by my side and our eyes met. We smiled at each other. This was so great. I bowed my head and said, "Thank you, God, for letting me see."

I lifted my head to thank Dr. Farris, but he was gone. I was not sure if he took offense to the fact that Ron was testing my eyes or if he wanted to be thanked first before God, or if he just wanted to give us a minute to enjoy the sight he had restored for me.

We flew home after a day or so in the hospital. Grandma Peterson had supper prepared when we got there. Chili, yes, good homemade chili. It looked beautiful in the bowl in front of me with crackers along the side. I could see the little holes in each cracker and the beautiful yellow-gold cheese. My prayer that night was full of awe and thankfulness. God does hear and answer prayers.

Heather, with her little pink pom poms made out of yarn, did her wrestling cheer for me. She jumped up and down and ran in place yelling "W-I-N! We want a pin! W-I-N! We want a pin!" She shook those little pom poms and yelled at the top of her voice. How sweet it was to be able to see her again. Chad, being a little older, showed me school papers and some of his action figures and other cars and toys. The Incredible Hulk, the Dukes of Hazzard and Evil Kneivel, who jumped everything from cars to the Grand Canyon with his motorcycle, were some of his favorites.

The next morning it was good to be able to walk through the house turning my head from one thing to another to make sure I hadn't missed anything. I opened the cupboard door to get a coffee cup. There in the upper cabinet on a double wide shelf, I saw prescription bottles. Ron was standing beside me as I looked at that shelf full of prescription drugs.

"Whose drugs are these?" I asked.

"Yours," Ron answered.

"What are they all for?"

"They are pain pills, muscle relaxers, nerve pills, that sort of stuff," he told me.

"Are any of them for my eyesight?"

"No," Ron said. "The new medications are in your case."

"We don't need these around here," I said. "Let's get rid of them."

That very day, I took all the bottles, the pain drugs, the muscle relaxers, all the addictive type drugs, and dumped them out.

With determination I stated, "I am not going to let anything control my life. I most certainly don't need them for life sustaining purposes. I can do without them."

I praised God for giving me the strength, and stubbornness, to stick to my decision. I now began reading myself to sleep instead of drugging myself. I was turning my life over to God, each and every part of it.

Buddy and Claire and their kids came up for the weekend. The series *Roots* was on TV. We sat down to watch it and they tested me to see how well I could see.

"What do you see in this scene?" they asked.

As I described what I could and couldn't see, it was amazing to be able to watch TV again. I had eyesight, but there were so many problems with adjustments to the implant. Rejection and risk of infection kept Ron busy running me back and forth to see Dr. Willcockson in Yankton. Also, I had to carry sterile Q-tips around to wipe off the drainage that ran over my implant and constantly obscured my vision.

Dr. Willcockson saw me in April for a routine checkup. He said, "I think you are trying to reject the implant, and if we don't get you back to New York to see Dr. Farris, I'm afraid you will lose your vision." He set up an appointment for me to see Dr. Farris. Ron had to get out of school for these days. Grandma and Grandpa Peterson stayed with Chad and Heather and we flew to New York again. Dr. Farris wanted to do surgery immediately. I reluctantly agreed. This vision was not as good as I wanted it to be. It was better than nothing but a bit of a hassle. On top of that, my eye looked like a chicken eye and not very attractive. My eye definitely was not normal in any way. When children saw me for the first time, they stared opened-mouthed, braces hanging on the edge of their teeth, unable to look away. I tried to smile at them for reassurance that it was 'okay', but some days I wondered. We went home after my surgery with my eyelids sewn shut. They would remain that way for a month. I didn't like it, but whatever it took to see again.

At the end of the school year, Ron came home and got Heather and me so we could be at Chad's first grade field day and picnic. The swelling in my eyelid had not gone down enough to allow my eyelid to open in the middle, so I couldn't see anything, but I was there. We walked arm in arm across the football field through the field day festivities to where Chad's class was participating. I got glimpses of light, bright light, and then green grass on the field. My eyelid started to open just enough so I could catch a peek of all the school kids out on the football field and track area, running races, participating in games, and just flat out having fun. Wonderful! Marvelous! My heart jumped with joy. I looked down and saw Heather's little form walking beside her daddy. I only got a quick glance, though, because for the most part my eyelid was still sewn shut, not allowing me to see anything clearly or for long periods of time. It depended on how my eyeball would move the little implant away from the opening in my eyelids. It reminded me of being in a dream when you see something so close you could touch it, but just as you reach out your hand, it either disappears or moves just out of reach again. I knew underneath the closed lids, there was sight, and I thanked God for that. Everything was going to be okay. Someday, we would get back to living normally again.

We returned to New York City to have the stitches removed. Dr. Farris assessed the situation then said, "I think we have stabilized the Cordona Implant, however, I am going to leave your eyelid sewn shut around it for extra support."

I was not happy with my eyelids sewn shut with just this Cordona Implant sticking out in the middle of them. But I could see, so what did it matter what it looked like. Well, it mattered to me. I wanted to have "normal" eyes. That didn't seem to be in God's plan for me.

Dr. Farris checked my vision on the eye chart. With the Cordona Implant, my vision was 20/20 distance and 20/25 reading. He was very pleased and released me to fly home.

Once again I had vision to see the faces of my loved ones. We flew home and it was so great to see the kids again. Heather was doing her cheer leading and Chad showed me all his action figures again.

Ron's parents had to go to Centerville for an anniversary celebration and to check on their house. They left on Friday since Ron would be home until Sunday. I was getting stronger all the time, and when they returned, I had fixed supper. We had roast, potatoes and carrots, but no gravy. They were surprised by my ability to do this, and after the kids were tucked in for the night, they began to discuss the possibility of their going home to stay.

"I can see you are doing lots better," Grandma Peterson said. "Do you think you can do the house chores by yourself now if Ronnie helps?"

"I think so," I said. "It is all I have to do, so even if it takes me all day, it shouldn't matter. Heather can help me too."

Grandpa and Grandma Peterson decided to go home in a day or so for good. It seemed like a lonely house without them. We had been so blessed by their patience and giving of themselves and their time. Hopefully, some day, we would be able to return the gift they gave to us.

I had pretty good vision with this implant, 20/25, but it was like looking down the barrel of a shotgun. So if I was not looking directly at something, I didn't see it.

It was springtime and Heather wanted to go outside. I instructed her not to leave the yard. I listened for her voice and talked to her often. Then it was quiet. I panicked.

"Heather, where are you?" I yelled out the door.

"I'm in the sandbox," she called as I heard her little feet pounding the ground as she ran back from the neighbor's yard. I made her come inside and lectured her on listening.

At my next regular appointment, Dr. Willcockson thought my implant was doing okay. He didn't feel the right eye was looking good and felt I should go to New York and have Dr. Farris look at it. Dr. Willcockson told us, "The eyelid is growing down to your eyeball and leaving less and less space for you to see. I fear eventually if we do nothing to stop the scar tissue, it will completely close your eye. I will call and talk to Dr. Farris and see what he suggests." After half an hour or so Dr. Willcockson came back.

"Dr. Farris thinks you need to come to Harkness Eye Institute. He will release the eyelid from the eye ball and make a scleral shell for you to wear all the time."

"How long will this take?" Ron asked.

"You will need to stay a month. Dr. Farris will have optics in the front of the shell and perhaps this will improve your ability to see also."

"Wow, another month away from the kids. When does this end?" I thought.

Dr. Willcockson instructed, "Bring your prescription from your eye glasses you used to wear when younger. They will use that for the optics."

"Will this help my balance? I seem to have trouble with steps and walking on uneven ground," I explained.

"I'll discuss this with Dr. Farris and we will see," he replied.

We called and set up flights for May after Ron was out of school.

May 28, 1977

We left Sioux Falls in a heavy fog. We landed at O'Hare and a wheelchair service picked us up and took us to TWA where we were served rolls, coffee, and fruit sections. Before boarding, there was a problem that some of our ticket receipts had been torn out of the book. Finally getting our tickets approved, we were on the plane where we were served lasagna for lunch. We landed at LaGuardia in New York. A very friendly lady, a New Yorker, sat beside us on the plane and offered her assistance if we needed it. We went straight to the Holiday Inn and found the prices just as outrageous as ever.

"We just paid $7.51 for lunch," Ron said, "and all we ate was a club sandwich each."

May 29-31, 1977

Ron and I took a cab to Rockefeller Center. We went to the top of the Empire State Building, Macy's Department Store, and Madison Square Garden. We were eating at Mama Leone's when Ron said, "It's way too dark in here, and this is more expensive than Holiday Inn."

We were waiting, like many others for a cab. A Japanese man, who stood by us, using sign language asked to share our cab. He too was going to the Holiday Inn. We agreed and he showed his appreciation once again with sign language.

Dr. Farris called to confirm my appointment on Tuesday at 12:15 p.m. Ron thanked him and said good-bye.

"What do you think of going on the Circle Line Tour tomorrow?" Ron said.

"Sure."

It rained in the night. We had breakfast downstairs. The Japanese man who shared our cab the day before saw us. He bowed slightly and gave Ron a gift of a small decorated fan to show his appreciation. We went back to the Holiday Inn by way of Times Square, 42nd Street, and Queens Midtown Tunnel. It was time to rest for my appointment the next day.

We arrived at the Harkness Eye Institute at 11:00 a.m. Ron had to take me to different floors for x-rays, blood tests, and an EKG. We finally saw Dr. Farris, who said he would not do anything to my left eye.

"I don't want to jeopardize the sight you already have," he said. "Your vision tested 20/20 distance and 20/25 reading. I am going to give you a prescription for glasses. You have fifteen percent side vision, or forty degrees. This is probably what is affecting your balance."

My surgery was set up for Wednesday at 2:20 that afternoon. It would consist of a conjunctival plasty with a scleral shell molding and possibly a mucus membrane graft in my right eye.

"I may or may not sew your lids shut," said Dr. Farris.

"Oh please," I prayed, *"oh please don't let them sew my eyelids closed. And Lord, if you are listening, please don't let them take skin from inside my lip for a membrane graft."*

"You will be here seven to ten days. When you are released, I want to see you every two to three days to check on the progress."

Ron and I agreed. I was admitted to the hospital for pre-surgical observation. Ron was not allowed to stay, so he got a room at the Holiday Inn in New Jersey.

June 1-14, 1977

Ron caught a ride to the hospital with Dr. Farris. We spent the morning playing cards and reading. I was in surgery for two hours and recovery for twenty minutes. I was in a lot of pain afterwards due to the doughnut ring under my eyelids. They didn't sew my lid shut or take any lining out of my mouth.

"Wow," I thought, "did God hear my silent prayer?"

Back in my room, they started giving me pain medications. I slept until 7:30 that evening.

The next morning, Dr. Farris came in to check my progress. When he took the patch off my eye, I saw pretty well. The pain was less.

He said to us, "The eye is kind of swollen but looks real clear."

"I can see everything," I said.

"I will be back this afternoon to look at it again."

When he checked my eye in the afternoon, I reported, "I'm seeing double."

"It may clear up."

He offered Ron a ride to the motel since it was on his way home.

Two days after surgery Ron took the bus just across the bridge into New York City and started walking. He got to the hospital but thought it may not have been a good idea to get off the bus there. He walked fourteen blocks through some areas that didn't look very safe. He kept his head down and walked fast like he knew where he was going.

"Don't do that again," I told him.

"I won't," Ron agreed.

I was in a bit of pain again. Ron went back with Dr. Farris again this afternoon. He told me he didn't think he would come over the next day. Dr. Farris thought I could get out of the hospital on Monday. Ron called me and we visited on the phone instead of him coming to the hospital.

The next day Ron came to the hospital in a cab. I wasn't experiencing much pain. He took a cab back to New Jersey in the afternoon.

Dr. Farris offered to pick Ron up on his way by the motel. We went to Oritanni Motor Hotel after I was released. I would be seen again Thursday. Ron went to get groceries.

"I about broke my arms carrying them back to the hotel," he said. "It's too cold to go swimming, but Bloomingdale's Shopping Center is just across the parking lot. Want to go there?"

"Let's go," I said.

I was tired before long and went back to the hotel. Ron went for a walk while I rested. There was a discount store beside our hotel that he browsed through.

Ron and I went out for lunch and a walk. Once again I was pretty tired before we got back to the hotel. My endurance for activities didn't last long.

My appointment was at 3:00 p.m. with Dr. Farris. He examined me, and after he moved the doughnut ring that was under my right eyelid, the pain began. I was in so much pain he decided to admit me to the hospital. We had problems being admitted due to the fact that it was not an eye hospital. However, there wasn't a room in the eye hospital. Ron went back to the hotel and packed our things.

He moved back to the Holiday Inn. I would be transferred to the Eye Institute as soon as a room became available.

Ron settled in at the Holiday Inn and came to the hospital. The doctor was ready to mold the lens for my eye. We went to my appointment.

Dr. Farris said, "We need you to look at a point and keep your eye as still as you can."

I found a point of light and looked at it.

"You are going to feel a little pinch," he said.

The needle in my eyebrow was more than a pinch, and the injected medication burned like a hot needle as it ran around my eye socket. Then he did the bottom lid too. I almost passed out. Dr. Farris put his hand on my shoulder and said, "You okay? You did great."

I begged to differ. The lens was slid under my eyelids. I couldn't see as well with it in but Dr. Farris said, "This is partially due to the scarring that is already starting to grow over your cornea."

I felt so disappointed. I wanted to see as clear as I had after surgery. The roller-coaster ride was tiresome, sight one minute and when I wake up, it's gone.

Dr. Farris was going to release me soon because I wasn't in pain. Ron left to go to his motel room. I was released on Monday, June 13, and we went back to the Holiday Inn. I had my next appointment on Wednesday, Heather's birthday. This was my little girl's second birthday I had missed. When was life going to get back to "normal" for our family? I woke up the morning of June 14 in quite a bit of pain again.

June 15, 1977 (Heather's 4th birthday)

Dr. Farris picked us up, and I was in so much pain once again he readmitted me to the hospital. I felt the pain was triggered by the insertion and removal of the lens. I was to wear it for an hour and then remove it for two hours. We called home and wished Heather a happy birthday. She was having a good time with Grandpa and Grandma and

Chad so that was good. My heart broke to think of not being there again.

I wore the lens for two-and–a-half hours. It didn't seem to matter whether the lens was in or out. I was still in pain.

"Everything looks good," Dr. Farris said. "We plan to mold an optic into the lens today or tomorrow. I want to trim a little off the lens so it will fit better."

After he put the lens in again, it didn't hurt. So far, so good.

The next day, Dr. Farris put the lens in my eye at 6:30 a.m., and when Ron came in at 3:30 in the afternoon, I still had it in my eye. It wasn't bothering me too much. There was slight pain, but nothing I couldn't deal with.

"I think you are gradually getting used to it."

"I think trimming it off helped a lot," I replied.

Ron relaxed at the motel and went swimming. I had pain when the lens was out after having worn it for over twenty-four hours.

"You'll just have to get used to it," said Dr. Farris. "Take it out to clean it, and put it back in if that's what feels better."

Ron came over on the bus in the morning and went back with Dr. Farris in the afternoon.

I told him, "I didn't have a very good night last night. The pain in my eye is off and on, but sometimes it's really bad."

Dr. Farris said, "It may take two to three weeks to get used to the lens. I think we will just keep you in the hospital until you go home on Friday. Tuesday, for sure, we are going to mold the optics into the lens before you leave for home."

"How long will putting the optics in my lens take?" I asked.

"You will be without the lens until Wednesday, and we hope to stop the pain medications before you go home."

I had a lot of pain all night. Even though Dr. Farris said everything looked good.

I asked him, "Then why do I have so much pain?"

100

He didn't seem to have the answer to this.

I didn't sleep well the night before I was to be released from the hospital, but was able to take a nap. I had the lens with optics in and tolerated it pretty well.

"Let's go to the Holiday Inn at LaGuardia for tonight," Ron suggested. "We will be right there by the airport, and tonight we can go watch the Mets and Yankees play at Shea Stadium."

"I don't care. Just get me out of the hospital," I told him.

I was not dismissed until 11:30 a.m. because Dr. Farris wanted to examine me one more time with the lens to see how it was fitting. I finally got discharged and Ron and I took a cab to LaGuardia Holiday Inn. My instructions were to wear the lens for four hours then take it out for one hour. By afternoon, I was too tired to go watch a baseball game. Ron went without me.

We flew out of LaGuardia at 11:00 in the morning and flew into Chicago where we were an hour late for the plane leaving for Sioux Falls. We finally got onto a flight into Sioux Falls and drove to Centerville to get the kids. We were going home again. Hopefully, this would end the crazy trips and hospital stays for a while. We were finally getting used to handling life with me being legally blind. I wasn't sure how God fit into this picture, but somehow I knew He was there with us. We had a plaque given to us with the Footprints poem on it. I could just visualize Jesus carrying us through the rough times and leaving only His footprints behind in the sand. It just said it all for me.

For the next few months, we lived pretty normally. Each morning Ron would ask, "How is your eye?"

My answer was usually, "I can still see."

The kids were growing like crazy, and I loved watching them do funny things. One morning at the breakfast table, Ron announced, "Time to go to school." Chad and Heather rode to school with Ron each morning because he taught in the same school.

Heather said, "I can't find my other sock."

They were red, and we needed to find a red sock. Not too hard to do, right? But we searched and hunted and looked beneath everything Heather might have come near that morning.

Ron was fretting about being late for school, so I said, "We will just put on different socks. That will be fine."

I reached down to take Heather's sock off. "We have to hurry or Daddy and you kids will be late. Hold your foot out here."

She slowly held her foot out to me, and when I pulled off one red sock, there was a second one underneath it.

"Heather, how long have you known that you put two socks on the same foot?"

Heather, who had always had trouble waking up in the morning, said in a very small voice, "I didn't want to get into trouble when I found it."

I hugged her. "It's okay. But you still need to hurry so you aren't all late for school. Next time, you just need to tell us so we don't have to look anymore, okay?"

I realized that we needed to change how we handled things when the kids made a mistake. Surely putting two socks on one foot because you are so sleepy that you can't get dressed properly was not something a child should be afraid to tell. I was thinking of how I would yell and scream over little things, taking my frustration of being blind out on Chad and Heather and probably Ron too. I needed to make a change.

In church that Sunday I heard the minister talking about taking Jesus home with us and that Jesus was present to witness our behavior not only in the pews but outside the doors of the church. I began to pray, "Dear Lord, help me to be a kinder, more understanding mom. Let me take Jesus everywhere with me." I was determined to practice better behavior.

A Christmas party for the teachers was coming up, and I thought it was not going to be much fun. I would just sit and not be able to see much of what was going on. But there was going to be a band, and I loved to dance, so maybe it would be okay. We hired a baby-sitter and got dressed for the party. In the bathroom, I was practicing my dancing. I grabbed the towel bar and took a step back, lost my balance, and ripped the towel bar off the wall.

Ron was at the door immediately. "Are you okay? What happened?"

"Nothing," I said. "The towel bar just came off the wall. I can get it back on."

That was when I realized I could actually fix something when it broke without help. I got the towel bar back on the brackets. I didn't practice dancing again.

We attended the party. During supper I was nervous. Who was watching me, and what might they think of how I ate? I was going to try not to spill anything. People around us were laughing and joking. One teacher in particular was funny, and along with everyone else I was laughing. Then the table got quiet. I didn't know why, but I put my hand out over my drink glass and a straw hit the back of my hand. The laughter started from down the table.

"You almost got it, Jake," was one comment.

I looked in the direction of the joking teacher and asked, "Were you trying to drink out of my glass with those straws?" The entire table laughed out loud. That was exactly what Jake was doing. It was one of the best acts of acceptance I had had since going blind. I loved it, someone who dared to pick on me as a blind person. This was who I wanted people to know. I could laugh at myself too.

The next day we drove to Centerville for Christmas. The roads were not very good, but we made it driving slowly. All festive gatherings were different for us now. I had trouble with picking out food, helping the kids, and lots of other things, even with limited vision. I hoped to get better. I tried to concentrate on the fact that Jesus Christ was born for us. And He gave our family Ron to take care of us all.

January 1978

The New Year came, and I was still seeing sporadically. One morning when we woke up Ron said, "How is your eye?"

I answered, "It feels a little different somehow. Not sure I can see as well either."

I called Dr. Willcockson, who agreed to see me that day. After the exam, he said, "You are right. Looks like you're starting to reject the implant."

My heart sank. I did not want any more trouble with this implant.

"What do we do?" I asked.

"I will talk to Dr. Farris and see what he thinks. He is probably going to want to see you soon though."

Dr. Willcockson came back and reported, "He wants to see you as soon as you can get flights, within the next week or so if possible."

Ron and I both felt worn down by all the traveling, expensive flights, and hotel rooms not to mention the turmoil this was causing our family, leaving Chad and Heather over and over again. Thank God for Ron's parents. They agreed to come and stay, and Ron's brother-in-law and sister, Dick and Priscilla, were going to fly with us.

We flew out of Sioux Falls for a January 26 appointment. We landed in bad weather at O'Hare in Chicago. The announcement came over the loud speaker that the airport was shutting down due to weather. We were shuttled downtown to the Palmer House. At first, there were no more rooms, but then a manager came over to speak to us.

"I have one room for all of you to stay in," he said. "Will that be okay?"

We said, "Yes, we just need a place to rest."

We were given a suite for the night and tickets for the buffet to have dinner.

January 27, 1978

We went to O'Hare International the next morning. Ron called and spoke to Dr. Farris. He said, "We land at LaGuardia Airport at 4:30 p.m."

Dr. Farris said, "We will plan to do surgery tomorrow then. Bring Jenny to the hospital tonight."

We got a cab and went back to New York to the Medical Center. As we crossed the George Washington Bridge, the cab lurched and made a horrific noise.

"What was that?" Ron asked.

The driver guided the limping cab over to the side and onto an off ramp.

"I think the wheel fell off," he said.

"What! You've got to be kidding me!"

"No, sir," said the cabbie. "The wheel is definitely off."

He called for another cab to pick us up, and we finally got to the Medical Center. I was checked in, and Ron went back to the motel.

January 28, 1978

Ron, Dick, and Priscilla got up and went down to eat breakfast. They were looking at the décor of the rooms when an entourage of people swept past them. Looking up, they saw Mrs. Jimmy Carter getting into an elevator. Priscilla looked at Dick. "Did you just see Mrs. Carter?"

"Wasn't that her getting on the elevator?" Dick replied. "You just never know who you will see in New York City."

"Dr. Farris will pick us up at 9:30 a.m.," said Ron, "and we will stay at Maxwell Hall tonight, closer to the hospital. I'll go down and get a paper and be back."

Ron returned to the room about half an hour later. "Do you know who I just saw leaving the motel?"

"Who, someone we should know?"

"Tiny Tim."

"You're kidding," Dick and Priscilla said together.

"No kidding. He was just coming out of the elevator as I was going in."

"Wow, he hasn't been heard from since he got married on the Johnny Carson Show."

"Dr. Farris is due outside in ten minutes so we have to hurry," Ron said to them.

As they rode over the bridge with Dr. Farris, Ron asked, "What does this surgery involve?"

"We are going to do a revision of the keratoprosthesis in the left eye, possibly covering it with periosteal transferred from the right leg with lid closing. I don't know how long the surgery will take. We won't know that until we open the lids."

After I went into surgery, Ron and Dick checked on their room at the Harkness Pavilion, which Dr. Farris said would be cheaper to stay in than a motel. Priscilla stayed in the surgical waiting room just in case. The Harkness Pavilion didn't have any rooms so Ron and Dick checked into a room at Maxwell Hall. They returned and told Priscilla about the trouble they had had getting a place to stay.

"Do you want to go get something to eat before Jenny is out of surgery?" Ron asked.

They agreed and went to eat at a restaurant and buy some groceries for the room.

I was out of surgery at about 3:30 in the afternoon but in recovery for two hours.

"She is doing well and the surgery went well," Dr. Farris told Ron. "We didn't have to remove any tissue from her leg. She might be able to go home by Tuesday or Wednesday."

"Okay," Ron said. "When do you need to see her again?"

"Perhaps Dr. Willcockson will be able to do the next surgery in Yankton. Then you won't have to fly out here just to open her lids. She should be able to see through them at that time."

Ron thanked Dr. Farris for doing the surgery on Saturday. Alone with Dick and Priscilla, he said, "Three months with her eye closed. Man, the ups and downs of this is about enough."

When I came out of recovery, I was sick to my stomach from the anesthesia.

"When was the last time she ate anything?" the nurse asked Ron.

"She hasn't eaten since yesterday on the plane. She probably doesn't have anything in her stomach to throw up."

The nurse agreed that I was only throwing up bile. The retching was causing more pain, so it was a vicious circle. Once I was in a room and not vomiting anymore, Ron told me all the instructions. "Dr. Farris doesn't want you to wipe the front of your eye with your finger anymore."

I rolled my eyes. Carrying the sterile Q-tips was a pain in the neck. I was constantly laying them down and losing them. I found them everywhere and since they had been exposed to the elements, they couldn't be used.

After Ron, Dick, and Priscilla went back to their room for the night, I was scared to death. I had a rash starting on my chest. I called Ron.

"I have a rash starting on my chest."

"What's it from? Are you having another reaction to something they gave you in surgery?"

"I don't know what it's from," I cried.

"We'll be right there," he said hanging up the phone.

The nurse came in and looked at it. Ron, Dick, and Priscilla had run through the tunnels of the hospital to get back to my room. As they came into my room panting from the run, the nurse was just saying, "I think it looks like where the heart monitor was taped on. It is probably from the tape."

We were all relieved to say the least. The last thing we needed was to go through another reaction to something. I maybe overreacted to the rash so from then on I would try to calmly figure out how serious a situation was before causing chaos again.

January 30, 1978

I called Ron's room and told him I could go home the following day. They would book reservations on TWA.

"We are going sightseeing today, if you are okay."

"That's fine," I said. "I'll just sleep most of the day anyway. Go see the sights."

They went downtown, spent the day sight-seeing and rode the train back to the hospital.

The next morning rounds brought Dr. Farris into my room. After his exam he said, "Jenny is not to lift anything heavy for two to three weeks. Dr. Willcockson can take the stitches out in three weeks, however, her eye will remain shut for three months."

Now I had to accept being blind again. At least my right eye had some light perception, so I was not in total darkness. Small blessings were just something to hang on to.

January 31, 1978

We got to the airport and had to run to get on the ten o'clock flight instead of the eleven o'clock flight. As we ran, Ron and Dick each had a hold of my arms.

I thought, "I can run, but I am not allowed to lift? Go figure."

We were served western omelets or steak and scrambled eggs on the flight, but I was too sick from running to eat. When we arrived in Sioux Falls, we thanked Dick and Priscilla, said our good-byes and then drove to DeSmet. We were home again, thank goodness. Yes, I had my eye sewn shut and I was not in the best of conditions, but we were home and our kids and Ron's parents were waiting for us. In three months, I would have sight again. Thank you, Dr. Farris. And thank you, God, for sustaining us in all of this. Now if I could just tolerate this blindness until I could see again.

Chad came to me and asked, "Mommy, have you seen my Evil Kneivel?"

I answered, "Yes, it is right there on the countertop in the bathroom. Don't you see it there?"

When he went in and found it exactly where I said it was, he came running out all excited and said, "Mommy, can you see through that wall?"

"Yep, so don't try to get away with any naughty stuff."

I was not sure whether he really believed me, but from that day on I tried to bluff my way through life, laughing instead of crying (well, most of the time), enjoying what I could and not worrying about the things I couldn't do. In my own way, I was laughing at myself before anyone else could laugh at me. It was my way of coping.

Some people asked me, "Do you have a bionic eye?" "Can you see for long distances?" or "Does your eye make the sound of the Bionic Woman's, like *zing, zing, zing,* when you look at things?"

I answered them, "No, I wish it would work that well, but that is not the case." I originally thought surgery would make my eyes "normal". I soon had to give up that hope and learn to be thankful to be able to see at all.

May 8, 1978

I was ready for this trip. To get my eye opened again would be great. Three months had passed, but not quickly enough. I don't know how I had continued to do anything, let alone the laundry, ironing, dishes, and most of the cold prep for cooking while having my eyelid closed over the optics. Bring on another surgery.

This trip, Julie Nelson, Ron's niece, and a good friend, Randy, went along. It was always nice to have someone go with us to help with me. While Ron was checking in at the airport, I was given the bags to "watch". If I needed to use the bathroom, I had a woman to help me. It was just little things. We were delayed an hour and a half taking off but arrived at LaGuardia in good shape. We were planning to go to Yankee Stadium, but the game got rained out.

I thought, "That is okay with me." But the others were disappointed. I had a 12:30 appointment the next day, so I tried to rest before then.

May 9, 1978

We slept in until ten o'clock then got ready to go to my appointment. We saw Dr. Farris and checked into the hospital. Ron, Randy, and Julie were staying at Georgian Apartments.

Dr. Farris explained the surgery to us. "It is an uncovering and elevation of keratoprosthesis in the left eye under general anesthesia. It should take only forty-five minutes to an hour. We may need to go through the eyelid, but once we get started, we will be able to decide."

"Okay," I said, but I was really thinking, "I hate not knowing what is going to happen."

I convinced Ron, Julie, and Randy to go do something. It didn't take much convincing since they would be going to see the New York Yankees play the Minnesota Twins.

Randy said, "I can't damn believe it. We came clear across the United States to watch a home town team. Well, close enough, the next state over."

It rained off and on throughout the game. They got back at one-thirty in the morning to go to bed. My surgery was that morning.

May 10, 1978

I had my thirty-minute surgery. Dr. Farris didn't have to go through my eyelid, so that was great news.

"Everything went well," he said. "You can probably go home on Friday. I am going to take off the patch in the morning and check your vision to see if you can actually see. You have to leave this patch on for two weeks after surgery. Dr. Willcockson will take it off for you in South Dakota."

We agreed, but I was thinking of the two more weeks of not seeing my kids again. I felt as though I was not asking the right questions. I most certainly was not getting all the

110

information I felt I should have had. Ron, Randy, and Julie were going downtown to do some sightseeing. I encouraged them to go.

"I feel like we should maybe hang around the hospital in case something happens," said Randy.

"There is no need for you three to waste time sitting here while I sleep," I said. "Just go see the sights. How often are you going to be in New York City?" So they went.

May 11, 1978

The three sightseers were at the hospital early, and my patch was taken off. Ron wrote in his journal, *"Jenny can see!"* We were all excited. I can't wait to go home and see the kids again.

We called home to speak to the kids but Chad had already left for school. Ron visited with his mom, dad, and Heather, who was too shy to talk.

Randy, Ron, and Julie once again thought they should stay with me, but what fun was that? I told them, "You need to take advantage of the next two days and see the sights." They reluctantly agreed. Morning and night they checked on me and enjoyed New York City during the day.

May 13, 1978

Ron, Randy and Julie showed up with their bags after they turned in their room key. We were checked out of the hospital and took a cab to LaGuardia. Our flight went to Chicago and then to Sioux Falls. This was our fifth trip to New York. We were met by Ron's parents, Chad, Heather, Buddy, Claire, and their boys, Jon and Joe. It was good to be in South Dakota again. We would eventually get back to normal, or what was normal for us now. I was going to do all I could to improve our home life. I wasn't sure how I would achieve this, but that was my goal and I was asking for God's help.

111

The summer of 1978, Heather and Chad turned 5 and 7 years old. They participated in summer swimming lessons, little league baseball and girls softball. The winter was basketball games, hoop shoots and kids wrestling. Heather even wanted to wrestle like her big brother. After her first match, she came off the mat crying. She had lost. She needed to wrestle again and win to continue to participate. After her second loss, she again was crying. She said, "Mommy, I think I'll be a cheer-leader next year." I agreed and was glad she had gotten the wrestling out of her system.

Ron did the Christmas shopping and grocery and clothes shopping for us. We finished the year without problems with my eye so could just continue adapting to my being legally blind.

April 19, 1979

My brother, Rick and friend, Kirk 'Sornie' Sorensen, started a band named Clay Creek Deaf Cowboy Band. With Rick on lead guitar and Sornie on bass they played gigs around their home town. They had a drummer, and my sister Vicki sang harmony. They played benefits and dances and had a great western sound. I loved listening to their band. My dad's Uncle Russell, who raised him, was fighting a battle with cancer. The fishermen and hunters around his community of Ute, Iowa, had decided to have a fish fry for Uncle Russel's birthday and the band would play later. All of my family from South Dakota planned to attend. I rode down with my brother, Royce, and his wife. Ron was in school with the kids and planned to come to Centerville after school for the weekend to pick me up. We went to Iowa in the morning and visited with Uncle Russell and Aunt Lily. When it was time to go to the fish fry, all my siblings and dad and mom were there. The fish fry was a huge success.

The band set up their equipment and was getting ready to play when a cousin of my mom's started to play the piano. She played an old schottische tune that Grandpa and

112

Grandma Leisinger used to dance to. My mom was teaching my sister, Vicki, how to do the steps when without any warning Mom fell to the floor. Medical people who were on the scene started CPR. There was a noise coming from Mom that sounded like a gurgle. An ambulance was called from another town, but due to road construction, it took them longer than usual to get to Ute. I knelt down beside my mom and touched her hand. She was cold. I knew right then that she had died. She was only forty-eight.

I got up and went to Dad. "We have to believe she is going to be okay, Dad. You know what a miracle we have had just with me surviving this disease. We have to keep believing she will be okay."

Dad had his head down on his arms on the table, his shoulders shook with sobs under my hand. He knew Mom was gone and was devastated by the loss. We followed the ambulance to Onawa, Iowa, where the hospital was located and were given the news. Mom had died. By the time we gathered and decided to drive home to South Dakota, it was really late. We arrived in Centerville at about five in the morning.

I went into the house, and Ron said, "Where have you been? What time is it?"

I said with a shaky voice, "Mom died tonight."

In disbelief, Ron put his arms around me, and we cried together.

Over the next week, reality set in, and we all moved around in a fog. The funeral and burial were hard, but then leaving Dad alone at the farm house without Mom was most devastating to me.

In the first part of May we stopped at the cemetery to see my Mom's headstone. I felt the urge to "talk" to her and tell her I had to go back to New York. As I started to speak, my voice started shaking. It was not a good idea. My kids were crying and Ron was stunned at what was happening. I stopped, hugged the kids and Ron and said, "Now that isn't going to happen again. We will come put

113

flowers on Grandma's grave but no talking to her from me anymore." I just talked to her in my heart.

May 26, 1979

It seemed like we were meeting ourselves coming and going to New York City. Ron felt more comfortable if someone went with us to help with carry-on bags, checking suitcases, and me. Julie, Randy, and his younger brother Doug went along this time. Doug was young, and his parents weren't sure they wanted him in New York City. But Randy felt this was an opportunity that Doug should not miss to see the Big Apple, so he went along.

We arrived in New York City without problems. My appointment with Dr. Farris wasn't until Tuesday, so I was going sight-seeing.

May 27-31, 1979

While Julie was getting her makeup on and Doug was showering, Randy, Ron, and I went downstairs for coffee. We had an Asian waiter whose pronunciation of coffee was quite different from ours. He came around and asked, "Coffee, more coffee?" Randy started chuckling and had tears running down his face because it sounded more like "Cahhee, more cahhee?" Randy's laughter was contagious, and before we knew it, we were all three laughing and trying not to let the waiter know that it was his accent causing our mirth. I needed this laughter. Walking around New York City with very limited vision was not my idea of fun. I went along so as not to cause concern to the others, and I especially didn't want to ruin the trip for the three coming along just to see the sights. I could at least enjoy being with all of them.

The next morning I had a checkup and was admitted to the hospital by Dr. Farris. Ron, Randy, Doug, and Julie went to the Georgian Apartments.

My surgery went well. I was in pain and nauseated coming out of surgery. The crew hung around the hospital.

Dr. Farris told Ron, "We did a revision in the keratoprosthesis combined with a conjunctival flap and lid adhesions of Jenny's left eye. I sewed the inside and outside eyelid shut and brought the prosthesis through the center. I feel surgery went well"

"Good. I'm glad it went well. Thank you," said Ron. He turned to Randy, Julie, and Doug. "We might as well go back to our room and rest. Jenny will sleep the night through now." They left.

In the morning I woke up hearing their conversation. "I think we should hang around here for at least half the day," Randy said to Ron.

I spoke up. "There is no sense in all of you just sitting around this hospital when you should be out seeing New York City. Don't worry about me. The nurses can take care of me, and I'll be just fine."

After a short discussion, they decide to go out into the city. I was basically pain free and doing fine. I would rest more if they were not there for me to visit with, so this worked for me.

June 1, 1979

Dr. Farris said, "You're doing fine."

"You can probably go home on Sunday if you continue to progress and have no problems."

"Good, I'm ready to get back home, back to normal, so I can be with my kids again."

When the sight-seers returned I told them, "I'm actually being discharged from the hospital Saturday now. Can we change our flights?"

"We are pretty much locked into Sunday for flights. We will stay at the Kennedy Airport Howard Johnson's and be right there for our flight on Sunday."

"Okay, that works. So tell me about your day"

Ron was excited over the day's events and said, "Radio City Music Hall for the debut of New York Summer was the best thing I've seen in New York City yet," said Ron. "We went to a baseball card collector on 59th Street and

115

then to Yankee Stadium to watch the Yankees and White Sox play. Yankees won 4-0 over the Sox."

June 2, 1979

I checked out of Columbian Presbyterian Hospital and we got a cab to take us to Howard Johnson's. On the way, the cab got a flat tire and we had to wait for the cabbie to change it. We stayed at the motel to rest. I especially needed the rest. We ordered pizza for supper. A huge pie was delivered, and after paying and tipping the delivery boy, we opened the pie box. The pizza was huge. Randy described it to me.

"You just have to see this, Jenny," he said, laughing. "This pizza is huge, and I mean huge. Fifteen to twenty inches across, and it has three pepperoni pieces on the entire pie."

Randy could barely stop laughing. We all laughed with him, partly because it was contagious and partly due to being tired. I loved laughter. It was truly the best medicine.

We'd all had better pizza, but it lifted our spirits. We settled in for a game on TV.

They watched the baseball game as I fell asleep, still worn out from surgery. Moving from the hospital to our motel and just being up all day was wearing on me. Now it was time to rest for tomorrow's trip home.

Back home we got into our own routine. I found I could do most things around our home without too much assistance. God was truly teaching me that I was strong and could do all things through Christ who strengthened me.

My mom always called on Wednesdays, so when it was close to ten o'clock on a Wednesday morning, I thought, "Oh, Mom will be calling soon." But then I remembered that she would never call again. It was sad to lose a parent, but I felt worse for my dad, who thought he would live out his life with Mom and no longer had that dream.

We continued to deal with everyday life and the problems that occurred. I asked God to help with

116

everything. Someone once told me, "You are not to pray for trivial things." But the Bible said, "Not even a hair from your head is unknown to God." So I prayed to God about everything.

With Heather in first grade, I had a lot of time on my hands. I needed to do something to fill my days. I just didn't know what. Then one evening a teacher called me.

"Would you be interested in taking care of my two children while I'm in school?" she asked.

"I'm sorry," I said. "I can't do that. I can't see."

She said without hesitation, "You take care of your own kids. I trust you to do this."

"Really? You would trust me with your kids?" I was amazed.

She said, "Let's just try it. I have had my kids to five different daycare people in town, and none of them have worked out."

"Wow," I thought. "This is scary, but I supposed it wouldn't hurt to try."

"When do you want to start bringing them?" I asked.

Very quickly she replied, "Tomorrow."

I was afraid. Putting my own kids in clothes and getting breakfast was one thing, but being in charge of someone else's children was quite another.

"Lord," I prayed, "please help me take care of these kids. Don't let anything happen to them while they are in my care."

The next morning, the kids showed up. They brought their breakfast along. I had coloring books and toys. They were good kids and gave me no trouble at all. My limited vision was enough to see them, and though I couldn't read or color, I could keep them safe and play games with them, with God's help. This started many wonderful memories of kids coming to stay with me while I otherwise would have had way too much time on my hands, time enough to feel sorry for myself. At least this way I could enjoy the little things of life. I felt useful, and it was great therapy, too.

Challenging but good. There was always a laugh with kids around.

Once again life got on an even keel for us. We lived life as normally as we could. Ron got the groceries, paid the bills, and drove us shopping where he then picked out our clothes. All the things I was doing for our family involved the household chores. I washed clothes, ironed them, made meals, vacuumed the floors, dusted, and did just everyday chores. We worked on this together and eventually got back to a somewhat normal home life.

Then in the fall of 1979, I sensed something was going wrong with my implant. I had horrible pain, and nothing seemed to stop it. The pain was one of the worst migraines I had ever had. I struggled with this for about a week. The medications I took for most of these migraine headaches didn't relieve it. The pain was located in my left eye. I finally went to the doctor, who admitted me to the hospital in DeSmet. He came into my room, and before I could even get undressed and gowned, he looked at my eye again.

"You have blood coming out of the eyelids around the implant."

"I do?"

"You need to go to the eye doctor and get his opinion. I'm pretty sure this is not a migraine."

We went to Dr. Willcockson in Yankton. He examined my eye and said, "Let's put a shot into the eye to relieve the pain."

He injected the back of my eye by putting a needle through my eyelids into my eye globe. Leaving the needle end in place, he attached another syringe with a different medication in it. This injection relieved the pain.

"I think what is happening here is that your optic nerve is detaching," said the doctor.

"What can we do?" I asked.

"I will call Dr. Farris and see whether he needs to see you."

He left the exam room and came back to report, "Yes, Dr. Farris wants to see you immediately."

We called Grandpa and Grandma Peterson to stay with the kids while we went to New York again. They came immediately. Ron thought it would be good for Chad to go along this trip. He would get to see the city and historic sites. We told Heather, "When we go on the next trip, you can go along, okay?"

We got tickets for the three of us to fly. The pilot allowed Chad to sit in his seat and wear his pilot's hat.

I had a day or two before my appointment, so we went sight-seeing with Chad. My appointment with Dr. Farris was not a good one. "Your optic nerve has been blown due to the glaucoma you now have. There is really no need for you to stay in New York City to have the implant removed. Dr. Willcockson can do that for you back in South Dakota," he informed us.

We called Dr. Willcockson and he agreed to do the minor surgery of removing the implant. As we left Dr. Farris' office, he gave me a hug and wished us the best. Ron, Chad, and I decided to see some of New York City before we flew home the next afternoon.

I had had the implant for about two-and-a-half years. There was no rush in having it removed. We would do it whenever Dr. Willcockson had an opening for the surgery. The implant no longer worked, and I was trying to see through a vascular-scarred cornea.

The little telescope, or optics, was removed, but part of the implant was left in my eye. The doctors thought it better to just close the eyelid over that implant instead of removing it. They thought because of the scar tissue, it would be very difficult just to get the eyelids open, not to mention trying to remove the implant without doing extensive surgery and perhaps even damaging the eyeball and eyelids. Now my eyelid was permanently closed.

"One eye opened, one eye closed," was what the kids I baby-sat always said.

There was no surgery to help improve the vision in my right eye, and I was not going to let them do another Cordona Implant. It was too much trouble in my opinion for the amount of vision I had. I had monthly appointments with Dr. Willcockson to check my right eye. I told his interns, "The Cordona Implant was a pain in the neck, more trouble than it was worth with all the running around to keep it stabilized. Be sure to continue working on some new procedure that will let me see again."

I was not sure anyone believed as much as I did that someday I would see again. This was all a part of how I got through life without being depressed all the time. I believed that, someday, I would see again. Depression did get me down for a few days at a time, and when that happened, I took my guitar into the bedroom, closed the door, and hammered out my frustrations on that old stringed instrument, singing at the top of my lungs until, eventually, I got my head around the whole blind thing again. I always found that, before I got done strumming and singing, I would be playing the old hymns or some new Christian praise songs that my sister, Cathy, taught me. God was bringing me back to Him, comforting me through the words of the songs.

Dr. Willcockson said, "I don't think there will ever be anything in my lifetime or yours that will help you see again."

"We'll see," I said.

No one could stop me from feeling that God was in control and someday...someday.

After losing the implant, I found that I could see a little through the scarring on my right eye. It was not good sight, but at least I could see colors and objects, though not clearly. I could see well enough to take care of the house and kids, do the cooking, and wash and iron clothes. Ron was still getting groceries and shopping for clothing for the kids. I thought Ron did just fine. If things weren't perfect, it didn't matter. We were together.

Getting into the routine of managing a household blind, I started by having spare staples in the cupboard. As I took the bag of flour out of the cupboard, I added it to the list for shopping. This way, I always knew there was an extra one in the cupboard so I wouldn't have to call someone to run to the store. It was less stressful on me and less demanding on Ron. Sometimes when sorting clothes for the wash, I would put whites with colors, but most of the time, I could see the colors and sort them accordingly. Ron never griped about what I couldn't do. Instead, he just took it in stride and helped me with the chore. Cleaning always had an interesting twist. I cleaned the bathroom, for instance, but then I asked him to look at it, and if it wasn't clean in a corner or along the bottom of the tub, I did it again. Sometimes, Ron even took over the scrubbing on a particularly stubborn stain. We worked as a team because this was how our home ran more smoothly. If I didn't do my part and would forget to put a grocery item on the list when I used it up, then we didn't have any when I needed it. Simple as that.

I got into the habit of making breakfast for Ron and the kids before school. Sometimes, I just took a roll of biscuits, cut the centers out, fried them, and dipped them in a glaze of powdered sugar frosting. The kids and Ron loved them. Otherwise, cereal or toast served them well.

Every time a new procedure was on the news, someone either sent us an article about it from a newspaper or called us to see whether perhaps this would help me to regain some of my sight. Each time, Ron took time off from his busy teaching schedule, and we would go for an appointment to see this doctor. One of the things we checked out was laser surgery. We were told after an exam, "It was good to meet you. I've never seen anyone with this degree of scarring on their cornea. I'm so glad you came in to let me look at you but, this will not work for you due to the fact that once the laser cuts into the vascular scarring on your cornea, the blood from the veins in the scarring will start to cover the surface of the eye, and the laser will not cut through blood or other fluids." Once again I was disappointed.

Every few years, we went somewhere to have another doctor check my eyes. Each time, we first felt the excitement of my possibly being able to see, but inevitably, we suffered the disappointment of not finding the answer to my problem after all. It always took me at least a few days to get my mind around the fact that I was going to remain blind and that I would just have to continue doing things as I was. I had to accept the fact that there was not a marvelous plan, and that I might never be able to do things as a sighted person again, like watch the kids perform in plays or participate in sports, or sing in school functions. Just being able to spread a pan of brownies or flip an egg without it slipping off the turner was not to be. Everyday things were nothing special, but I just wanted them with sight.

Most nights, as I was sitting in the bleachers listening to singing coming from the group of teenagers that my kids were a part of, I would pray to God to just let me see them. I would be at one of the kids' ball games or listening to the cheer-leading in between halves, and I would be praying that same prayer. I so wanted to be able to watch and actually see instead of just listening, but that was not how it was. So instead of making each year of the kids' activities be about what I couldn't do, I tried to concentrate on what I could do. I praised them on how talented they were. I was thankful that I was alive to enjoy everything they were involved in. At least when Ron had to be gone for coaching or meetings, the kids had an adult at home in case of an emergency. I could get help if we needed it. That was why living in a community of wonderful, caring people was so special to us. It didn't matter what we needed. If we needed help, I could call someone and they would come. The security of living in small-town America was wonderful.

Traveling out of town to meets and games was also a challenge. But several of the parents going to the event offered to give the kids and me a ride. It was so awesome to share these wonderful times riding back and forth with other parents. Being there for our kids was so important to them and to me. Even if I couldn't see them clearly through binoculars I constantly carried, I wanted to show my support by being in the stands.

God worked in our lives every day. I would ask Him for help before giving up on a project. In high school, our daughter, Heather, was involved in cheer-leading, volleyball, basketball, plays, choir, and church events. One day, as she ran to catch her ride to school, she realized that she needed her letter sewn onto her cheer-leading sweater before the end of the day. Panicking, she said, "Mom do you think you will have time to sew the letter on my sweater?" Not 'can you', but 'will you' have time? Our kids had grown up watching me do things that their friends' moms did, except for driving a car, of course.

"Can you thread a needle before you leave for school?" I asked.

Later, when I sat down to sew the letter onto her sweater, the thread came out of the needle. I was frustrated but immediately thought, "Maybe if I just hold the thread very close to the end, I can manage to get it through the eye of the needle." After trying this until my arms ached, the thought came to me to ask for God's help.

I bowed my head and said, "Lord, you know I need to sew this letter on for Heather. Please help me to thread this needle."

I picked up the piece of thread, got the thread right to the end of my fingers as close as I could while still hanging onto it, picked up the needle, and tried to line up the thread with the eye of the needle. I took hold of the end of the thread with my teeth and pulled. I couldn't believe it. The thread went through the eye of the needle! I was amazed and smiled and bowed my head again.

"Thank you, Lord, thank you for helping me."

I sewed the letter on for Heather as carefully as I could, making sure the thread didn't come out of the needle again.

Slowly, I learned to trust that God was working in our lives. Each day, if I didn't like my reaction to something that was said or done, I tried to think of a different response I could make or a better way to deal with the problem. Little by little, I started to behave in a much nicer way in all areas, although I sometimes still blew my top and responded in ways I was not proud of.

Each time I struggled with something, asking for God's help came to me a little quicker. No matter how small the task or how big the project, I asked God and knew that He heard me.

One evening, I was preparing supper while listening to a book. I was making salad by ripping lettuce into bowls. I went to pick up a bowl and found it empty. The lettuce was stacked in a very neat pile right next to the bowl on the counter. The edge of the bowl that I had my hand against to make sure the lettuce was going into the bowl was actually the outside edge, so the lettuce ended up on the counter. I just shook my head at my mistake and moved the lettuce into the bowl.

Making soup was a great adventure at times. I had a full kettle of hamburger soup that contained, of course, browned ground beef, onion, carrots, potatoes, and celery. Lots of good things. I thought it needed a little more garlic salt, so I opened the lid and smelled it to make sure it was actually garlic. I shook the bottle vigorously over the pan and there was a big splash. I just realized I had picked up the dried minced garlic with no shaker lid on the bottle. Instead of shaking a little seasoning into the pan, I had dumped an entire bottle of dried minced garlic into the soup making it inedible—way too much garlic! So we had hotdogs or grilled cheese instead.

One other cold stormy wintry day, I decided to make soup. Checking to make sure the shaker lids were all in place, I seasoned the soup to perfection. Sometimes I liked to make dumplings for the soup. It not only tasted good, but it also gave the soup a little thickening in the broth. As I mixed up the dumplings, I thought, "This flour is not mixing in properly." I went ahead and added the dumplings to the soup, thinking it would be okay anyway. When Ron came in to taste the soup, there were little bugs floating on the top of the broth. The flour was buggy, and I had ruined another pot of soup. Yuck. We decided to keep flour in the freezer from then on. I left just a small amount in the canister and checked to make sure it was not infested before using it.

Shopping was not my favorite thing to do as a blind woman, but once again Ron stepped up to the plate. I needed a blue-green shirt to go with my slacks, so we went to a department store to search for that color and possibly a style that would look good on me. Ron went down one side of a rack of shirts, and I went down the other. I felt my way along, going very slowly so as not to run into another shopper. Out of the corner of my eye, I saw the exact color I needed. Because I was legally blind, color did show up, but not necessarily anything else. As I called to Ron and reached out for the shirt and grabbed the corner to pull it off the rack, I felt warm heat coming from under my fingers. As Ron shouted my name, I pulled my hand back. I realized I had just grabbed hold of the front of a man's shirt with the man in it! Apologizing, I moved toward Ron, who hustled me out of that store like we were on a mission. Lesson learned: Don't be grabbing things off a rack if you can't see clearly that the rack is a human! I laughed because I thought it was funny, but Ron was not amused.

I embarrassed him many times without really planning to. I felt that if we continued to try to be productive people in our world that had changed so dramatically, things were going to happen that we didn't necessarily want to. But I found that laughing at myself was the best fix.

One winter day driving down the interstate, Ron got way too warm in the vehicle. He had a sweatshirt on that needed to come off.

"Can you pull it over your head?" I asked.

"Not here." By this time he is sweating.

"Well, if you just pull your arms out first, and take off your glasses, I think you can pull the sweatshirt up over your head without much of a problem."

The thing was, I didn't know that this particular sweatshirt had a very tight neck. Ron prepared to pull the sweatshirt up over his face. He gave it a quick, hard tug to pull it off quickly but it got stuck on his chin and up in front of his face. We were flying down the interstate with me trying to watch for traffic while Ron scrambled to tug the sweatshirt off his face. I was laughing, but Ron didn't think this was funny at all. I always laughed nervously when it came to that type of situation. Seeing the humor in situations kept me from going crazy about it. Ron just went crazy.

After one of the disappointing trips to get my vision restored, or at least improved, I had a very hard time getting my feet under me again. As I was going to do laundry, Heather met me in the hallway. She looked at my face and then put her arms around me. As soon as she touched me, I started to cry. She held me. "It's going to be okay," she said. "You are still a good mom. You have never given up, and you just need to get your positive attitude back again."

"You're right," I said. "But I am so tired of all the times we check out a new procedure and it never seems to be the one to help me see better."

"It will someday, Mom. Just keep believing."

For reasons like this, I tried to keep my faith and spirits up. It affected my entire family when I did not. I would be positive.

Ron and I attended every school activity we could as the kids grew up. As their graduations approached, I was nervous as to how we were going to handle it. With so many people in our home for the celebration, I was not able to get around. And to greet people, well, I just left that up to Ron and the kids. I wanted to do more, but Ron took care of setting up pictures and memorabilia, and my sister Cathy and other family members once again came to my rescue and helped me out in the kitchen.

Chad graduated in 1988 and Heather in 1991. They both attended the University of South Dakota where Ron had also graduated. Ron and I had lots of time on our hands. Ron still attended sporting events and school functions, and I enjoyed the musical productions at the school, but I felt that we needed something else to fill the void of not having our children at home. Then our children began to add spouses to our family group.

Chad married Denise Olsen in 1992. It was a Christmas wedding, and I was nervous about buying the right dress and getting my hair just right for this most important day, so I prayed about it. My friend LaVonne stepped up and helped me shop. We went to a big mall, and she found a dress that I could afford that was actually red for a Christmas wedding. I appreciated all that she did to help me. Now all I had to do was get my hair to behave itself.

Then, wonder of wonders, Denise, who was a hairstylist asked, "Would you like one of the girls in the shop to do your hair?"

"Wonderful," I said. "I only ask that I not look like I'm trying to be a teenager. Just myself done up for a wedding."

"Done deal," said Denise.

I gave every concern to God, and He sent someone in to help me.

One evening in the 1990's, while Ron and I were sitting at home, the phone rang. It was Buddy and Claire calling to tell us about an article in their local paper about a woman in Canada. The article stated that this woman had been blind and was given her sight back through the use of a stem cell transplant and a donor cornea transplant. They wondered if maybe this would be something that could help improve my vision.

I wrote down the woman's name and called information for Canada. I got her phone number. When she answered the phone, I explained, "I am calling because your name was in a local paper stating that you have gotten your vision restored with surgery. Can you tell me more about it and who performed the surgery?"

"My doctor is from St. Paul, Minnesota. His name is Dr. Edward Holland."

She gave me his number at the University of Minnesota and said, "I really think he could at least take a look at you, and maybe even help you. After surgery," she continued, "I was instructed to go to the mall, walk around and look at everything. I am sitting and watching the snowflakes fall out my front window," she said, "and they are beautiful."

I was very excited for her. I thought how wonderful it would be when, someday, I too would be able to see the snowflakes falling.

"Wow," I thought. "How long had it been since I could just look at anything without struggling to see what I was looking at?"

I thanked her for speaking with me and for the information. I hung up with my mind already starting to create scenarios of things I would be able to do when I could see again. Even though I told myself not to get my hopes up, I couldn't help it. My brain was speeding over the joy of being able to see colors clearly again and whether there was something on the floor in front of the vacuum. I thought about not having to touch the cookie sheet and measure with my hand when putting cookie dough down to make sure they weren't touching and that they had enough space to bake properly. What fun that was going to be! But most of all, I was going to get to see my kids, my husband, and my family, just everyday things. I didn't want anything special. I just wanted to be able to do normal things in a normal way.

I called the University of Minnesota and got an appointment. We had had lots of rain, and most of the roads were under water or washed out between us and the University of Minnesota. I was still excited over the possibility of seeing again.

"I'm not getting my hopes up," I told Ron, but I am sure he could see that I was.

It was June. Ron and I drove up to Minnesota and got rooms at a motel downtown not far from the university so we could get to my appointment the next morning. We got to the university, and I was called in. We went from the waiting room to the exam room. The moisture content in my eye was checked.

Dr. Holland examined my eye. "I have never seen anyone with this much damage to their corneas. There is just no moisture in your eye due to the scarring over of the tear ducts." I could tell by the tone of the conversation that this was not good news. "I don't think there is anything we can do to help you," he said. "If you would like, I can take a look at you in a couple of years and make sure there isn't anything bad going on. I would be willing to do that. Just give me a call and set something up."

As my voice began to shake, my lips quivered, and Ron and I both thanked him for seeing us. As we walked out of his office arm in arm, Ron felt my entire body shaking. I was so disappointed. We had both hoped for a little something encouraging for this appointment, hope of some kind that maybe *someday*, but that was not to be.

"Are you going to be okay?" Ron asked.

As my spirit rose up to take a hold of God's hand, though my shaking voice and tears and disappointment made it difficult to speak, I said, "Yep, once I get my feet under me again, I'm going to be just fine. God has a plan for my life, and that is good. We will do things like we have done for all these years, and it will be okay."

Dr. Holland had told us to call him every couple of years, just to see if something new was being developed that would possibly work for me. I agreed to do that.

We arrived home, spread the news that nothing could be done, and I took my frustrations out on my old six-string. Singing loud and playing fast, I sang county rock and old standbys. Before I was done playing, my heart and soul went back to singing praises to God. It sustained me and let me know He was with me, and that it would be all right.

At first, I called every two years, hoping and also believing that some new procedure would help restore my vision. Each time I called, I was told that nothing new had been developed and there was no need for me to come and see Dr. Holland. They suggested, "Just continue to check in every couple of years by phone."

1992

I called the University of Minnesota to see whether Dr. Holland was working on any new procedures that might help to improve my vision, and the receptionist told me, "Dr. Holland no longer works here."

"Where has he gone?"

She told me that he moved to Cincinnati to work in a huge research clinic/hospital. She asked, "Can I refer you to one of our other doctors?"

"Thank you, but I think I will check in with Dr. Holland and see if he has any new procedure developed over the last few years. If I want to see one of the doctors still on staff at U of M, I will call back."

I called the Cincinnati Eye Institute after getting the number from information. The receptionist transferred my call to Dr. Holland's surgical nurse. I explained my previous examination by Dr. Holland in Minnesota. The surgical nurse said, "If you haven't seen Dr. Holland in five years, you should really come down and let him examine your eyes. He is doing some new and exciting procedures that are helping a lot of people get improved vision."

Again, I tried not to get my hopes up. I tried not to think about being able to see the flowers clearly once again, to be able to fill my own plate at a family picnic, or just to see to go into a public bathroom on my own where I could see toilet stalls, sinks, and paper towels. Nothing extraordinary, just simple everyday life things. I couldn't even think about what it would be like to see my family again. It would be too much of a disappointment if that didn't happen.

I got an appointment in the next couple of weeks, and Ron and I got flights this time since it was a fifteen hour drive one way, and the time element didn't work out. Then, an amazing thing happened. When people in our community heard that we were making this trip and perhaps getting a chance to restore some of my vision, they took up a collection of money to help defray the cost of travel and motel. Ron and I were both in tears but agreed that we couldn't take the money. This was just an appointment, not a surgery. I called the man who had collected the money. "This is just an appointment. There is no surgery, no guarantee that they can do anything to even help improve my sight."

The man replied, "We know, but we want to help."

"We have to give this money back. We can't have people paying for a doctor appointment every time we have one."

He laughed and said, "We can't give money back when people want to help. You just need to accept it and have a safe trip, and good luck at the doctor appointment."

We were overwhelmed.

This is amazing. All these years, I didn't even believe that most people realized I was still around. Sure, some called or spoke to me, but most people didn't know what to say. They didn't know that I joked my way through life, and just loved to visit with other people. They didn't know that just because I was blind didn't mean I couldn't think, hold a conversation, or just flat-out live everyday life. I just needed a little help once in a while. Then to have them do this and prove me so wrong.

We flew down to Cincinnati and drove to our motel. My appointment was the next morning. Dr. Holland came in to examine my eyes. I was trying not to be too nervous, but hope had sprung up in my heart once again. Hope was singing that I was going to see again. The testing was done and the exam finished, Dr. Holland said, "I've done about a hundred surgeries involving the stem cells and donor cornea. Out of the one hundred surgeries, about eighty percent of the patients have improved sight. The neat thing about this surgery is that, if the vision is not improved for the patient, at least it doesn't make their sight any worse. The problem with your eye is the dryness. There is not enough moisture to sustain and keep a donor cornea healthy and alive. My fear is that even if the stem cells are successfully transplanted and do their job, that is only a small part of the procedure. The big thing will be to keep enough moisture on the new cornea. I don't see any way to do that. I don't think this is going to work for you yet."

I could barely speak.

Dr. Holland advised me to call and check to see if there were any new developments instead of flying down again.

"There is really no need to make the trip when we can keep in touch over the phone."

We thanked him for seeing us.

As Ron and I walked arm in arm out of his office, Ron could feel me shaking with disappointment, withholding sobs because I'd just had my feet swept out from under me again.

"Are you going to be okay?"

Through trembling lips, I said, "Yes, God has a plan for my life, and if that means I will never see again, it's okay. I know God isn't done with me yet, so we will have to wait a little longer."

We flew back home, and the word spread through town that there had been no help for me at this appointment.

Our lives got back to what we considered normal. We attended church whenever we were home and not sick. I found peace of mind while listening to the singing, hearing God's promises for our lives in the readings, and all we had to do was accept Jesus Christ as our Savior and try our best to follow in the way He would have us live. Sounded easy enough, but I had to get my feet under me again. Stop dreaming of doing the everyday things of life with sight and do them as I had been.

Although I was very, very disappointed by the news Dr. Holland gave me, I felt in my heart God was not done with me yet. He had a plan, and I just had to keep believing.

Generally, this was how I dealt with things that were difficult. I'd make a joke about myself before someone else could do it. I didn't think being blind was funny, but I did realize that no one wanted to hang around a down, depressed and somber person, so I continued to get back on my feet and laugh again. This was just my personality, standing by my belief that someday something good would happen, and that meant staying close to God and not giving up hope.

I noticed that my vision was not as clear as it had been. I still saw Dr. Willcockson on a regular basis. He examined my eye and said, "It is probably just normal aging. I really don't understand how you see through the scar at all. I don't know how your eye is under the scar because I can't see back there. Continue doing what you are doing."

I felt God had a hand in helping me see through the scarring.

As the aging process continued to affect my vision, I knew that eventually I would have to stop doing daycare out of my home. I needed something to occupy my time while Ron was out coaching or going to school events and activities that I did not attend. I started to study medical transcription via correspondence. I studied, took tests, and actually passed them. I didn't know if I would ever use this information but found the study very interesting, and for the first time I enjoyed studying.

1995

Heather was about to graduate from college with a business administration degree. She and her fiance decided to get married the same month. Crazy, yes. I wasn't sure how much I could actually do to help, but I would do what I could.

We met her in Sioux Falls and shopped for dresses on Saturday. It was cold and windy, wintertime in South Dakota. We walked into our first dress shop about ten o'clock in the morning. Heather tried on several dresses. The salesclerk was very helpful.

Heather came out in the first gown.

"Can you see it at all, Mom?"

"I can see a lot of white and the shape against the dark wall, but not the pattern of the dress or the material."

We left the shop and huddled down in our coats to run to the car. Ron didn't have the keys. In our hurry to get out of the weather he had locked them in the car. "I always carry an extra set just for this reason," I said. As I dug in the bottom of my oversized purse, my fingers closed over the keys to the car. "Got 'em," I said. I gave a quick "thank you" that God had given me the foresight to carry a spare key, even though I wasn't driving.

We didn't find a dress Heather really liked that day, but she was going shopping with her fiancé's mother the next weekend. She found a dress in Iowa she liked. If she liked it and it didn't cost too much, I was good with it.

Heather did most of the planning for her wedding. We helped by keeping the checkbook handy and meeting her whenever and wherever to look and shop for flowers and decorations and so forth. When we went in to check on the flowers Heather had ordered, she was quiet. We got back in the car and she said, "They aren't my flowers."

"What do you mean they aren't your flowers?" we asked.

"The flowers we just looked at aren't the flowers I ordered."

"You should have just said that when we were in the shop," I said. "Don't ever take something you haven't ordered and don't even like."

Back into the store we went. We explained the situation to the saleswoman making the flowers for Heather's wedding. She took down the order a second time and promised the correct flowers would be ready by the wedding day. We hoped so.

The one thing I could do for Heather's wedding was put birdseed into netting and tie them with ribbon. I did this while the kids in my daycare were napping. It went pretty well, even though I was not sure what each looked like. I was so excited and pleased when I could help in any way.

The wedding was planned and the kids married, and I was relieved to not have to try to plan any more huge events. Doing this as a legally blind person was not my idea of fun. Just attending these events was more work for Ron, so the actual being involved behind the scenes of the event was stressful.

A group of ladies from Cathy's church were going to Des Moines, Iowa for a bus trip to Women of Faith. The two-day event consisted of women giving their testimonies, singing, laughter and a message of how God was always in the midst of life in general.

Cathy called me, "Jen, do you want to go with me?"

"Yes, that sounds like fun."

"I'll get the tickets. Maybe Ron can bring you halfway to meet me and I will bring you back so he can pick you up."

"Okay, let's go," I agreed.

The first night where the keynote speakers get up and tell a little about their message was wonderful and we couldn't wait to spend the next day celebrating together.

Our motel phone rang at 4:00 a.m. It was Ron. His brother, Buddy had passed away. I felt I needed to go home immediately. Cathy spent the next four hours calling airlines and buses to get me home. Then, Heather's husband called and his step-father and mother lived in Des Moines. I would ride with them halfway back and Heather and her husband would pick me up and get me to Ron.

My heart ached for Claire and the kids. Buddy was so full of life. He would be missed.

1998

I decided that I needed to close my daycare and not put any of these little ones in jeopardy due to my vision growing much worse. I knew that I would miss the excitement of the first days outside in the spring, the after school snacks when kids came off the bus to my house, and especially all the funny things kids said. There was always one of them who could make me smile during the day, just by being so innocent and unassuming. I loved them.

One evening, I was visiting with a friend who is a nurse. She asked, "What have you been doing?"

"I'm studying medical transcription, terms and all that."

"That sounds great. If I hear of anyone who needs a medical transcriptionist, I will let you know."

I laughed and said, "Okay, you do that." But I was thinking that I was not really studying to be a transcriptionist, just doing it to fill time and learn.

About four months later my friend called and said, "The group of clinics I work for is looking for a transcriptionist. Are you interested?"

"Well, I am not really done studying yet," I said.

"Do you want to come for an interview tomorrow?" I hesitated, and she said, "Well, do you or not?"

"Yes."

Ron dropped me off at the downtown office for my interview with the CEO, Mr. Horsemeyer. The girls working at this clinic said, "Mr. Horsemeyer is grumpy today, but if he isn't nice to you, we are going to talk to him about it."

I smiled and said, "It will be fine."

I went in shaking in my shoes. I hadn't been on an interview for so long. Mr. Horsemeyer asked, "What format do you use to transcribe?"

136

"I don't use any since I don't transcribe for anyone. I am only studying and have a couple of lessons left."

"We use SOAP format," he started. He then proceeded to give me other information about wages, etc. Before I knew it, he had hired me. I was amazed. I wasn't sure what had just happened. I got up to leave the office, thanked him, and turned and ran right into the filing cabinet.

"Oh, I'm sorry," I said.

He said, "You're okay."

I got out of there as fast as I could without walking into anything else.

The girls in the office helped me to the door where Ron met me. I sat down in the car stunned.

"I got the job," I told Ron.

"Good deal," Ron said. "Congratulations!"

I worked from home as a transcriptionist. I thought to myself, "It's ironic how, if we prepare for something, God will take care of the rest."

The state of South Dakota helped me get the programs so that my computer would speak the words I typed and enlarge the print on the screen. I purchased a closed-circuit TV myself to help me look up words and medicines. Wonderful technology that we had. It truly opened up a whole new dimension in life for a handicapped person.

I worked both as a daycare provider and a transcriptionist for the first year because there wasn't much transcription work for me at first. My days were full though with daycare during the day and transcribing medical notes in the evenings. Then I had an opportunity for more work as a transcriptionist, enough for full time. I was so sad to not have kids in my home any longer. I would truly miss the laughter of children each and every day.

I worked for eleven years doing medical transcribing. At times, I was very busy, and then other times I was just busy enough. Self-employment had always been my way of working. I loved working at my own pace, taking breaks when I needed them, and being at home.

Our family picture for the church directory 1973.

Ron, Chad and Heather in my ICU room.

Owens Packs covering wrist.

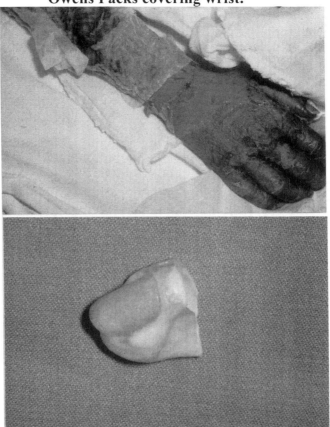

Sloughed fingernail with skin up to first knuckle.

Blister on my back.

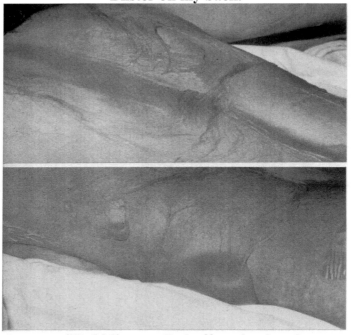

A water-filled blister rolled off my back to hang on my side.

The blister on my wrist just above my IV.

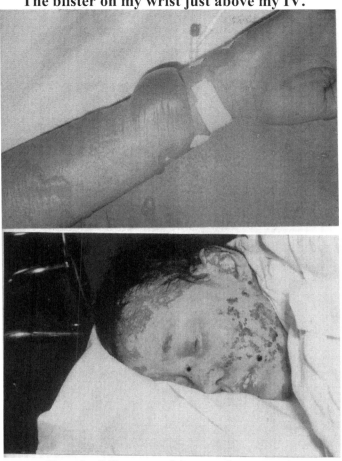

I'm shedding my skin patches at a time.

Chad and Heather, ages 3 and 6.

Connor and Jenna, our grandchildren, ages 5 and 7.

Our first little cabin.

The remains of our cabin after the forest fire burned through our property. I was thanking God for the good He would bring from this ruin.

And this cabin has come up from the ruins.
God is good.

The problem with working from home was that, many times, the work came in after 5:00 p.m. If the ironing was done, clothes were folded, and dishes cleaned up, I checked out how much work I had on my computer. I felt like I needed to keep ahead of the work, so I would transcribe it at night. Sometimes, I worked fifteen to eighteen-hour days. Yes, long days, but I loved it when my computer worked properly.

The kids said, "Mom, you need a lock on your office door so at five o'clock it closes until the next morning."

"I like my job, so when I'm tired, I quit."

Every couple of years, I called Cincinnati to check and see whether there were any new developments that might work for me. After a while, time between calls became longer, more like three to four years instead of every two years because the new developments weren't happening, and I didn't want to be told that again. I kept busy and tried not to think of the fact that my eyesight was getting worse. I just continued to believe that God was not done with me yet and kept my faith in Him strong. For more than twenty years, I kept a positive twist on my statements. I frequently said, "*When I get my sight back...*", not "*if*". But then I started saying, "*If I ever get my sight back...*" I knew God had a plan for me but I wasn't sure it included letting me see again.

Heather and I were visiting on the phone one day, and I said, "If I ever get my sight back again."

"Mom, I hear you becoming negative, and it's just not like you. I want to hear that positive mom that I grew up with."

"You're right, Heather, I have started saying "*if*" instead of "*when*". I just have a hard time right now staying positive. My vision is worse, and every time doctors see me, they find my case interesting but don't have any procedure that will help improve my eyesight. I guess I just need to get back to God."

Chad and Denise were working hard and taking trips to Disney World. They had no children so it was fun for them. Ron and I of course were waiting patiently to be grandparents. Heather was following her husband to many different states and helping him build his career in the Army. We tried to travel to each of their homes to visit them. Ron helped me in and around their homes until I was familiar enough to move around a little on my own. Otherwise, I sat in a chair visiting, talking while everyone else was making food, or listening to whatever sport Ron, Chad, and Heather were watching. Denise and I were not sports fans. I still was not able to see, but I wanted to. I wouldn't let blindness stop me from going to visit our children or anything else I wanted to do.

While riding in a vehicle seven to eight hours, I felt trapped inside. If I had to go to the bathroom, Ron would take me to the door of the women's restroom. Once inside, if I heard the voices of too many women, I just backed out and waited in the hallway for Ron to come get me. If it was quiet, I ran my hands along a wall or tapped my cane around to find an open stall. After using the facility, if I couldn't find the sink or there were too many women in the restroom, I simply washed my hands with Wet Ones and hand purifier in the vehicle. It was easier than trying to find the sink, the towels, and then the door again. If we were close enough to our destination and I was unable to navigate a restroom, I just backed out of it and told Ron, "I'll wait until we get home." It became a joke between us. Sometimes, a woman in the restroom would offer assistance to me and I appreciated this, but I hated it too. I hated with a passion not being able to do simple everyday things. At home, I could do most things because I knew where everything was. If I didn't remember where something was, I had no problem going through closets until I found what I was looking for. This was a good way to get the closets reorganized and reminded me where things were. Sometimes I just waited until Ron got home, and he either knew where the item was or helped me find it. Frustrating at times, and yet I liked being at home where I was in my own space. My self-reliant, independent self didn't like asking anyone for help, but over the years I had to.

Ron and I still went to church and still believed there was a God watching over us. And I knew in my heart that someday God had something awesome for me. Waiting was the hard part.

One Sunday after church Ron and I were visiting on the couch. I asked him, "Is there anything you have ever wanted or wished you could have?"

"I have always wanted a place in the Black Hills."

"I never knew you felt that way. Okay, let's start looking for one. Then by the time we retire, it will be paid for."

"How are we going to pay for it?"

"I need to build up my credit score," I said, "so I'll pay for it."

We started contacting realtors and looked for two years to find just what we wanted, a one-room hunting cabin with no running water, no electricity, and nothing to do but enjoy. We purchased it in 1994 and spent many wonderful summer days there. The kids came once to visit us there, and we had a long weekend together. We always enjoyed our times with our adult children. Laughter was abundant. Usually, if there was a game that they wanted to play, I just told them, "Play it. I'll just sit and listen." Most of the time they chose a question and answer game so I could participate. Each of these events just made me want to see all the more. After one such weekend, I especially wanted to be able to see to do things with the family. This usually triggered my contacting Dr. Holland again about any new developments in eye surgeries.

2000

In the heat of the summer, a forest fire burned in the Jewel Cave area. It came within a mile of our cabin. At that time we discussed whether or not we should insure our property.

"What do you think?" Ron asked.

147

"We need to insure the little cabin, even if it isn't much. We can't rebuild it if it burns."

Ron called our insurance agent, who said, "Is there a fire burning in the Hills now?"

Ron said, "I think there is always a fire burning this time of year out there."

"You have to wait until there are no fires before we are allowed to write a policy for you."

"We'll wait until winter," I said, "then get the cabin covered."

2001

Spring came and Ron started golf practices for the high school team and was busy. The cabin insurance kept coming to my mind, but we still hadn't gotten coverage on it. I thought, "This is God nudging me to get the cabin insured." One day at the end of June, I called our insurance agent and asked him, "Can you insure our property in the Black Hills?"

"I need to check whether there are any fires burning in the Hills presently, and I'll get back to you."

His return call affirmed no fires were burning, and we started insurance coverage on our little cabin in the Hills. Ron and I felt sure that we would never need to put in a claim on it.

Two months later, in August, Ron had finished with the summer recreation program he was in charge of in DeSmet. I took time off from work, and we spent a wonderful week at the cabin. It was so peaceful there. Ron cut up trees that had fallen and trimmed dead branches from others. He read out in the hammock and enjoyed nature. Ron told me the golden eagles were flying around floating on the wind currents. It was soon time for us to leave the cabin and go home.

Summer storms built in the hot days of August, and a lightning strike started a fire about four miles southeast of our cabin. The news was sketchy about details of where the fire actually was but gave a web-site and the number of

148

the fire control team if anyone wanted to check on their property. Ron got in contact with forestry and neighbors who lived in the area to keep track of where the fire was burning.

A few days later, we heard on the news that the fire had jumped Pass Creek Road and a structure was lost to it. Ron called and spoke to our neighbor about our cabin.

Roger said, "The firefighters have foamed most of the structures. Your place is good."

The next day, Ron called again to check on the progress of the fire. Roger's wife answered the phone.

"How is the fire doing?"

"It has moved over the west ridge and is seventy-five percent contained."

"So is our cabin okay then?"

She hesitated and said, "Didn't Roger tell you?"

"Roger told me they foamed it and the cabin is okay."

"No," she said, "I'm pretty sure your place is gone."

"Is there anything left?" Ron asked.

"No, it's on the ground, nothing left."

Ron thanked her for telling him. I was standing close to Ron.

"What did she say?"

He replied in a shaky and stunned voice, "It has burned to the ground."

We were devastated and could not believe it really burned down. Ron called our insurance agent and reported the loss. The insurance company would send an adjuster to check it out. We decided to go see for ourselves at Ron's first break in the school year.

We drove out and met the adjuster in Rapid City. He had already been to our cabin site and taken pictures.

"Would you like to see them?"

Ron looked, and when the insurance agent handed them to me, I said, "I'm legally blind and won't be able to see pictures. Thanks anyway."

I could hear in Ron's voice that it wasn't good when he asked, "Is there anything left?"

The adjuster said, "It's a total loss."

We continued on to our cabin in shock, wondering what we would find. I said, "Maybe it would be a good idea to stop in town and buy hand-wipes and paper towels to clean up with after we walk around."

We drove in, and the area actually looked good. We couldn't really see that there had been a fire. Ron drove around the corner of the road. "Here is where the fire has burned," he described it to me. "It looks like the fire started on our property line. The trees are blackened and the earth is charred down to the dirt. All five acres of our property looks like a war zone. Only a few trees are left standing on the south and east of the cabin. Everything north and west is black and dead."

We got out of the pickup, and the smell was the first thing I noticed. It was hard to describe. The area was dead silent. No birds, or wind in the trees, no sound whatsoever.

Ron said, "It looks like a bomb has gone off here." His voice had a quiver in it.

"There is absolutely no wildlife," I said. "Listen, no birds, no squirrels, nothing alive."

We walked into the yard arm in arm to where the cabin had once stood. With tears in my voice, I said, "I don't know how and I don't know when, but God will make something good from this mess."

Ron continued to describe it to me. "Trees in the front to the south are maybe still alive, but behind the cabin to the north it is leveled to the ground. The trees are now blackened toothpicks sticking up from a blackened earth."

We were sad, very sad.

Ron took pictures and we left to find a motel in which to spend the night.

September 11, 2001

We returned home the next mourning. We decided to leave the property awhile untouched, then plan what to do after seeing how it came back from the fire in a year or so.

We were back going through our regular routines. Ron was gone to school when our phone rang. It was Heather.

"Mom, turn on the TV. The Twin Towers are being attacked."

I turned on the television and listened to the reports of the devastating attack on New York City and our country. My heart went out to them, and when Ron returned home from school, I told him what I had been thinking. "Ron, this really puts the loss of our little cabin into perspective, doesn't it? After all, it is just a cabin, not our lives, not thousands of lives."

Ron agreed. We can take our time deciding what to do with what is left of this little cabin we loved. The lives lost in the 9-11 terrorist attack were far more devastating than the loss of our little cabin.

September 2, 2003

We listened to the news and updates on the recovery efforts in New York City each evening. This particular evening on a health segment the reporter told of a new procedure being done in Boston by Dr. Rozell. I called and spoke to a receptionist at the Boston Clinic. Previously, clinics would request that records be sent before they would schedule an appointment. I wrote to Dr. Holland, and several other eye doctors that had seen me over the years, to have records sent out to Massachusetts.

My local doctors responded promptly. I sent the information to Boston and received a response from Dr. Rozell a few weeks later:

Dear Ms. Peterson,
After reviewing your records, I feel the procedure we are doing for our patients will not be beneficial to you at this time. Keep in contact if you have any further questions.
Sincerely,
Dr. Rozell

"Why does this not surprise me?" I said to Ron. "I guess I will continue to do what I'm doing. I don't like it, but what choice do I have? God will find a fix for me someday. My chances seem to be better if I go out into a thunder storm and get struck by lightning than a procedure being developed to help me."

Ron didn't reply.

February 2005

I went to see Dr. John Willcockson. He said, "I see no change in your eye."

I asked him, "Is there any new procedure that might help improve my vision?"

He said, "When you first came to me we were both a lot younger. Honestly, I don't think there will ever be anything that will help you regain any measurable vision in your lifetime or mine."

I looked in his direction and said, "You've told me that before, but we'll see."

I still had my hands outstretched to God, and the Bible tells me nothing is impossible for God and I believed it.

2006

I called for an appointment and was told by the receptionist, "Dr. Willcockson has retired, but we can set you up to see our new doctor. He is very good."

I accepted the appointment to see a doctor in that clinic, but Ron and I talked it over.

"Dr. Willcockson has been seeing me for nearly twenty years with no better or worse results," I said. "Not really anything better or worse for probably twenty years. I'm not sure I even need to be seen anymore."

I cancelled my appointment. I would see an eye doctor as needed.

Ron and I got into a regular routine over the next few years. He went to school each day. I was working out of our home as a medical transcriptionist. My vision continued to get worse each year, but most days I could still see colors and shapes, light and dark. Ron did chores and helped with cooking. If I couldn't do it, Ron did it. We worked as a team, with Ron taking the lead. Basically, God was good to us. We were healthy. Our children had jobs and were doing well. We were content, but I still prayed that God would let me see my family again.

Ron and I had been dealing with this blindness for thirty years, and each day it seemed I turned to God more and more often for every little thing I struggled with. He was always there just in the nick of time. If I was feeling useless, I prayed, "Dear Lord, make me feel useful." The phone would ring in the next couple of days or even hours and someone would ask, "Could you give your testimony for our group?" I knew God always had a message for at least one person in the audience, and I was eager to do His bidding. One time, though, I remembered being called to give my testimony, and I just could not find enough strength to do it, so I declined. I regretted refusing the offer, and did not repeat my negative answer to God's call again.

Most of my evenings were spent listening to books on tape from the South Dakota State Library for the Blind and Handicapped. The stories took me beyond myself and allowed me to picture in my mind beautiful countrysides, wonderful houses, and excitement of all sorts. When Ron was home, we usually ended up reading or he would watch TV and I would read. We did nothing too extraordinary. We got together with friends and played trivia or watched the Super Bowl, but otherwise, my ability to play games was more limited than ever. Visiting was a great thing, and friends learned to accept me as a legally blind person, helping me if I needed help, joking about some of the things going on, just being friends. Sometimes we were not invited to events due to my blindness because the event was not something in which I could participate.

In the spring of 2006 Heather was living in Kansas after a divorce. Chad and Denise lived in Vermillion. One evening, mid-winter, Chad and Denise were channel

153

surfing to find something to watch on TV. A preview for a show called *The Miracle Worker* came on. One segment showed a young man with horrible scarring on his eyes, which sounded to them like my problem, so they decided to call us.

"Mom, there's this show on TV tonight. A man has eye problems that sound a lot like yours. We think this is going to turn out good, or they wouldn't put it on TV. We are going to watch it, and thought you might be interested in it too."

"Yeah, that sounds like something interesting to watch," I said. "I will try to remember to turn the TV on at 8:00."

Not being used to listening to much TV, when the phone rang Chad said, "Mom, are you watching the show?"

I replied, "No, I forgot about it."

"Hurry, you need to see this."

Ron turned the channel on, and I heard the medical assistant helping a young male patient to fill out his chart. His sister was also being interviewed because she was going to be his stem cell donor. Then the doctor came into the exam room to introduce himself to the patient.

"Hi, I'm Dr. Edward Holland," he said.

I don't know what happened in the next few minutes of the show. I grabbed my phone and called Chad and Denise.

"Chad, that's my doctor!"

"Where?" he asked.

"On TV. That's Dr. Edward Holland."

"Here we go, Mom," he said. "This is what we've been waiting for."

We finished watching the show, and with each minute that passed, my hopes soared. At the end of the show, this young man stood at the edge of the ocean and watched the whales blow and the dolphins jump. "Amazing," I said. "But I am not going to get my hopes up again. Dr. Holland couldn't do anything for me when I last saw him, so he probably can't do anything to help me now. Only God knows what to do for my blindness."

We discussed whether I should call Dr. Holland. "It has been three years since I've checked with his office," I told the kids. "He told me to check in every two to three years just to see if anything new has been developed that might help me. I just don't want to have the rug pulled out from under me again."

I was just not sure I could pick myself up one more time. Ron and I were getting along fine like we were. But I so wanted to see again. It was so tempting.

The show dramatized the surgery by saying that the stem cell donor had a chance of losing vision in the eye from which the stem cells were taken. The stem cells formed a line or barrier around the iris to keep the blood vessels from growing over the front of the new cornea. I was excited for this patient but nervous, and not sure what I should do.

I knew Dr. Holland would be busy with calls after *The Miracle Worker* aired. If I didn't call, then I would have wasted years that I could have been seeing if this surgery would work to restore my sight. So I called.

The receptionist told me, "The Cincinnati Eye Institute (CEI) is changing its filing system over to digital, and I am not finding your name in our records. I will continue to look for your records and get back to you."

A week later, I had not heard back from her. I called again. She said, "I am still checking, but I have not found your chart yet. It could be in transit from the old facility and might take a couple of days, so could you check back with me the first of next week?"

I think, "Well, I've been blind for thirty years, so what's a few more days of waiting to get an appointment? No big deal."

Over the next couple of weeks, I called CEI eight times. I had learned through listening to sermons and my Bible that God wanted us to be persistent. The eighth time I called, the receptionist told me, "Your chart seems to be missing."

I replied, "I know you have my social security number. How about looking for my chart using that?"

The receptionist was surprised that I was willing give out my social security number, but she typed it in as I recited it. Lo and behold, she found my chart. She said, with surprise in her voice, "Well, there you are! You're Jenny."

"Yes," I replied.

She said slightly sheepishly, "I have to tell you, I've been looking for Jennifer this whole time."

"No, I'm just plain, ordinary Jenny."

There was nothing special about me. I was just an ordinary South Dakota girl who didn't really understand why God had chosen to hold me in His arms and save my life, but I know He did.

The receptionist scheduled me for an appointment in July 2006. Ron and I were deciding whether to drive or fly. The kids announced that they all wanted to go to this appointment. Ron and I were very surprised because over the last thirty years, Chad and Heather, for one reason or another, had not gone to one of my appointments. So when they announced to us that all three, Chad, Denise and Heather, were planning to go with us, we were very surprised to say the least. Heather drove up from Manhattan, Kansas to Chad and Denise's home near Vermillion to meet us. We drove down from our home to Chad and Denise's. The people of DeSmet were all wishing us well and praying for restored sight for me. We were about to have dinner when Chad and Denise brought out gifts for each of us.

"You kids need to stop buying gifts all the time and save your money for a rainy day," I said. But they assured us that it was just something little. We opened our gifts. My gift bag contained a baby bib and a book. I heard Heather reading out loud, "If you think I'm cute, you should see my Auntie Heather."

Ron said, "I got a card and it says, 'You're going to be a Grandpa'."

There were many hugs and laughter over the news that Chad and Denise were expecting their first child. After fifteen years of marriage and ten years of waiting to become pregnant, they were ecstatic. We were thrilled for them. I was standing by my chair, waiting for someone to come to me. I heard them laughing then Chad came over to me. Chad hugged me and tears ran down his face onto mine.

"We weren't going to tell anyone quite yet, but Denise isn't feeling well and she certainly isn't staying home. She wants to be there for the good news too."

"Congratulations," I said. "I am so happy for you both. When is the baby due?"

"March," Denise said as she gave me a hug.

I told them all, "My appointment will probably be about fifteen minutes long, and we can maybe make it halfway home the same day."

"We'll see," the kids replied.

I had been telling the kids and Ron "We'll see" for many years. Now, they had picked up on that line and were feeding it back to me.

We traveled in Chad and Denise's vehicle to Cincinnati, a fifteen-hour drive. My appointment with Dr. Holland lasted a little longer than fifteen minutes. We told him we had seen the show on TV.

"Is that why you came to see me?"

I reminded him, "I've seen you several times before, starting when you were at the University of Minnesota."

After examining my eyes, he asked, "Have you ever seen our plastic surgeon?"

"No."

"I want you to see the plastic surgeon. I'll check and see if he has any time today."

As he left the exam room, I turned to Ron and the kids, "I think he's talking about doing surgery," I said.

Chad spoke up, "Yeah, don't you want that?"

157

I hesitantly answered, "Well, I guess so." But I wasn't so sure.

The plastic surgeon had time to examine me. He started by telling me what he was going to do. I hadn't signed any papers, nor had I agreed to anything yet, but he told Chad and Heather they were a fifty percent match to me for stem cell donor. When the kids heard this, they huddled in the corner of the exam room doing paper, rock, and scissors to see which one of them got to be the donor. They were wonderful kids. Not that there hadn't been a few bumps in the road of their growing up years, like with many other families, but they had made us proud to be their parents.

I was lucky to have Ron too. Many had seen Ron in the grocery store or walking arm in arm with me to sporting events, concerts, and church. He was what we called in South Dakota "a keeper". From the day I got sick, he had been there taking care of things I couldn't do either for myself, our children, or our home. He hadn't taken one step backwards from my becoming blind. He hadn't always had enough energy to take on some of the things I asked of him, and I was willing to wait if possible for the shopping trip, catalog order, or grocery store run. But Ron had been a wonderful life partner to me.

I told him, "God knew you would take care of me, and that is why He gave us to each other."

At this extended appointment, the plastic surgeon said, "I will need to have an ENT surgeon remove tissue from your turbinate in your nose to be placed under your eyelid to help produce more moisture in the eye. The nasal tissue is the most moisture-producing tissue of the body, and that is why we choose it."

We went for an appointment with the ENT surgeon, who also thought this surgery would possibly improve my vision. I was basically in shock. I was more used to the letdown, getting myself back on my feet, having Ron ask me after a disappointing appointment, "Are you going to be okay?" I was definitely not used to hearing, "We think this may help you."

We were all smiling from ear to ear, excited to be able to have success this time.

I kept thinking, there was no risk to what vision I had so let's give this a try. It would only be a few surgeries and then either it works or it doesn't. If not, we go back to what we know. The ride home went quickly and the excitement carried into our home town and families. Newspapers carried the story and television had a clip about it. Prayer chains in over half the United States had my name on them.

Due to all of the interest in what was happening to maybe get my sight restored, I decided to write a note for our church bulletin. I knew we needed God in control if anything was going to go right.

August 2006
UPDATE ON PEOPLE WE ARE PRAYING FOR.
This is Jenny Peterson. I am being scheduled for surgery in Cincinnati, Ohio. This may take six weeks up to three months because it involves two surgeons: a plastic surgeon, and an ear, nose, and throat surgeon. The ENT surgeon will be removing tissue from a middle part of my nose, and the plastic surgeon will be removing scar tissue from inside my upper eyelid and placing the tissue from my nose on the inside of the upper eyelid. This is a very moisture-producing tissue and hopefully will adhere itself and grow into the eyelid to replace the scarring. Also the plastic surgeon will be relining the edges of my upper and lower eyelids. This is to remove any eyelashes or nubs of eyelashes to prevent irritation to the new cornea when the time comes for that. This is what will be done for the first of four surgeries. If this surgery is successful, then the second surgery will be performed in about three months. If the first surgery is not successful, there will be no further surgeries performed. The important thing in these surgeries is that if they fail to restore my vision, it does not ruin my eye for future developing procedures. The surgeries will all be performed in Cincinnati, Ohio.

Thank you all for your prayers. During the last thirty years, I have tried to look at life with my glass half full, not half empty. I pray that God continues to control each aspect of my life, including the upcoming surgical procedures, and that His will be done in this. May God bless the surgeons and use their skills to work a miracle in our lives. God bless you all.
Jenny and Ron Peterson

In August, not only did I have checkups, but Ron, too, had his annual checkup before school started. A week later, we got a call that Ron's PSA was elevated. This was not an alarming level until the doctors saw that the jump in one year was over 2.0. The doctor thought Ron should have a biopsy. I called to tell my Dad the news and I said, "I am going to be so pissed off if Ron has cancer."

"I bet you will be," my Dad answered.

I called my family, and I was crying because after all we had been through, why did Ron need to be sick? Didn't God know I needed Ron? I needed Ron who had always helped me with things. Most of all, I was thinking that I was just getting my sight back, and this was our chance to enjoy doing things together, and now, if Ron had cancer, it was not fair, not fair at all.

Then my sister Vicki said, "You're just scared. It will be okay."

And with that statement, I realized that she was right. I was afraid, afraid of losing the person who had been through it all with me, afraid I wouldn't be there for him like he had been for me, afraid of so many unknown things. So once again, I turned it all over to God.

By August, my siblings had heard that Chad and Heather were an automatic fifty percent match to me for stem cell donors. The doctors told us that one of my siblings might be an even closer match, and if they were willing to be tested, we could find the closest match and give me the best chance to not reject the stem cells and let them do their job. Two of my friends, LaVonne and Susan, drove me to the lab in Sioux Falls where our blood would be drawn for testing. Meeting me there were my five siblings, two brothers and three sisters. Each one was hoping to be the closest match and help give me sight again. It took several months, but we were finally informed that Vicki was going to be my donor.

At the same time we were waiting for the match results, we waited for a call from Ron's urologist. Then the call came and the nurse reported, "Some cancer was found in one lobe on the biopsy. The doctor wants you to come in and discuss options with him."

An appointment for consultation with Ron's urologist was set for September 19, 2006. We were given options, and after the discussion we decided that removing the prostate was best. Get rid of the cancer, and then don't worry about it again until the next checkup. A surgical date would be sent to Ron.

October 2006

My first surgery in Ohio was set. We were to stay six days this trip. As a gift, we received warm socks for the hospital stay and a journal to keep notes. Wonderful idea! Ron wrote on October 8, 2006, "I am going to have to write like hell if I am going to fill this up before we go home."

I had a plan in my head of when I could get these surgeries done and could see. One surgery, three months healing, second surgery, three more months healing, third surgery and then the stem cells and corneal transplant then voila, vision. Yes! "By the birth date of our first grandchild I should be able to see," I thought.

Ron's surgery was set for October 18, 2006 to be done in a Sioux Falls Hospital with a three to four-day stay. I would stay with Claire and Bob, who lived in Sioux Falls. They would take me to the hospital and back to their home at night. The old adage of life being like railroad tracks running together, some good and some bad is true. We had the excitement of me possibly getting to see, and then the scare that Ron had cancer. We needed time to absorb it all.

While waiting for Ron's surgery I was also concerned about the expense of flying, motels and meals that would add up during my surgeries in Ohio. I started to check into familiar places that I had heard would house people going through extreme surgical procedures. I was worrying about hotel costs, so I decided to check with the Ronald McDonald House to see if they knew of any programs that housed people who had to stay extended lengths of time in Ohio.

"I do not know of anything like that," a representative said. "All I have are numbers for airlines that help people get to their appointments."

"Really? That's amazing! Can I have that number, please?" I said.

Here I was worried about hotel prices, but I hadn't yet thought of the cost of flights to get there.

She gave me several phone numbers of airlines and also the web-site where I could download forms to be filled out by doctors with medical information stating that I needed a companion to fly with me. It did take paperwork, but the clinics and doctors in DeSmet were more than happy to help me. Again small town living was a blessing.

October 5, 2006

We drove to Chad and Denise's to stay since we were flying from Omaha to Dallas and then into Cincinnati. Kind of a round-about way, but we flew any way that Miracle Flights could get us there. Another blessing!

At my appointment, I was found to have right upper and lower lid entropion (curling in toward the eyeball), which needed to be fixed by doing a right upper lid reconstruction, and a right upper lid buccal mucosa membrane graft. Also, pre-op pictures were taken.

October 6-10, 2006

My surgery was scheduled for 7:30 a.m. The tissue was removed from my middle turbinate by 8:30 that morning. During this first surgery, the ENT surgeon and the plastic surgeon worked together. The plastic surgeon also placed a blepharon ring underneath my eyelids to prevent the scar tissue from growing the eyelid back down to my eyeball during the healing process.

After surgery, my nose was swollen and my right eye looked like someone had punched me, but the pain wasn't bad. It was going to be okay. I wanted to see my family again so whatever it took would be worth it. I needed to sleep with my head elevated for ten days to help prevent swelling, so I put pillows up behind me in the bed and tried to get some rest. We were told to expect some drainage and that the bruising might go down as far as my jaw area. No blowing my nose. My eye actually started bleeding the next day. We went to the hospital and were given more patches.

At my appointment the next morning, Dr. Holland reported, "The cause of the bleeding is a large blood clot that is stuck underneath the eyelids, which are so swollen and with the blepharon ring in place it could not be washed out."

Dr. Kersten said, "The stitches are holding the harvested tissue in place. Let's put a numbing drop in your eye and see if we can open your eyelids a little."

I held my breath. He pulled on my eyelids, and the pain started to build.

Dr. Kersten said, "Let's see if I can remove this blood clot with tweezers."

Again, I held my breath. "Okay, that's it. Now, you shouldn't have any more dripping blood. The outside of the eye looks good. The swelling should be down in a few weeks, and I would like to see you in a few weeks, after the membrane graft has had time to heal. The ring is in good position. Right now, you have epithelial tissue or skin for the front of your eye."

"Can she do exercises?" Ron asked.

"You can walk or use an elliptical machine without much tension, but no jumping rope or rowing machine, nothing that puts pressure on the eye itself."

I was started on five days of Cipro and Vicodin as needed. I only took Vicodin the first day as scheduled, then one tablet each of the following two days.

I thought, "Only take as much as you need and then less if possible. I'm not going down the addiction road again." Ibuprofen took care of any discomfort thereafter. Sleeping upright leaning against pillows was not the best, but I was willing to do whatever was necessary to see again.

Dr. Holland examined me and looked at Dr. Kersten's notes.

He said, "The healing process in a month's time will help us to know how it really looks. As long as Dr. Kersten likes what he sees, that is good. I will see you when you come back to see him again. Your next appointment is November 7."

We found out early in the process of setting up appointments that both doctors were in the Cincinnati Eye Institute Clinic on Tuesdays, so we made my appointments on Tuesday instead of having to travel into Kentucky to see one of them where they also practiced. We flew home to South Dakota. Now it was time to get Ron healthy.

October 18, 2006

Ron had surgery for his prostate cancer. Chad was there, along with other members of our families. Heather would be up on the weekend to check on her dad. Friends stopped in, and the vicar from our home church was there to visit and pray with us. The surgery went well, and Chad and I were allowed up to see him in recovery.

Ron was so funny. He held up his finger with the pulsometer on it and asked, "Did I break my finger?"

Chad laughed and said, "No, it's fine."

He made jokes until the anesthesia wore off, then it wasn't funny. Ron had an abdominal incision from just below his sternum to the pubic bone. Lots of staples were used to close the wound. The rehab started almost immediately, and Ron worked very hard at it, walking down the halls of the hospital as many times a day as he could to get stronger and having less pain with each step.

Three days after Ron's surgery the doctor said, "We are releasing you tomorrow."

Ron said, "I'm not ready to go home yet."

The doctor replied, "You are at greater risk for infection if you stay here. We are sending you home." We went home and Ron did fine. Recuperation takes time.

November 6–7, 2006

While Ron recuperated from his surgery, Chad volunteered to travel with me to Cincinnati. My appointment was the morning of the 7th. The plastic surgeon found that scar tissue had grown over the edge of the blepharon ring.

Dr. Kersten said, "I think we should set up surgery for tomorrow to remove the ring from under your lids." He continued his exam.

"Can't you just cut through the new tissue today?" I asked. "We have a plane to catch this afternoon."

"We may be able to do that. Let me check and see if there is a minor surgical suite open."

He found one free then administered a couple of numbing drops to my eye. Dr. Kersten led the way to a minor surgery room as Chad and I, walking arm in arm, followed. I didn't really want to have that minor surgery done while I was awake, but the hassle it took to get the airline tickets changed was enough to make me take the chance that it would be okay. Dr. Kersten, with local anesthesia and a very sharp scalpel, sliced right through the new tissue and removed the blepharon ring. We left the minor surgery room, and went to my appointment with Dr. Holland next.

After examining my eye, he said, "Without the blepharon ring, your eyelids may start to curl again. We

165

will see if that happens with the new tissue on your next visit. Have you set that up with Dr. Kersten yet?"

"No, we usually wait to set it up to see you both here on a Tuesday, less running around that way."

"Good deal," he replied. "We will see you in December. Have a safe trip home."

"Thank you," I told him as we gathered my purse and Chad came to lead me out.

Chad told me on the way to the airport, "When the first doctor said you needed surgery the next day to remove that ring, I had already put my head back on the chair to think about what we needed to do. You know, things like, book a room for another night in the motel, keep the rental car for another day and switch airline tickets. When you asked the doctor to cut it out while you were awake, I picked my head up off the back of the chair, looked at you and the doctor, and thought, 'You've got to be kidding me. You want to have that ring cut out while you're awake?' I can't believe you'd suggest he do that."

I said, "It saves us time and trouble of changing everything. If the ring can be removed in five minutes, why take an extra day to do it?"

I heard a chuckle in Chad's voice, along with a little disbelief.

"Now, if only my eyelids don't curl inward again. Let's pray for healing for both your dad and my eye and uncurled lids."

At the airport Chad and I were pulled aside, and our bags were dumped and checked. One of the security men stood with his arms crossed and just watched me. I looked up and smiled toward him because I could see a shadow of a man standing about four feet away. I told him, "I am having surgeries to restore my vision."

He said nothing. Then he put my shoes down in front of me except he set them down the opposite way of which they went. I found that out when I tried to slip my foot into one shoe and they were backwards. I just shook my head at the ignorance of some people.

166

"Ridiculous to do that to someone who has one eye stitched shut and the other one barely open," Chad fumed.

"I supposed terrorists would do anything to get their bombs set off in an airplane," I replied. We were only trying to get my sight back.

Ron and I spent the next month recuperating from our surgeries. Neighbors, friends, church members, and family took care of us, not only through prayer but also physically.

December 18, 2006

After two months Ron's healing process was coming along well, so we flew to Cincinnati.

Dr. Holland examined me and said, "The eye is well lubricated. It doesn't seem inflamed, which is good for surgery of stem cells. There are some eyelashes yet on the inside corner, but the eyelid closure is good. I want Dr. Kersten to take a look and see what he thinks. To me, it seems okay, but not ideal yet."

Dr. Kersten examined my eye next. "There is some swelling in the conjunctival tissue, but the margins of the eyelids are setting together well. The globe is stuck to the eyelid again because the blepharon ring was removed. So I think we should do another surgery on the eyelids to get better opening for the stem cells. We will do right entropion repair with insertion of a blepharon ring on January 19, 2007."

I made my calls to family, and the word spread once again across the country through emails and texts. My progress was being followed in many prayer circles and churches. I was pushing forward with whatever the doctors in Cincinnati told me was needed. I wanted to see again so badly. I thought this would be a six-month process and I would be able to see, but three months had gone by, and I was still not getting my stem cells.

January 19, 2007

This surgery was more of the same, lining the edge of the eyelid with tissue from inside my lower lip this time. It was officially called right upper eyelid resurface with mucous membrane graft. I was waking up from this surgery while the doctor was still putting stitches in my eyelid. My arm itched, and I started to rub it against my side.

"Could you please lie still?"

"My arm itches."

The nurse turned my arm outward, and there was a rash running up my arm from the IV line.

"Benadryl 50mg IV," said the doctor, "and add another antibiotic allergy to your list. Intravenous Cipro this time. You have to stop all Ciprofloxacin eye drops and don't take any oral Cipro that is prescribed in the future."

They were pleased with the outcome of the surgery. I, on the other hand, woke up with a strip of tissue from the inside of my lower lip removed. It stung like crazy, and I couldn't keep my tongue off it. The only thing I could get in my mouth was a tiny spoon of malt the first day, then soft foods. The next morning, I soaked a pancake up in enough syrup to make it mushy and very carefully spooned it in behind my teeth. All I had to do was swallow it. After flying home it took ten days for my mouth to heal. I most certainly prayed that would be the last time I would have to have that done.

January 29, 2007

We made a quick trip down to Cincinnati for a checkup on the healing process of my last surgery. Ron was starting to feel he should maybe not get out of school to travel with me so much, and furthermore he felt like he was not properly doing his job as a teacher leaving every month and sometimes every two weeks for my appointments. That was where my sister, Cathy, came in.

"If there is any time Ron can't go for some reason, I am here for you. I have never flown before and I don't know the first thing about getting through airports, but I am willing to try if it will help."

"Ron probably should not leave school as often as he has been to go to Cincinnati with me," I replied, even though the school had told Ron he was okay to take leave and not worry about it, he was covered.

I told Cathy, "I'll keep you posted if we need you to fly with me. Thanks for the offer. It means a lot to know we have a backup travel companion."

Cathy started traveling with me then. She and I were dropped off at the airport by her husband, Dave. She led me into the airport. We each had a carry-on bag.

I told her, "First, we need to look for the screens where the info for flights is posted. Then we need to check in at a kiosk. Next, we go through security. We need to take our shoes and coats off and put them in bins with our purses."

The phrase "blind leading the blind" came to mind. We made it to our gate on time and I told Cathy, "You did an awesome job."

We had grown in our Christian faith together and also closer as friends and sisters. When our plane landed late and our next connecting flight was on time we needed the gate for our next flight to be close, so we prayed. God answered our prayers. Many times that next gate for our connecting flight was just across the concourse. We felt so blessed.

Cathy would experience severe motion sickness unless she was the driver or was on Dramamine. When we got on the first plane, she said, "Wow, this is small. I can't believe how they pack people into these planes."

"Will you be okay with your motion sickness pill?" I asked.

"I took half of one."

"You'll need to take a whole one since the next plane we fly on will probably be smaller." And it was. So she took my advice.

At my appointment Dr. Kersten said, "I am happy with your eye, but there are a few eyelashes on the lower lid that need to be removed before the stem cell transplant."

I saw Dr. Holland after that, and he was also pleased with the condition of my eye. He said, "I will wait for Dr. Kersten's surgery to see what to do next. This will take about three months with healing and all."

February 23, 2007

After school on Friday, Ron and I drove to Omaha to get away from a snow storm that was coming to our area. We would fly on Sunday, and my surgery was scheduled for February 26. This was a lower lid recess with mucus membrane graft to the right eye. It went well, according to Dr. Kersten. He gave Ron instructions: "Put ointment in the right eye four times a day. Keep it moist."

The eye doctor in Brookings could check on the progress the following week. We flew home the next morning.

March 3, 2007

I especially wanted sight by now, the time my little grandson was due, but that wasn't to be. I still hadn't had a corneal transplant, so I could barely see the little face of our first little grandchild, Connor Ray.

As Chad placed this little five-pound baby in my arms, I started to cry tears of joy, frustration, and doubt. I said to Chad and Denise, "I am so sorry. This is such a happy time, and I am crying."

They both assured me, "We had our tears of joy, and it is perfectly okay with us if you cry a little."

I was still having preparatory surgeries to get ready for the corneal and stem cell transplants. I found this frustrating to say the least. I had a plan and wanted to follow it. Surgery, healing, surgery, healing, surgery, and sight in six months! It didn't happen.

With each trip to Cincinnati, I sent out a mass email to report the results. Family and friends forwarded my

170

message across the country so that at least one person in each of the fifty states was following my progress. Many added me to their church or personal prayer line. That was where our strength came from, all of the prayers offered up on our behalf. I was amazed with the response and encouraging words from far and wide.

Word got out that I would be speaking at a church in the Centerville area. As I tried to practice what I wanted to say, I just couldn't get my testimony to come together. I couldn't seem to stay on track or get my mind around how to work every important thing into a forty-five minute speech to tell people how God was so very loving and just waiting to answer our prayers.

Finally, I told Ron, "It will be okay if I forget something. No one will know but me, God, and a few others, and God will take care of this."

In conversation, I mentioned to Julie, Ron's niece that I was going to be speaking.

She asked, "Can anyone come? Send me details."

The following emails were a result of the news of that upcoming speaking engagement:

Sent: Monday, March 12, 2007
Julie,
I am not sure how many churches they are inviting from the area but I am speaking March 31st. I think a 10:00 start is planned. I can't wait to put a new ending onto God's story of my life.
Love,
Jenny

From Julie to Joni, another of Ron's nieces:
Sent: Monday, March 12, 2007
Joni,
I talked to the event coordinator yesterday and they are having a Guest Day. I told her to put me down for two. I think they want numbers, and I think anyone is welcome. Talk later, Julie

Hi Julie, thanks for forwarding Jenny's message about her speaking date. That would be fun to go to. I see it is on a Saturday so I will plan to attend.
Talk later. Joni

When Ron dropped me off at the church where I was to speak, Cathy met our car. It was pouring rain and the parking lot was a sloppy mess. Cathy led me under the carport and into the church.

After we had eaten and family members started coming over to greet me, I was amazed at how many of our family were present. Now I was nervous. I started to pray inside my head and inside my heart, "O God, please use me to give your message for those present today."

While the women were moving into the sanctuary, I decided to give a VHS tape of *The Miracle Worker* show to my sister, Vicki. She was to be my stem cell donor. Before we went into the sanctuary, I told her, "The show is dramatized by saying the sister has a chance of losing her vision in the donor eye, but I spoke to the doctor about this and he said it is not true. No one has ever lost sight by being a stem cell donor."

Vicki said, "I don't care. I have another eye. I will give up one eye if it gives you a chance to see again."

I could barely believe my ears. I had no clue anyone felt that way, and on top of it, I didn't want my sister to lose her eye sight. I didn't want anyone to go through that difficult situation. All I could do was hug her tight and thank her.

My thought was, "If our sisters and brothers love us this much, how much do you think God loves us?"

The youth of the church gave a dramatic mime of *Watch the Lamb*. I couldn't see what was going on, but just listening made me emotional. When I was introduced, my sister, Cathy, helped me up to the podium. With guitar strap around my neck and shoulder, I started to speak. My voice was shaky from the amazing portrayal of Christ's crucifixion. On top of that, knowing that between one hundred fifty and one hundred seventy-five family members and other women were sitting there, waiting for me to tell them how God had been working in my life, was overwhelming for me. As I started, I felt a strange calm come over me. It was so amazing. The time went by, and God's story was told through me. As I ended my testimony, there was applause, and I stood at the podium and waited until Cathy took my arm. We got back to our seats, and my other two sisters each greeted me with "that was awesome," "great job," "wonderful," to which I replied almost in a daze, "That was God."

When practicing my testimony, if it doesn't fall into place, I let God tell His story through me. I simply had to stand up front and give Him control. All I could say was having the Holy Spirit work through me was a wonderful experience.

March 19, 2007

Ron and I met Cathy and Dave for lunch, and I went home with them. Cathy and I were on our way back to Ohio and Kentucky for yet another checkup. My appointment was on March 20, 2007. Both doctors agreed that my eye looked good.

"Let's give your eye another two months of healing time, and if all still looks good, we will schedule the stem cell surgery."

I was frustrated with all the waiting and yet relieved to have two months before another trip. How many eyelash removal surgeries could you do and still not get all the lashes out? It was seven long months of flights, planning for the next flight, paperwork, getting my job done, and on and on. I was praying along with many others that this worked and we would survive the rigors of the trips. Many times the doctors seemed to tell me the same things. More eyelashes to be removed or the eyelids are not closing properly.

May 21, 2007

Ron and I were on our way to Ohio to see whether my eye was ready for the stem cell transplant. My appointment was at 9:40 in the morning with Dr. Kersten. He examined my eye.

"I am delighted with how well you are doing," he said.

"Is it normal for my sight to get better even if I haven't had the corneal transplant yet?"

"Yes," he answered. "The surface of your cornea looks smoother, so that explains why you seem to be seeing more clearly. Let's see what Dr. Holland thinks about your eye before we plan anything."

Ron saw Dr. Kersten and Dr. Holland conferencing. He asked, "Do you suppose they are discussing your case?"

"Probably not," I said. "They have so many patients, what are the chances?"

We were called in to see Dr. Holland an hour later. "Your eye closes nicely and easily. I think we are good to go for the stem cell transplant. The transplant coordinator, Stacy, will call you. This is a big step. Follow-ups are critical."

Ron asked, "What are the major problems with this surgery?"

Dr. Holland explained, "Infection, of course, is major, if the skin does not heal. Too dry is a real problem. If the surgery does not work, we will let it scar over again like it wants to and stitch the eye shut. We'll see you in a month, remove stitches, and your eye will be back to where we started, no worse than what you have now."

"Okay, that sounds good," Ron said.

"Stacy will call you to coordinate immune suppressant therapy and get you set up for that."

"Thank you for all you are doing to help people like me have a chance at seeing," I said.

"You're welcome," he answered. "We all do what we can."

Stacy told me, "You should have sight after this next surgery."

"Are you sure this surgery is when I should be able to see if it works?"

I'm thinking, "I don't think I am supposed to be able to see before the corneal transplant surgery is done," so I continued to question her.

She continued to tell me, "Yes, if the surgery is a success, you will see after this surgery."

I might have been confused, but I thought the cornea was to help me see.

Ron and I flew to Sioux Falls, drove in the pouring rain, and got to DeSmet at 11:30 that night. The next day, Stacy, the surgical coordinator, phoned me. We discussed my blood pressure and medications. "There will be blood drawn at your local hospital, and the results will be faxed to us. We will then adjust your dosages of anti-immune medications according to the blood work results. You will be started on a high dose of steroids, 40-60mg daily. These can cause weight gain, so be careful with your diet. Dr. Holland will start them after surgery in August. The anti-immune medications will be started a week prior to surgery."

"Okay," I said.

"We will mail you a copy of these instructions, any questions?"

"No," I answered. "Not yet."

June 2007

A fundraiser bake sale was held during the Old Settler's Day parade in DeSmet to help us with some of the expenses of traveling to Cincinnati and Kentucky. We had made nine trips so far, and I hadn't even had my stem cell surgery yet. The amount of bake goods delivered was unbelievable, and we were very touched to see the response to this bake sale. Many people donated, and many more came and bought baked goods, homemade jellies, and snack mix. The money raised was three times what was expected, and a third of this was matched by a Lutheran fundraising company. Chad, Denise, and Connor

175

Ray came up for the weekend. Connor was only three months old. Everyone could see how much he looked like his daddy. I was still patiently waiting to have the stem cell transplant to see that for myself.

Also that summer, a couple of Ron's former golfers decided to hold a golf tournament benefit, and the money raised would also be matched by Thrivent and would help once again with motels, meals and other expenses. Ron and I visited with people who attended. My chin was quivering. I could barely stop the tears of gratitude for everything these caring people were doing for us. We wouldn't have to sell any of our possessions to pay for these trips thanks to their giving hearts.

July 2007

I was sent an appointment to see the doctor who would manage my anti-immune medications. They wanted to see me in the Kentucky office. I made some phone calls and got the flights set up.

Finally, the time had arrived when I was to start immunosuppressant medications. The doctor instructed me that I needed to be seen in the Kentucky Clinic to test and make sure I was healthy enough to take the immunosuppressants. After flying down and getting lost in a not-very-safe part of town, we arrived at my appointment. I was weighed, blood was taken, and my blood pressure was checked. The doctor spoke to me about immunosuppressant therapy then I was free to go.

I said to Ron, "This seems to me to be a wasted trip. Blood work, weight and blood pressure checked. All that could be done at home and faxed down. The doctor could have easily made prescription and dosage recommendations without us making the trip to his office in Ohio."

We were frustrated and felt this truly was an unnecessary trip. We arrived back home and waited for our next appointment date. I received the surgical date of August 8, 2007. Once again, I called the flight company and got our flights set up. I also called Vicki. It was time for her to go donate the stem cells. She was ready and excited to do this for me.

August 6, 2007

For this trip, Cathy, Vicki, Ron, and I all flew to Cincinnati. Vicki was my stem cell donor, and Cathy would accompany her on the way home because she would have limited lifting and one-eye vision. We were delayed until midnight at Chicago's airport due to weather. We arrived in Kentucky and found all the car rental businesses closed. One shuttle was charging fifty dollars per person one way to take us to Cincinnati. We got a cab, and he drove like a maniac.

After safely arriving at our motel, we opened our luggage to get ready for bed and found most of our clothes were wet. Our luggage had been left out on the tarmac in the pouring rain during the storms in Chicago. The rain had seeped through the zippers on our luggage and soaked our clothes. We found a few dry t-shirts to wear to bed.

The next morning, Vicki and I had our pre-op appointments. She was instructed for post-op activities to be off of work one week due to her job in a paper envelope factory and all the dust from it. Otherwise, she was good to do her normal activity. I needed pre-op photos and stopped the Erythromycin the night before surgery. Post-op there was a 50/50 chance that Dr. Kersten would have to put a stitch in my eyelid. I would have a patch on my eye after surgery.

August 8, 2007

Vicki and I were both prepped for surgery. Vicki's surgery was at 1:15p.m. and mine was at 1:45p.m. We were taken to connecting surgical rooms. This allowed the stem cells to be removed from Vicki's eye and brought directly to me for transplanting. It was a success, but I couldn't see.

I said to Dr. Holland, "I was told I would be able to see after this surgery."

"Who told you that?"

"Stacy did. Chad, Denise, Connor, Heather, all my children, and grandson are flying down here due to her telling me that if this surgery is a success, I will see."

"I'll visit with her about this," said Dr. Holland.

We were all disappointed. Not only were the kids, my sisters, and my husband all present, but my first little grandson that I had never seen was there. I wanted to see now!

Dr. Holland told Ron, "Jenny's eye is soft after surgery, but that is better than hard. She will need another surgery, the corneal transplant, before she will be able to see."

Ron was in shock. Dr. Holland said, "The eyelid is free to move now. We peeled off part of the old cornea and put a new layer of skin over it."

Chad called saying that they had landed at the airport. Ron went to meet them. We ordered pizza. I got sick during the night from the anesthesia. My eye pain was better, but I had a big headache.

August 9, 2007

At my appointment, Dr. Holland said, "The eye moves well, and the pressure is good. A successful first surgery allows the second, which is the corneal transplant. I need to break some adhesions because the eyelid is trying to stick to the new cells."

Ron said, "He is going to see if Dr. Kersten has a donut ring to put in under your lids. Are you okay?"

"Yes," I answered.

Dr. Holland came in. "Here is the plan. Go to CEI. Dr. Kersten will put in the ring and place a stitch on the outside of your eyelid to hold it in place. The stem cell surgery was a success. Things went well. Don't get any water in your eye for a week. Wear the metal shield at night for a month, okay?"

I wasn't sure if it was okay. He had ordered my eyelid sewn shut, and that was not what I wanted.

Vicki's checkup went well. Her eye looked good, and she had to put drops in for a week. Her vision was 20/20. I was so glad the stem cell harvest did not damage her eye. Cathy and Vicki flew home after Vicki's checkup. Heather, Chad, Denise, and Connor Ray all stayed. I was not able to do much. My eye hurt to try and open it, and light caused great pain. It felt like I had something in my eye all the time.

From Ron's journal:
PRAY
August 9, 2007
Dr. Kersten is going to put a conformer or donut ring in Jenny's eye. Looks like he is not very careful, pushes pretty hard with a q-tip. Dr. Kersten puts three sutures on the outside and three on the inside of lids. One more shot to deaden, one more shot to deaden again. Will put ring in but not leave in. Dr. Kersten decides not to put ring in because it may stick to stem cells from yesterday. He will go only with stitches. I watched the whole procedure.

From Ron's journal:
PRAY
August 10, 2007
Go to Dr. Holland's office in Edgewood, Kentucky. Eye: no pain, some headache, lights bother still, asked about Jenny's medications again. Jenny still feels like sleeping all the time. Can see a hand moving in front of her up and down, side to side but no fingers. Worst sight Jenny has ever had.

The doctor trainee said, "The surgery was to keep your eye alive for the next surgery. Your eye probably won't clear up before you have the corneal transplant. What Dr. Kersten did yesterday worked well. Your sight may go back to what it was before surgery, so you will have okay walking-around sight. Two eyelashes were going in the wrong direction, so we pulled them out. Your sight is not good now because of surgery. Some sections of the stem cells are starting to grow already. Keep doing what you are doing. The pain is probably because of how extensive the scarring was. Surgery and stress can cause the headache. You need patience."

I wanted to say, "Listen here, buddy, we have had patience for long enough. Now get my sight fixed." But of course I didn't. I continued to pray that someday I would be able to see.

August 11-13, 2007

Chad, Denise, Connor Ray, and Heather left for the airport the next morning. Chad called and said, "Our flight has been canceled, so we are now leaving at 11:45 a.m. Heather's flight was okay, and she is in the air."

Until now most of the trips had been going for a checkup and returning home the same day, or at least the next day. For this trip, we stayed nine days. The longest stay before this was six days when I had the first surgery. Crazy, but we just kept thinking that it would all be worth it when I could see again. Each day, we had an appointment for the doctors to adjust something with my eye.

The assistant doctor came in. "How are you doing today?" he asked cheerily.

"I'm not sure. I have a lot of pain, and can't keep my eye open. It feels like there is something in it."

"Let's put in a drop to numb your eye and take a look," he responded. As soon as the numbing drop hit my eye, I could open it without pain. The exam began. After he examined my eye, he didn't tell me anything except, "Dr. Holland will be in soon."

Another forty-five minutes passed before Dr. Holland came in to examine my eye. "The upper right corner of your eye has inflammation, and the healing process is in progress. That is why you have pain."

180

He ordered an ultrasound of the back of my eye to make sure that the retina was not part of the pain problem. "Your eye is very dry," he said. "The transplanted cells are starting to work, however."

"How long before my sight comes back to where it was," I asked. "All I see now is mostly red."

"That's hard to determine. Each patient is different. The eye is extremely complicated. I see one adhesion that we need to break; otherwise, everything looks good. Let's put another numbing drop in your eye. I'm going to pull out some lashes."

"I thought I had all those lashes taken care of by Dr. Kersten," I said.

"That is a very difficult procedure to do. They continue to come back," Dr. Holland said.

"Your blink rate is down, and that leaves your eye to dry out. I think we need Dr. Kersten to put a couple of stitches in the outer corner of your eye."

"I don't really want my eye sewn shut."

"It won't be closed that much. We need to keep moisture on your transplant. Do you have any other questions?"

"Can I have some of the numbing drops until this healing is farther along?"

"That will only slow down the healing process and viability of the stem cells." he said. "Anything else?"

"Yes, I really don't want my eyelids closed."

"It will only be one or two stitches, not that much," he reassured me.

"Okay, I guess," I said.

Ron and I went to the waiting room until Dr. Kersten called us in to put a stitch in my eyelid. He said, "I think we can go with fifty percent closure, and that should work."

I told him, "I don't want to do this, have my eyelid sewn shut. Dr. Holland said one stitch."

"Dr. Holland will not go any further with this surgical process unless he can get the eyelids closed."

181

With a very shaky and angry voice, I said, "During my very first appointment back in July of 2006 with you, I made it clear that I did not want my right eyelids sewn shut. My left eyelid has been surgically closed for thirty years now, and one eye closed is enough."

"It's up to you," Dr. Kersten said abruptly, "but Dr. Holland is not going to go any further with this process unless your eyelids are closed."

"How long will my eyelids remain closed?" I asked.

"They will be closed permanently until Dr. Holland thinks we can open them. It's your choice?"

I pouted, I fumed. I was not a happy camper, but I agreed to the closure, and as soon as the stitching was done, Dr. Kersten ripped a sticky-backed piece of paper off my face none too gently. I sat up. The nurse tried to make sure I was okay, not dizzy, not feeling lightheaded, but I told Ron, "Just get me out of here." I was so mad I could have flown home without a plane. I needed to leave this place regardless of whether I felt sick or not.

The stitches closed fifty percent of my eyelid. I was taking twenty pills a day and doing drops four times a day and nothing was getting better.

From Ron's journal:
PRAY
August 13, 2007
The longer we stay the worse this trip gets. This is too damn much to go through, this reminds me of all the trips to New York City, all the pain and shit Jenny had to go through.

I kept thinking, "If I could see, if only I could see again."

I told Ron, "Remember when Dr. Kersten said, 'If there is a need for closure of the lid, it will not be that much, just a little on the corners and will not interfere with your being able to see'. Do you remember that? They have now sewn my eye halfway closed. I can't see anything but red. I can't even keep my eye open. How is that better?"

I was angry, frustrated, and tired of all the procedures, and my sight was just getting worse. "Do you realize, Ron, that all the surgeries that were done to build the edge of my eyelids up to give more closure to my lids are what Dr. Kersten just cut off? I don't think they plan to ever open my eyelids. What could I do? If I didn't allow the eyelids to be closed, I would have a chance of losing my eye."

I was praying with every thought, that God would help me. In between praying, I was crying. I didn't even know what to pray anymore. I just knew I needed to keep God close in this mess. He was the only one who understood me and knew what would happen. I needed Him in control. We would fly home the next day. I would get to go through airports with less vision than ever. I wouldn't drink much, so I wouldn't have to use a restroom during flights. It was just too complicated in airport bathrooms and with too many people in a hurry. May God help us all. My next appointment was to be in September, and hopefully I would be able to see more by then.

September 2007

The stories of my surgeries and progress to regain vision were being published in local newspapers in Iowa because my aunt and uncle lived there. Our family hadn't been back since our Mom died. My aunt asked my brother, Rick, and his band to come down to play on a Sunday afternoon.

She said, "The people who have been praying for success of your procedures want to meet Jenny."

Before we knew what happened, this family picnic turned into a bake sale and benefit for us. My brother's band provided music, and a bake sale auction was held. The people were bidding crazy. Thirty-five dollars was bid for a small loaf of bread and twenty dollars for a dozen buns because people wanted to be able to help. It was a fun time. Everyone who heard of my attempt to regain my sight after thirty-three years wanted to help.

All the money raised from the benefits in both states was put into a bank account specifically used for travel, meals, rooms and medication expenses. We could not have paid for all of these trips without the help from these benefits generously supported by local people and family members. It was amazing to be the recipient of such generosity. The flight companies were a great help to us also.

My cost for one medication per month was two thousand dollars. The rest of the costs added up fast. There was no way we could afford all that on our own. God's work and people's hands were what made the difference.

September 10, 2007

Up until now, the flight companies had been helping me and whoever flew as my companion, get flights to Ohio. Cathy and I booked our own flights for this trip. The flight companies were not always able to help us due to finances being short. Cathy paid for her own ticket to help out with expenses. We landed in Ohio without any problems, drove to our motel and tried to rest for my appointment in the morning.

Dr. Holland examined my eye and said, "It is normal that light bothers your eye. I can hardly see the stem cells because of the scarring. The cells are growing, lids are sticking to where we put the stem cells, and there are cells everywhere. No erosion. Cells have grown and healed, so that's good."

I asked on behalf of my sister Vicki. "If the stitches have not absorbed, can they be removed by a doctor at home?"

"Yes, Vicki doesn't need to use drops any longer. All should be well."

Dr. Kersten examined my eye, too. "This is a tough disease. The eyelid is sticking to the eyeball. We are not

184

going to do any surgery now until everything has quieted down."

"How long will that be?" I asked.

The answer was not what I want to hear. "Six to nine months."

Dr. Holland said, "The post-surgical scarring is bad news. We are going to wait and see what the scarring does over the next six to nine months. By then, the cells will be completely covered on the surface, and the surface needs to be better before we do a corneal transplant. Your lid function was better on your last visit. There needs to be better blinking function to keep moisture on your eye. The lower lid is sticking, so it is not closing as well as it was."

"When will I get my sight back?"

Again, the answer is not what I wanted to hear, "Not until we can do something else. You should get back the sight you had before surgery. Let's put the ring back in your eye for awhile."

I took a deep breath and put one foot in front of the other. It was all I could do except pray.

Cathy and I drove to the airport and flew home.

October 2007

It had been one year since we started this crazy journey of flying every two to four weeks, and nothing seemed to be better. However, the corneal doctor and plastic surgeon were telling me my eye was more stable now than when we started.

But I thought, "So, I'm not seeing better, and not even as good at times."

October 23, 2007

Ron flew with me to Ohio. I was having more surgery to remove eyelashes. Do they really come back after this many removal surgeries? Dr. Kersten wanted to see me again on October 30.

Ron said, "He thinks you live across the street. The good news is the surgery went well, but how long does it take to remove eyelash follicles? You were only in surgery for twenty minutes. I sometimes wish we had never started this whole thing."

I said, "But Ron, I want to see so badly. We just have to trust that they are doing what they say."

We stayed in Blue Ash until the October 30 appointment with Dr. Kersten. Ron was learning the area more each trip, and we ventured out just to kill time. Now, to take the cake, Dr. Kersten said, "I am moving to Denver the first of December. My replacement plastic surgeon is very good. He is not in the Blue Ash office the same day as Dr. Holland, however, so you will actually need to see him in the Kentucky office."

In the middle of the process, I had to have a new plastic surgeon, and he was not in the office on the same day as Dr. Holland, which meant more days in Cincinnati. It felt like a marathon, and we were not winning. We didn't know what to do. Only God could lead us.

December 3–5, 2007

This was my final checkup of the year. Dr. Holland said, "There is more moisture in the eye than before, so that is good. It is less inflamed, and that is good, too. If your eye looks like this or even better in March, we will set you up for a corneal surgery."

I was beaming. I couldn't wait, and neither could anyone else who had been praying for a successful process all these months. "What is the percentage of the corneal transplant being successful and giving me sight?" I asked Dr. Holland.

"Probably fifty-fifty," he answered.

I thought it was better than none, and if I just went back to where I started, we might as well do it.

Ron and I tried to survive the months until my corneal transplant surgery. It was difficult. At times I would fall asleep at the breakfast table due to low blood levels from too high of a dose of medications. I went to have blood drawn two to three times a week and adjustments in my dosages were made. The medications were very expensive and I didn't have any better vision.

March 17-18, 2008

This was our sixteenth trip in our quest to have my sight restored. Cathy and I traveled together. She was becoming a seasoned traveler, learning about standbys, printing our boarding passes the night before our flights, and taking empty water bottles through security to fill them at a water fountain later. Cathy and I missed our plane one morning due to icy roads. We spent many hours in the airport. I was wearing a mask due to my lowered immune system and the H1N1 flu season. Dr. Holland wanted to wait until spring to do my corneal transplant when not so much heat would be running in homes and cars, which could cause drying to my cornea. "It will need all the moisture we can keep on it," he said.

During my appointment, Dr. Holland asked, "Are you willing to take a risk of losing your vision altogether?"

I was shocked. "What?" I said, "You said there was no risk to my vision."

"Yes, with the first surgeries. Now there is a risk you need to think about. You will need to decide if you are willing to take it."

After all of the trips and all of the surgeries, I thought it would be stupid to stop, but the risk of losing my vision totally was scarier than anything I could have imagined. I began to think of seeing again.

"What do you think I should do?"

He said, "There is a chance of losing your sight totally, so you need to make this decision."

"I was told at the beginning of the surgeries that there was no risk, but this is new information. I have not been told of the risk after all the preparation surgeries."

Cathy said, "Jen, you can't see that much now."

She was right about that. So I decided to take the chance. It seemed like my only option. I felt that if I stopped the surgeries now, it would be like quitting in the

187

middle of a race. It didn't seem like the right thing to do. I decided to take the risk.

"Okay, let's do the corneal transplant," I decided.

Dr. Holland said, "The decision of a human cornea versus an artificial one will be made at a later date."

I was not sure whether I would regret this decision but prayed God would be with us and the surgeons. My corneal transplant surgery was set up for May 5, 2008. I was excited and scared. Everyone who received the emails was praying for a successful turnout.

Ron and I traveled to Cincinnati, Ohio, on May 4, 2008 and on May 5, I had my corneal transplant. The surgery went well. We were to start applying drops after four hours.

From Ron's journal:
PRAY
Corneal Transplant:
Surgery date and time: May 5th, 2008 12:15
Human donor cornea is used. 90% of scarring is removed so as to not perforate the eye and have less chance of infection. Length of surgical procedure: 2 hours, was only to be 1 hour but due to the amount of scarring and not doing a full corneal transplant it took longer. A clear plastic shell called a bandage lens was put over the front of Jenny's eye to cover the cornea also for prevention of drying out. Surgery is outpatient.

After I was out of recovery, with a patch over my eye, I was sent with Ron to care for me back to our motel. Four hours later, Ron and I were ready to remove the dressing and apply drops to my eye. Ron removed the tape from one side of my eye patch. I was sitting on the edge of the bed, very still, not moving my head so as not to cause any harm to what might be under the patch. Ron was taking his time getting the tape off my face, trying not to remove any skin. Then with a swish, the loosened side of the eye patch fell down, and over the top of it I saw Ron. His glasses

188

hung on the end of his nose. He was concentrating on getting the tape free from my skin when I said to him with a shaky voice, "Hi, it's good to see you." He stopped what he was doing and put his arm around my head and hugged me close, carefully, very carefully. We were both crying. I could hardly believe the color of his eyes was the very same. As a matter of fact, he looked pretty much the same as he did thirty-two years ago, just better. The bedspread had big pink cabbage roses all over it. The flowering shrubs were in bloom outside along the walkways. This was so wonderful! We could hardly believe it. God had blessed us! The doctors had done what they said, even though it took longer than any of us wanted. And my eyelid was open again! We thanked God immediately after coming to our senses. Ron put my drops in and we started making calls. Everyone was excited. We could barely speak, and we just kept thanking God and praising the surgeons. They had done it! Many tears were shed during those phone calls.

Ron said, "Want to go shopping?" I smiled. "I just want to see everything. Let's go." We walked around a department store, and it was so much fun, just to see all the colors clearly again. To me, everything looked good. I couldn't decide what I liked and what I didn't like. Everything I saw was beautiful: people, purses, trees, street lights, Ron, yes, everything. I peeked out from behind a rack at Ron. From two racks over, I waved at him, happy to be able to see him looking back at me. It was wonderful!

We had to return to the clinic every couple of days for checkups and new instructions. By the next day, my vision was down again.

From Ron's journal:
PRAY
May 7, 2008
It is coffee time. Jenny is reading headlines in US Today. Easier to see when eye is dry, put drops or moisture in and sight isn't as good.

After a few days of walking around, we decided to go to the ball game at Reds Stadium. I was so overwhelmed by the things I could see. I couldn't say how we even got to the ball park, let alone which direction we walked into the stadium. After Ron and I entered the stadium and walked up to the top where we entered the seating area, I stood still. The sight of all those red seats against the green playing field was more beautiful than I ever could have dreamed, all that color springing back into focus once again.

I thought it a good idea to use the bathroom before taking our seats. Ron asked, "Can you find your way around in the bathroom okay?"

"Yes."

I walked into the first door, and I could see why at times I couldn't find a bathroom stall. The first room was actually only sinks. There was a second door through which the actual bathroom stalls were. I walked to one all by myself as I felt tears start to form. I looked to see if anyone was occupying the stall. By now, I felt my eyes and nose getting hot. I still didn't make tears to actually run down my cheeks, but my emotions were high. I was actually in a state of euphoria. It was unbelievable. I washed my hands and left the bathroom.

Back in the corridor, I found Ron waiting for me as always. I could barely speak but managed to say, "Ron, I found my way through two rooms in that huge bathroom without any help. I can't believe this. It's a miracle."

Ron put his arm around my neck and pulled me to him. Emotions ran high for us both. Crying came easy.

May 8, 2008

I had a one o'clock appointment with Dr. Holland. Everything still looked good with my eye. I was able to see two fingers from four feet away. It was amazing. No words could express how wonderful it was to see. I absolutely couldn't wait to get home and see my kids, our families, but most of all, my little grandson, Connor Ray. I knew he was going to be so big by now. I wouldn't be able to lift him, and I didn't care, because I could see! Thank you God for all the days you lifted my spirits. Thank you for leading us to Ohio.

Dr. Holland said, "I can see the back of your eye for the first time ever. It looks good. I want to leave the bandage contact on to help keep moisture on your eye. Your blink is only closing ten percent."

An associate of Dr. Holland's spoke to us. He looked too young to be a doctor. I started to smile at him and said, "I am sorry for not being able to hear what you are saying due to the fact I can see you."

Ron said, "He looks about eighteen years old."

"How much better will my vision get?" I asked.

"It will continue to clear over the next month, and that probably will be it," Dr. Holland said. "Don't get water in your eye for a month, and no lifting over twenty-five pounds."

Rules, rules, rules, but I had my sight back, and it would be okay.

Then Dr. Holland said, "I think due to the ten percent lid closing, we need to stitch your eyelid shut a little, about fifty percent."

I said, "No, not again. How can I see if you close my lids?"

I was sick at heart and angry. Just before I was going to go home, Dr. Holland was going to close my eyelids over my sight. "Oh God, I don't want this! Please don't do this," I prayed. But they did. What good was vision if my eyelids were closed over it? Frustrating! My eyelid was swollen from the anesthesia injected into it. Actually, they ended up closing my eyelid about sixty percent. I only had a little corner towards my nose of my eyelid open to look through. Due to the injection of Lidocaine and swelling from the trimming of my eyelid, once again, my vision was not as good.

I felt a sickness in my stomach when my vision was taken so quickly and realized I could be totally blind just that fast. We had all asked God to grant His blessing upon me and give me my eyesight back, and now I trusted Him for that.

When we got to the airport back home, our families were waiting. It was so good to see all of them again even if it wasn't clear. My sight was so much better than it had been in thirty years.

Since it was Mother's Day weekend, Chad, Denise, Connor and Heather were all coming home with us. When we pulled onto our street in DeSmet, we found balloons in front of our garage. People brought in food for our lunch. The entire town was celebrating my restored vision. After church, Ron put the finishing touches on lunch. Then he got a great idea. "Why don't you kids go out on the deck and stand in the sunshine to see if Mom can see you better?" We all filed out the sliding glass doors. Chad stood before me and said, "Can you see me, Mom?"

"No," I said. I was turning my head side to side to try to get the little space in the corner of my eye to line up with my cornea so I could see. I then thought about the moisture drops I was to put in my eye. I said, "I have these little drops. Maybe if I put one in my eye it will clear it and I can see you better."

I got out the little vial and put a drop in my eye. With one blink, my son, whom I had not seen this clearly in over thirty years, came into view.

I said to him, "You grew up."

"Yes, I did," he said.

"You look just like your dad."

Chad said, "That's what they tell me." Then he said, "Now it's time to see Connor Ray."

I was already starting to cry, I had waited so long to see and now God was letting me see Connor Ray. Chad turned and picked up Connor, who was standing at the sliding doors looking in at Heather's puppy, Riley. Chad said, "Connor, look at Grandma."

He turned his little face toward me, and I am trying to keep my head still so I can see. There was the face of the little son I had left behind so many years ago. Connor looked just like his daddy. It was so wonderful to see him. Chad motioned for Denise to come over. She was wiping tears from her face and said to me, "I was going to bring you a box of tissues for Mother's Day, but I forgot them on the counter."

I told her, "It's fine. The doctor says moisture is good for our eyes, and tears are moisture, so not to worry."

She was a beautiful woman, a good wife and mommy. It was so good to put faces to voices. Finally, Heather stepped in front of me. Many people over the years had said to me, "Do you realize how beautiful Heather is?" To which I would reply, "No, tell me." Not one person even came close. When my little daughter, now all grown up, stood in front of me, I saw in her beautiful face the little three year old that I had not seen for all of those years. She was hiding behind the grown woman she'd become. Many times, Heather had tested me over the years, and she tested me again now. "Okay, Mom, what can you see?"

"I can see your teeth, your smile lines, but not quite your blue/green eyes that people have been telling me about. But Dr. Holland said it would take up to thirty days for my vision to improve to where it is going to be at its best, so we are not going to worry about that. I will wait to see the color of your eyes."

Over the next ten days, I enjoyed everything. My friends stopped in with flowers. Even frying eggs in a skillet and watching the whites turn color against the yellow of the yolk was beautiful. I had a plaque hanging in the bathroom which read, *"You hold your children's hands for just awhile but their hearts forever"*. I read this every morning, judging the improvement of my vision by how far away I could stand and still read the words. Life was so wonderful. I looked out the window at the trees, the birds and the green grass.

Moisture seemed to be the most important factor of keeping the cornea healthy, so we put a humidifier in our bedroom to run all night. I put saran wrap over my right eye with ointment under it when I slept, and I continuously put Systane eye drops in. It was all a pain in the neck, but I would do anything to keep my sight.

Then, on day ten of having vision, I noticed that I couldn't read the plaque in the bathroom. I knew what it said, but I couldn't see the words.

"Something is wrong with my vision," I told Ron.

"What do you think you need to do?"

"I need to call Dr. Holland," I said.

I called CEI and was asked to see a Sioux Falls eye surgeon for a check of what might be happening. Dr. Hohm thought that I had an infection. I needed to return to Ohio. We made arrangements to fly to Cincinnati in June 2008. An exam by Dr. Holland showed that my cornea was hazing over on the top. "I think your eye looks good as far as there not being any infection," he said. "The cornea is hazed over halfway down. The cornea has healed nicely, however." Dr. Holland removed the stitches from my eyelids, but the lids had now grown shut. He said, "I want to give this four to five months to clear, and if it doesn't, we can do another surgery, possibly with an artificial cornea or donor again."

In the meantime, I was going to have little to no vision. I was not liking this one bit.

I was switched to a compound antibiotic that was about forty dollars a bottle and had to be mixed at a compound company.

I sent an email to Stacy to discuss this.

From: Jenny Peterson
Sent: Wed 6/11/2008
To: Stacy
Subject: Vanco
Stacy,

In SD they have a compounding company so I will get the drops mixed there. If you could fax a script to them I would appreciate it since it is quicker than me getting this written script to them.
I will get the first bottle through Kentucky but try to change after that.
Thanks
Jenny

From: Stacy
To: Jenny Peterson
Sent: Thursday, June 12, 2008
Subject: RE: Vanco
No problem! I will fax a script over this morning.
Have a great day!

Email from Jenny to family and friends:

Date: June 12, 2008
Hello all,
Here is what has happened since my May 5th corneal transplant.
You may remember the doctors left my own cornea with 10% of the scarring on it. This was done as to not open my eye up to any infection. Also to see how I would accept a cornea. Looks like I am accepting the corneal transplant, the doctors say it looks good. I just can't see through it. It is my own corneal layer that is hazing over, getting cloudy. They have seen this happen before and it does sometimes clear up after a couple of months. If it does not clear up we will then discuss another corneal transplant, only a full thickness one this time. That means they will take my cornea off completely, opening my eye up to infection which could cost me all the vision I have if that would happen. We trust God is not going to let that happen so we go forward. We would at that time decide whether a plastic or human donor cornea would be used. Only if my own cornea does not clear within 4 months or so will the full

thickness surgery be done. The haziness on my cornea is the reason I have not been seeing as well as I thought I was at first. Part of the problem is the narrowed space in my eyelids that I look through. My stitches have been removed but my eyelid is grown shut so I still have my lid shut most of the way, we have put a humidifier in our bedroom for moisture at night to help my eye remain moist. Also some patients have stuck saran wrap over their eye at night to keep moisture in. I am doing this too. Anything to help the cornea heal properly is what I will do. I am not in any pain. The doctors pulled out a few eyelashes so the foreign body sensation is also gone for the most part.

Thank you all for your continued prayers. We will be going back to Cincinnati August 11th for an August 12th appointment. We will be seen in Sioux Falls in a month's time for a check with the local doctor.

I think that is all I can remember for now. God has blessed Ron and me with a sister who is able and willing to drop her own life's work to travel with me when Ron can't go and we can't thank her enough for that. We thank you Cathy and Dave also for that gift.

Love you,
Jenny and Ron

June 30, 2008
Good morning Stacy,
Just wondering if Dr. Holland would know how bad my vision will get before it starts to clear, if it is going to get clear.
At this time I am barely seeing light. I am seeing Dr. Hohm in Sioux Falls on July 10th.
Jenny

In July 2008, Cathy and I flew to Cincinnati for another appointment. I saw, Dr. Megalo, who was managing my anti-rejection drugs. He asked about lesions, and I pulled up my jeans leg and showed him my legs. I had just had eight or ten spots removed or frozen. He asked, "Have you lost weight."

I said, "Yes, I have lost about fifteen pounds."

Cathy said, "This is due to eating more carrots and apples instead of carrot cake and apple pie than anything else."

Dr. Megalo said, "Immediately stop taking Valcyte and Prograf."

"I just filled the one. It cost me two thousand dollars a month."

He replied, "I know, ridiculous isn't it? But stop the medications."

I was only on CellCept and needed to decrease the Prograf for one month before stopping it.

He asked, "Have you had a colonoscopy, pelvic exam, or mammogram lately?"

"Well, two out of three isn't bad. I will be scheduled for a colonoscopy soon."

One moderate concern was of the medications causing cancer. Maybe for me the risk was higher.

August 2008

Ron and I traveled to Ohio. We had made twenty trips to Cincinnati now, and my vision was nothing special. I could see a hand moving from eight to ten inches in front of my face and that was all. What a letdown. Surely, this "miracle worker" would come up with a solution for my problem.

Dr. Holland said, "Everything is clear except your cornea, which is pacified. I may do a full thickness transplant since you might reject partial thickness. The clouding of your own cornea is not common to what has happened to other patients."

"Imagine that!" I thought. Nothing that happened to me was ever common as to what happened to other patients. I hoped that meant that when good things did come, they too would be extraordinary.

Ron and I were not getting that fuzzy warm feeling this trip. Our motel was having water problems. There was no hot water, and our room had no TV. We visited with a gentleman outside our room. After Ron told him our story, he asked if he might add me to his church's prayer list. Of course, believing prayers were answered, we agreed. The more, the better. I knew God had a plan for us to run into this gentleman. He still called every once in a while to check on our situation and visit. He was truly a caring Christian man.

On August 13, 2008 I had surgery again. Dr. Holland did a partial, not a full thickness removal of my cornea. My eye was left open, and he would close it later, if needed. I was so glad to have my eyelids open again, I could only pray Dr. Holland could leave it open. Ron and I got back to our motel room. Four hours later, Ron was to take my patch off and instill drops into my eye. That night, we discovered that Dr. Holland had done it again! The patch came off, and I could see! We gave thanks and made at least fifty phone calls to share the good news once again with family and friends. I looked at some of the pictures of Connor that Ron had brought along just in case. He also brought photos of Chad and Heather. I could read signs on TV, at Fenway Park and some post-op papers. Thank you, God. This was so wonderful again. Dr. Holland was a miracle worker.

August 14–17, 2008

Oh my, for the pain. I was awakened at about 4:00 a.m. with the worst pain in my head. I took two Tylenol. It was around my eye, temple area, and above and below the eye. I woke Ron by getting out of bed.

"What's wrong?" he asked.

It was so painful, I could barely walk. "I have a headache," I mumbled.

"What do you want me to do?"

"Call the emergency room."

We were instructed by the on-call person to administer Travatan eye drops every five minutes for three doses. I took three Ibuprofen tablets two hours after the Tylenol but there was no relief. Dr. Holland wouldn't be in the office until 7:00 a.m. I was suffering with this pain. Ron drove us to the office. Other patients at the door asked if we needed a wheelchair.

Ron said, "No, she just needs to see Dr. Holland."

The assistant put drops in my eye and checked it with the machine. The assistant could not tell us what they saw of course. Dr. Holland came in at 7:30 a.m.

He said, "Your pressure must be up." He felt my eye. "I think it is around forty. You now have glaucoma. The cornea looks good however."

I was given medications to lower the pressure and drops to dilate the pupil. He told me the pain should only be temporary. They put in more dilating drops. The pain was starting to recede, giving some relief. Now that I could think again, Dr. Holland examined my eye.

"Ron," I said, "since I am not taking the Valcyte, CellCept or Prograf anymore, what do you think about giving it to Dr. Holland's office to see if another patient of his could use them?"

Ron said, "Just give them away?"

"I know they were expensive. We paid two thousand dollars just for the one medication, and instead of throwing them out, maybe we can help another patient if they would be willing to take them from us."

The cost was ridiculous, but throwing them out would be even more of a waste so we gave them to another patient. I was started on Diamox, for glaucoma. This was a new disease to deal with now. Wow, what next?

The contact that Dr. Holland had on my eye was a bandage contact, one that was soft and collected protein, so within ten days it was as clouded over as a glass with heavy water spots. It needed to be changed by a doctor. Dr. Hohm had changed it for me, and Dr. Kersten could also change it out in Denver where he now practiced. Dr.

Holland was pulling out lashes, up to ten total. The next day, Dr. Null, an assistant to Dr. Holland, pulled out five more lashes.

"What were all the surgeries for to get rid of the lashes? Did they not work? Was it even done?" I asked Ron.

I had shadowy vision and light sensitivity. Upon examination, Dr. Holland saw that my cornea and the donor cornea were not growing together, and he thought he needed to put a bubble in the middle of them. There was a fold in the cornea also. Man, would the problems never stop? We had been on the run between doctor appointments, surgeries, and airports, and it was all very draining. Ron and I were both exhausted.

Dr. Holland told Ron, "If you see her sleeping and her eye is open, you need to tape it shut. Let me show you how." Dr. Holland taped my eye, and when he moved away, it opened. He taped it another way, moved back, and my eye opened again under the tape. He said, "Just use the saran wrap and ointment on it."

Both Ron and Chad were wishing we would have never started these procedures. They, like many of us, had a gut feeling that this was going downhill fast. Still, I was depending on God. He had a plan, I was just sure He did and I trusted Him.

Stacy sent us to the hospital close by for my blood work, so we didn't have to drive into Blue Ash to have it done. I napped in the afternoon. I wasn't sure if I was just tired or if depression from all the ups and downs was starting to set in.

We went to a restaurant to eat. When we left Ron said, "That was a killer joint. We were a little out of our element in there. Some of the patrons in that restaurant could have been carrying guns." It felt that way to me too. We went to another baseball game. It was hot, and we tried to move to shade, but there wasn't much around us. Back at the motel I took a nap while Ron swam, then we went for a bite to eat. In the evening, we played six-card rummy. I thought I had oral thrush from a medication or surgery. I could see fingers from two feet away and hands from five feet away. My eye was still sensitive to light.

"I can feel the lens when I blink," I told Dr. Null. The wrinkle was still there along with the two corneas that were not adhering to each other. Otherwise, the eye looked good.

Dr. Holland said, "Pressure is good. The eye is staying moist, the cornea looks good. I do want to wait to put an air bubble in between the corneas. Maybe we can do that next time."

"When do you want to see me again?" I asked.

Dr. Holland looked at my eye through the machine and said, "I see a cataract that I haven't seen before. It is small and needs to come off, but we can do that at a later date. I can give you a script for the thrush since that is what it looks like to me also. I will see you tomorrow in Blue Ash."

Not only did I have glaucoma, but now there was a cataract forming on my lens that Dr. Holland had not seen before. "Lord, what next? Would we never get my sight fixed? What is your plan, O God?"

August 19, 2008

At each appointment, someone pulled out lashes. I continued to wonder if the surgeries were done at all to take care of this lash problem. Dr. Null saw me first. "The wrinkle looks less to me, but you need to see Dr. Holland to have him check it."

Labs were drawn. Stacy said, "The Rapamune level is 3.3. Increase the dose and check again in a week to ten days at home. They can fax the results, and we will adjust the dose if needed."

Dr. Holland checked my eye. "The cornea is starting to attach on the outside, and that is a good sign. It might attach completely if we give it enough time. The tissue underneath looks good. I am going to take out the contact bandage and put a new one on. Leave it in longer this time. I will give you another one, size sixteen, to take with you.

201

One of your doctors closer to home can change it for you. Do not jump rope. You can walk as much as you like, however. We will see you in September, and if the cornea is attached, we won't do anything to it. If not, we will put a bubble in between the two layers."

"Okay, thank you," I said, and he left. We left for the airport and home.

Ron and I understood the need for security at the airports. What we didn't understand was why all our items had been dumped out of our carry-on bags into a big bin, then one of the security guards noticed the time and we were free to go. We were left to sort out and pack up our belongings again.

Ron said to me, "I heard someone say to our two security men that they could go on break just after they dumped our stuff into the bin. They didn't even look at any of it."

We were both frustrated with this airport thing. I said to Ron, "It is difficult enough for people who can see to have all of their things in a backpack or roller bag to sort through and find something. When security does this to a blind person and then walks away because it is their break time, that makes my back go straight and my chin come up. I am fighting mad, but just throw it all in the bag and we will try to sort through it later. Don't sweat the small stuff, Ron. We'll make it okay."

"All the security guys are worried about is getting a donut down their throat," he said. He made me laugh.

I had carried a half empty tube of toothpaste with me for over two years now. Yes, it started out as a larger tube, but it was flattened to less than half its size. Not one security guard ever pulled that tube to question it. Over twenty trips through the airports, and I had made all the changes to keep from being pulled out of line for a search. The questioning of this half tube of toothpaste just about broke me. One security woman told me, "This toothpaste is too large to pass inspection."

"It's over three-fourths gone. The tube is flat," I said.

The security woman said, "We know, but it started out as too large a tube."

"Look, that tube of toothpaste has passed inspection for over two years now, and if it bothers you that much, just throw the damn thing away."

The inspector said, "I can call my supervisor."

I told Ron, "Just leave it. Get our shoes, and let's walk away."

Give me a break here. I wondered, "Does she really think I am a terrorist?" I really don't need one more hassle after over two years of traveling through airports. I was so fed up with the roller coaster of "Yes, this is good but one thing needs a little more fixing," and airport rules if anything, made it more difficult to deal with life in general.

It seemed our tickets kept getting marked SSSS across them regularly. I finally asked a worker in security, "Why are our tickets always being pulled?"

"Get your ID updated, and that will stop it, for the most part."

So, it was due to my invalid ID. I still carried my old driver's license for an ID. It had expired, but since I couldn't drive, I hadn't thought to renew it. I went to get a new ID. I followed the rules when I knew what the problem was.

After my next trip I sent this email:

Sunday, September 21, 2008
Hello all,
I just got home tonight again from Cincinnati/Kentucky. Cathy and I left on Tuesday morning at 4:15 a.m. from her house. Our plane left at 6 a.m. and we flew to Chicago and then to Cincinnati. My appointment was on Wednesday morning. I had to go in as if I were having surgery, fasting. The decision was to be made by Dr. Holland that morning after he checked my cornea. Of course he decided that my corneas, mine and the transplanted one, are not fusing

together and he wanted to put an air bubble in between the two corneas. (the 2 corneas are one layer of my own which is still in place with very little scarring on it and the new donor cornea which is my second cornea transplant). My surgery was set for noon. I didn't get in until 1:00 p.m., but within an hour Dr. Holland had the bubble in place and I was laying flat on my back with my nose pointing to the ceiling for an hour in recovery. Then I had to stay that way for the rest of the day and night except for potty breaks and to eat something quick. Not fun, I didn't really want to do it. I also did not want to mess up two years of surgeries just to have my own way about how I would sleep. So, I told myself to buck up and get my nose pointed in the right direction. I survived it with Cathy going out for French fries and chocolate malts to keep me fed. She's great and has been truly Ron's helping hand to travel with me when Ron is at school. We try to fit in some fun whenever we can during these trips.

My appointment for recheck on Thursday morning at 7:30 was exciting as Dr. Null, Dr. Holland's intern, said "Fabulous" as she looked at the position of the air bubble and cornea. When Dr. Holland came in and looked at it you could hear the triumph in his voice. He said, "It's just where I wanted it. This was a little tricky you know."

I said, "You didn't tell me that!"

He said, "I didn't want to worry you."

Hmmmm, we know he is the top of the line and knows what he is doing but I am a 'need to know' person, need to know what to pray about.

Also during this surgery he was planning to take out a few stitches and give me a shot to stop the blood vessels from trying to grow through the stem cells. He put on a new bandage contact. The air bubble should be out of my corneal layers within 3 to 4 days although one doctor said weeks. Dr. Holland said days and I am going with that. I will have to wait for the swelling in the cornea to go down to help clear my vision even more. He did suggest that I may have to see the plastic surgeon again as my upper

204

eyelid wants to curl under. We will deal with that when the time comes.

My sight now is a little blurry but seems to clear more each day. As always we thank you, each one for the prayers since that is what sustains us through these trying times. God is still working on me and my faith grows with each bump in the road. My next appointment is October 24th in Cincinnati. I do have to go to Sioux Falls this week but just for a look see to make sure things are okay.

Hope all is well with you and yours,

Ron and Jenny

October 23, 2008

Ron and I had a return visit to Ohio where they were still pulling lashes out. Overall, the entire eye looked good. The cornea was not adhering in the middle, so my vision was cloudy. Dr. Holland said, "Wow, the cataract looks huge today. It really grew in a hurry."

The bandage contact was no longer in my eye, so that was why it hadn't been bothering me.

I told Dr. Holland, "Darn. I thought I was just getting used to it."

Dr. Holland said, "The cataract is more of a problem than the detached cornea. The top third of the cornea is clear. We need to do something about the cataract. The stem cells look good. There is no inflammation. You need to get a flu shot due to your lowered immune status."

"Okay," I said.

I knew Ron was taking notes.

Dr. Holland said, "Here's what we will do: take the cataract off, and do an artificial cornea transplant. First, you need to see Dr. Kersten. The problem is that your right upper lid rolls over itself instead of blinking. We need to get more function of the upper lid, more strength in the lid. We need the lid to move a little more."

He continued, "I want you to go to Denver to see Dr. Kersten before I do another procedure. Your eye pressure is now twenty-seven, and I want it lower than that, so I am adding another drop twice a day."

I was not sure how many drops that made. Ron kept track of that, too. We left the office and flew home the next day. Disheartening, never ending problems and very frustrating. When would I have sight that lasted?

I sent this email out Monday, October 27, 2008:

We are not sure what God has planned or why we are going to Denver when it would be just as easy to see a different plastic surgeon in Cincinnati, but where Dr. Holland wants us to go, we will, thinking God has this reason you see.
Take care,
Jenny

Since May 2008, my vision had diminished farther than ever before. My faith in God and His plan for my life continued to grow and flourish. I would not falter in my faith. I knew that God was in control, and I was trying to follow where He led. Two years of traveling and surgeries was almost more than I could endure. The ones traveling with me were also getting worn out. But we were not going to give up. We were going to do everything that it took to give me the best shot of seeing again.

I would have rather had God just lay His hands on me and heal me. I believed He could just touch me and heal my eyes but didn't know if that was His plan for me, so I continued with the surgeries.

I sent this email on Friday, October 31, 2008:

Subject: appointment in Colorado
I have an appointment in Colorado on November 24th Dr. Kersten is the plastic surgeon that has done all the work on my eye up to this point. We will have him look at me and see if he can get a better blink on my upper eyelid.

November 2008

Life could get anyone down, even when trying to follow God's plan. I knew in my heart that God was not done with me. I didn't know what or when He would allow something good to happen. Sometimes life was just hard to deal with. One week before my dad's seventy-ninth birthday party was to be held in our home, my vision started to cloud over again. I just couldn't believe I would really have no sight within the next five days or so, but it happened. I could barely talk or think of anything else. Everything I did reminded me that I couldn't see, and that I was going to have twenty people coming to our home. These family members always pitched in and helped, but just walking across a room with extra people in it and not seeing them was a challenge. It wasn't as if I hadn't done it before. This time, however, I had started to think how fun it was going to be to have all of my family here and be able to see them. So when my vision was not good, it was disappointing!

Chad, Denise, and Connor Ray came up on Friday night to help prepare for our Sunday gathering. We were ready for the meal, and family started to show up around 9:00 that morning. We always prayed before our family meals, and I offered the prayer of thankfulness for all the Lord had given the past year, and for my Dad celebrating his birthday, and that we were all coming together for that celebration. Then my voice started to break. I knew I was not going to be able to hold back the tears. There was silence as we all stood, hands folded, heads bowed, awaiting the blessing God had ready to pour out upon us. I finally got myself under control enough to get out something of a prayer through a voice full of anguish for all of the ups and downs and setbacks we all had gone through over the last year. My disappointment was obvious. My dad gave me a hug as we all finished with "Amen."

I said into his shoulder, "If they would just leave me alone now, I would be okay."

Cathy's husband, Dave, squeezed my hands as I stumbled by him. I knew that these ups and downs and my emotional prayer had an effect on my entire family. In a way, by letting them know that I had times when I couldn't deal and couldn't seem to fight through the disappointment again and again, showed them that I'm human. I thought that was okay, too, that my family saw the struggles and anguish of yet another setback. I just wanted it to stop.

Before we left for my November appointment in Denver, I sent this email out:

Hello, I am just keeping you posted on another appointment. We go to Denver, Colorado this trip to see the plastic surgeon. If he can fix my upper eyelid again, that will be great. If not we will see what Dr. Holland wants to do then.
Thanks again for your continued prayer. We also keep you all in our prayers.
Ron and Jenny

Since a winter storm was predicted for our area, Ron and I drove to Omaha two days prior to our scheduled flight to Denver.

November 24, 2008
Ron and I got to Dr. Kersten's office. He checked me thoroughly to see what was holding my eyelid up and stopping it from closing. There was an adhesion growing from my eyelid to the eyeball, and he believed he could release that.

"I want to put in a blepharon ring for six months."

"The last blepharon ring was only in for a month before it had grown in," I said.

To that he said, "I am doing this for better closure of the eyelids. I may leave the eyelid closed over the ring. Not

208

sure how much yet. The closure could be partial or all the way. We will wait to decide. I have no idea what to use to keep scar tissue from growing over everything. I am going to call Dr. Holland before making any decision. Sit tight, I'll be back."

This email was sent, after our trip to Denver:

November 25, 2008
Hello,
Well, here I am again letting you know what I don't even know myself. Here are some details though:
We went to Denver to see the plastic surgeon, Dr. Kersten. He moved there from Cincinnati and did all of my previous plastic surgeries. He wants to do a removal of scar tissue with taking tissue from inside my lip and putting it underneath the upper eyelid. Sound familiar? Well that is because they did this same surgery in 2006. It did not work. So if they haven't made any improvements to it I may cancel the surgery which has been set up for Dec. 9th. Also he mentioned to me that the risk of having the muscle in my eyelid cut is 5%. This is a new risk to me. Never before mentioned and one I don't like thus I am asking for other options. They would also put a blepharon ring underneath my eyelids for 6 months. I'm not liking this more and more. I especially don't like it since I have a gut feeling that they want the eyelid shut over this and they feel the easiest way to convince me of that is when I am unconscious.
Dr. Holland has not called me back yet. He says he doesn't need to see me for six months in Cincinnati until this procedure is done. I have a call in to both doctors and need more answers before going into any surgical room with either one of them.
Pray for God to lead me in this. I feel someone is not being above board and I don't think it's me.
Love to all,
Jenny

November 26, 2008 happened to be the date of our 39th wedding anniversary. What I wrote was not in celebration of this date. It was due to the fact that I had lost what vision I had had over the last thirty-three years. I had not yet gotten a handle on this rock in the road of life. I started to type out my frustration, and before I was done, my feisty self reared its head, and I was standing ready to fight, with God's strength present once again. Thus the following:

I am in the depths of despair. Satan has me on the run and I am struggling to catch the tail of God's robe, to hang on and gravitate to the Light. Is this a test? . . . If Satan thinks for one minute he can win me over, he has another think coming!!!! I am God's child . . . I am the one He saved to sing His praises and spread the word about His good works. I am the one He chose to stand strong against Satan and God will fill me with the power of His Holy Spirit so I am not afraid. I am going to stand strong and firm in the Light that God shines around each of us to bring us out of darkness and away from Satan's grasp and that is exactly where I am heading . . . to the Light. To see again my husband . . . my children . . . my grandchildren . . my dad, my sisters, my brothers, my family each and every one for that is what I desire and that is what God has for me, my heart's desires and more, much more.

December 9, 2008.

Ron wrote in his journal, *"This is like starting all over."*

Ron had parent-teacher conferences in December, so Cathy and I flew to Denver. I was nervous over what Dr. Kersten was going to do. We got to Colorado in fine shape. Three to five inches of snow fell overnight, but we made it to the clinic in time for my appointment. Dr. Kersten was one-and-a-half hours late for surgeries. I felt like he would be rushed when he wasn't at the clinic on time. It felt wrong somehow, and yet I didn't know what else to do.

Dr. Holland needed to have my eyelid closing better to do the next surgery, so I sat still, waiting for surgery and praying. Dr. Kersten finally arrived at the surgical center. I was taken into surgery. Not long after, I was returned to my cubicle.

Dr. Kersten told Cathy and me, "Right away, we found a big defect in front of your cornea. The front part of your right eye has had a leak and is flat. There is scar tissue too close to the optic nerve, and I didn't want to risk cutting into the optic nerve. I stitched your eye two thirds of the way closed and left a small corner by your nose open for you to put drops in. There is no more I can do for you. Dr. Holland needs to see you next week. Do you have any questions?"

Questions? We were both in shock. How were we to think of what we needed answers to? I was thinking, "Get me back to Dr. Holland. He will know what to do."

While still in recovery, the nurse asked the patient next to me, "Are you nervous?"

I replied to him through the dividing curtain, "You had better be because once they put you out they do whatever they want to you."

I was so upset. One reason was because Dr. Kersten was always the one who sewed my eyelid closed. And secondly, he said he couldn't do anything for me. I was shaking with disappointment. I was holding back sobs.

Cathy said, "It's okay to cry. This is too much to hold inside."

The nurse with me kept saying, "I know how you feel. This is so upsetting. I know what you're going through."

Cathy said to her in her most stern voice, "You have no idea what she has been through."

The nurse quit trying to console me. Cathy and I were both devastated.

Cathy drove us to our motel and asked, "What do you want to do? Should we stay or go home?"

I handed her my credit card, "Just book us flights, I need to get home."

I called Ron and told him the news and that we would be flying home immediately.

Cathy and I arrived at the Denver airport. I was pulled over for a body search.

Cathy said, "She has just had bad news from her doctor, can you just let her be?"

The airport employee said, "You can appeal the search with one of the airport security officials."

I told them both, "Never mind, just get it done, I don't care anymore."

I wanted to crawl under a blanket and never come out. I needed to get back to where I knew the exact place of each thing in our home. I needed to have Ron give me a hug and let me cry. I needed to have a little talk with Jesus and ask God to take me home. I needed Him to take control of everything in my life. I knew in my gut that things were not going well. I knew that God had the answer, and that He was the answer. Yet, I was scared. After returning home I called Dr. Holland's office. He said, "There is no hurry. Come for an appointment after Christmas. That will work too."

I was relieved and yet unsure why there was no hurry to get to Dr. Holland's office.

People asked me, "What will he do now?"

And I told them, "I don't know, but he is the "miracle worker", so he will have something he can do. He told us he has not left anyone with less sight than they started with, so at the very least he will remove the cataract and put my scleral shell back in under my eyelids. I will have the same sight I started with."

'No hurry to see me' is not good news. That should have been a red flag, but I was trying to ignore it. I just kept thinking that Dr. Holland would come up with something else. I knew it was going to be okay.

I sent this message to Dr. Holland's nurse December 21, 2008:

Stacy,
I am wondering if you could find out how long I have to be
on the Cyclosporin?
Is Dr. M. planning to stop all anti-rejection drugs some
time in 2009?

From: Stacy,
To: Jenny Peterson
Sent: Sunday, December 21, 2008
Subject: RE: Cyclosporin
Jenny,
It really depends on what Dr. Holland recommends. I
heard about the perforation of your cornea during the
surgery with Dr. Kersten and I am so sorry for you. Let's
wait until your follow up appointment before making any
changes. I do not want to jeopardize the viability of the
stem cells if there is still a chance that he can proceed with
a cornea transplant. If he feels that we cannot proceed,
then he will stop the cyclosporin at that time.
Try to hang in there a little longer :)

I wish you and your family a Merry Christmas and hope
that 2009 will be a better year for you!
Stacy

I did not remember anything being said about my eye
being perforated during surgery. I responded as follows:

To: Stacy
From: Jenny
I was not informed of this . . . I am in shock . . . should I
not have been told that my cornea was perforated? I am
not sure what to say or what question to ask. Jenny

I told Ron about this message, and he checked the notes
he wrote down from speaking to me after my surgery. In
the notes was something about the perforation. I was under
the influence of anesthesia and didn't remember any of the

conversation. Thankfully, Ron had taken notes as we visited on the phone.

From: Jenny Peterson
To: Stacy
Sent: Tuesday, December 30, 2008
Subject: blood draw
Stacy,
First of all I want to tell you that Dr. Kersten must have mentioned the perforation of my cornea to me since Ron has written it down but I do not remember it at all yet. Something that the drug they give to me after surgery does to me I guess
Anyway, I was told about the perforation but do not remember. So I'm sorry if I gave you a heart palpitation over it.
Now on Friday, January 2nd I am getting my blood work drawn. Is that the same order that I got drawn the last time?
Jenny

From: Stacy
To: Jenny Peterson
Sent: Friday, January 02, 2009
Subject: new order
Jenny,
The last order for blood work was with a Rapamune level. I will fax a new one to the hospital for the Cyclosporin level, thanks.
Stacy

I called CEI and got an appointment for January 8, 2009. I was informing everyone by email what was to happen next:

Sent: Saturday January 3, 2009
Dear family and friends,
We fly out on Wednesday to Cincinnati to see what is next
for me. Dr. Holland will have a plan soon after he sees me.
Happy New Year to all of you.
Ron and Jenny

Thanks for your continue prayers, they work miracles.
Jenny

I was so sure Dr. Holland could and would fix whatever was wrong. I was once again confident in his abilities to help me regain my pre-surgical sight at least. We received many messages like the following one:

To: Ron and Jenny P.
Sent: Saturday, January 3, 2009
Subject: Hi
Hi,
I'm keeping you in my prayers, Jenny, as you prepare for
your trip to Cincinnati this next week.

This email message was sent to me from our daughter. I received it just before my appointment with Dr. Holland on January 8, 2009.

From: Heather
To: Jenny Peterson
Sent: Tuesday, January 06, 2009
Subject: just a little help and encouragement
A friend sent this to me:
God grant me the serenity to accept the things I cannot
change; courage to change the things I can; and wisdom
to know the difference.
Living one day at a time; Enjoying one moment at a time;
Accepting hardships as the pathway to peace; Taking, as
He did, this sinful world as it is, not as I would have it;
Trusting that He will make all things right if I surrender to

His Will; That I may be reasonably happy in this life and supremely happy with Him Forever in the next.
Amen.

From Jenny Peterson
To: Heather
And all God's people said "Amen."

As I read this message from my daughter, tears formed behind closed eyelids and never reached my cheeks. I felt defeated but would not give up. I needed to find my guitar and yell out my frustrations. I needed to find my Bible on tape and hear His message to me.

My appointment with Dr. Holland was January 8, 2009. He said we had to have better lid function for further surgeries. That wasn't sounding too good. My body was dehydrated since I was not drinking enough water. Dr. Null said, "Lid function is key to everything else. We can't do anything with the cornea until lid function is good."

I asked, "Can the cataract be taken off?"

"We have to take the cornea off to get the cataract off, and there is a risk of infection getting into the eye, thus losing the eye completely. The lid has to be closed to protect the cornea or it will dry out and fail."

Dr. Holland explained, "The opacification of the cornea cannot be stopped because there is no lid function. A full thickness transplant has an increased risk of infection with it."

"What more can you do?"

"Nothing. There is no more I can do."

Ron's journal:
January 8, 2009
"Sad day!"

Dr. Holland asked, "What do you want me to do for you?"

216

I had a list. "First, I want my eyelids opened again, like they were when we started this process. Second, I want the cataract taken off so at least I can see whether the sun is shining and where I am in the house by looking for the light from the windows. Third, I want the sclera shell back under my eyelids so they will not scar down to my eyeball again. I want the vision I had when we started this process twenty-five trips and fourteen surgeries ago. After all, you told me and my family that you had never left anyone with worse vision than what they started with."

"But you have this huge cataract that formed during the last six months, and I am not going to risk your only eye to remove it. That is part of the reason you are not seeing light. You won't be able to see through the opacified cornea even if we do remove the cataract."

I reached down for my purse to show him the conformer I used to wear, but I couldn't get my hand on it, and out of frustration I said, "Shit."

"Maybe I can find a plastic surgeon closer to you at home to help you get the conformer back under your eyelids," Dr. Holland offered.

With that comment, he left the exam room. The nurse was still in with us, but after quite a few minutes, she too left to see what was going on and why Dr. Holland had not returned.

Ron came over to me and leaned into my face and asked quietly, "Isn't he going to do any more surgeries?"

"No, they are going to leave me like this."

Ron came a step closer to me and said again, "What? They aren't going to do anything to help you?"

I reached out my hand to feel where Ron was. My hand rested on his chest. Curling my fingers into his shirt, and consequently into his chest hairs, I pulled Ron towards me and he quickly followed.

I said in a very shaky voice, pausing between each word, "They are going to leave me like this."

I then felt the white Light that had surrounded me over thirty years ago once again put His arms around me and I calmed.

I uncurled my fingers and smoothed out Ron's shirt and said in a voice filled with assurance, "These doctors may be done with me, Ron, but my God is not. I don't know what He has planned for me, but I do know that He has a plan, and whatever God wants of my life, I am a willing servant."

Dr. Holland never came back into my exam room. The nurse came in and told us that we did not need another appointment, but if there was anything we needed, we should call. I was not really sure what she said, something about stopping some medications or continuing other medications.

I just said, "What's the use?"

She said, "Please, continue the drops."

Once again Ron was taking notes, instructions, so we knew what medications to stop and which ones to continue. Dr. Holland did not give us follow-up advice or who to see as far as a plastic surgeon. Nor did he tell us what might happen to my eye if we left it alone. We had lots of unanswered questions as we returned to our motel room.

We were left grieving, not just Ron and I, but everyone who had been praying over the last three years. Everyone who thought this was the "miracle worker" who could restore my sight and allow me to see my family and new grandchild, who was going to be two years old in March. I would never be able to see pictures, flowers, my beloved Ron, my own children, my siblings, or my dad. They had all been so accepting of me just the way I was, seeing or not. We enjoyed each others company and modified whatever we did together so I could join in. Now I had to learn to live again as a blind person, pull myself up by my boots straps, and find a way to live in a world that had become darker over the last three years than it had ever been before.

Back in our motel room, we started making calls. My voice shook as I let people know that Dr. Holland was not going to "fix" me. He was actually leaving me like I was. After a couple of calls, I put down my cell phone. I felt my way along the wall and into the bathroom. I put a towel over my mouth, trying to block out the noise that was boiling up from inside me. I was not sure if it was rage or disappointment, but most assuredly it was grief. We had lost the dream we had built up in our minds. We had built up dreams of how it would be for me to be able to see again and enjoy watching birds fly, flowers bloom, and tree branches dancing in the wind. I knew now that I was not going to get to see the snowflakes I had so long desired to see. The thing I most needed to do was get back to God and the feeling of peace and comfort that only He could give, and for that I needed to be home. I needed to start to do the things I could do, like ironing, washing clothes, filling and emptying the dishwasher, vacuuming, and everyday cleaning. When I had gotten control of myself again and came out of the bathroom, Ron was there to hold me in his arms and cry with me as we mourned our lost dreams. The "miracle worker" couldn't help me.

After a while, I realized what I had just thought. Miracle worker? No, not really. Dr. Holland was just a man, doing the best he could with the knowledge he had gained over the years. We had lost our way, thinking he was the miracle worker. There's only one miracle worker and that was Jesus Christ, Son of God and of man. The Perfect Physician was the only One to help me now, and I was not even sure what His plan was. But one thing I did believe and know in my soul was that He was my God. He loved me as His child, and whatever His plan was, I knew that was what was best for me.

I called Cathy as soon as I could speak again. I told her, "I am not going to have any more surgeries. I am going to be left with a cataract covering my eye. The cornea on my eye clouds what light I might have gotten through the cataract, which is slim to none."

219

I was crying and she said, "It's going to be okay Jen. You are still a good person and we can still go places and have lots of fun."

"Oh no, I'm not going to be a good person anymore. I am going to start drinking, smoking, and running wild."

Cathy paused then said, "Well, I will be your DD then, and we'll still be together."

I started to laugh because I needed to make a joke out of this pitiful situation. My laughter didn't hold for long.

We flew home, and over the next couple of days people tried to call and see if I was okay. At first, I didn't answer the phone. I needed time to get my feet under me again.

Tears were aplenty over the next days, but before too many weeks had passed, God gave me strength once again. When I told my pastor about my conversation with Cathy about drinking, smoking and going wild, he said, "No, I don't believe that of you. You are going to stay just like you have been, strong in your faith, close to God."

And that was truly where I belonged, regardless of what happened in life. God had my back. He was right there on my team, leading the way to the Light, giving us the way to escape from the turmoil, the sadness, and the grief. God knew our every desire, and when we turned everything, every little thing, over to Him, no matter what our circumstances in life were, He could make good out of bad events for those who believed in Him, loved Him and served Him. We needed to laugh at Satan and kick him to the curb because my God was all powerful and was not wringing His hands over these little things that go wrong in life. God knew what was going to happen before it happened, and it was all for His good, for His purpose. If we trusted Him, even in the most horrible of circumstances, He would bring us through, and something good would come of it for those who loved Him.

Then, as I started to answer phone calls, sometimes we cried, sometimes we just talked about other things, but eventually I did get my feet under me again. With a shaky emotional voice I started telling everyone, "It's going to be okay. God is not done with me. Let's watch His power now!"

I told this to my brother, Rick, and he said, "If you say so, sis, I will believe it for you too."

I said, "It is not me who said it, but God who will do it for me. Watch His power now. He is not done with me."

I had to believe this. I told Ron's sister, "It's going to be okay. Even if I never get my sight back, God is in my life, and that makes it okay. I'm going to be the same person, just with less sight now than I have been for thirty-three years." Sometimes I had to say this through my tears, but nevertheless I believed it.

I started to deal with the facts of this failed procedure, not the emotions. Messages and questions came to mind, and I sent the following emails:

From: Jenny Peterson
Subject: failed procedure
Date: Friday, January 9, 2009,
Hi all,
I am sorry to tell you all that Dr. Holland is not going to do any more to my eye. I will need to get a plastic surgeon to open it and put my old shell in it to keep the scarring from growing the eyelid down to my eyeball anymore than it already is. Actually the two doctors are looking into that and I may go back to Denver for that. Not sure yet.
The problem is this:
1) the scarring is holding my eyelid up from closing and lets the corneas dry out, simple as that.
2) in order to get the cataract removed the cornea has to be removed first and that opens my eye up to infection, which has not been done yet and Dr. Holland is not comfortable taking that risk for no gain in vision and just to have another cornea dry out.
3) the cornea I have is opaque or clouded over so between that and the cataract I have light perception only.
I am going to try to continue working but am not sure I can make that work so God must have a plan for me other than

typing medical info. Let go and let God, I will let go of the devastation and disappointment as soon as I can and let God take control of my life again and see where He leads me.
Love to all,
Ron and Jenny

The following were some of the responses we received back:

From: Jon Peterson
To: Jenny Peterson
Sent: Friday, January 09, 2009
Subject: Re: failed procedure
We are so sorry to hear this news. We will continue to keep praying for you and remembering that God is in control and He has a plan. We are so thankful that He gave you the opportunity to see your family and hopefully, in the near future, there will be something more the doctors can do to give you back your vision. Your strength and faith have been such an inspiration to us all!
Our Love and Prayers,
Jon and Kathy

Sent: Friday, January 09, 2009
Subject: FWD: messages from Bell Med
Jenny, I am so sorry to hear this news. We will continue to pray for you. It may not be for what we want, but I guess for the patience to deal with this for now, and to deal with the disappointment you must be feeling. I am disappointed and that isn't me. Thinking of you! Lindy

Message #2:
I'm sorry to hear that jenny...I'm sure there's something else they can do...we will continue to pray...keep being strong...
Andrew

The following were some of the correspondence I sent to Dr. Holland's office:

From: Jenny Peterson
To: Stacy
Sent: Friday, January 09, 2009
Subject: meds
Stacy,
I just want to be sure I have the dosages correct on the eyedrops.
Vigamox twice a day
Prednisone 4 times a day
Travatan once a day
Combigan twice a day
Diamox once daily 500mg
How often will I need to have my pressure checked by Dr. Hohm?
Will I need any other blood work being on the Diamox?

From: Jenny Peterson
To: Stacy
Sent: Saturday, January 10, 2009
Subject: for Dr. Holland
Is there anyway to use an ultrasound guide or something like that to remove the cataract?
Can stem cells be used to replace the tissue underneath my eyelids to get rid of the scarring?
Also a problem that I am having since the surgery with Dr. Kersten is whenever I do an activity such as cleaning the shower walls or exercise or something like that my eye gets purple underneath it, similar to a black eye. The discoloration is there most of the time but worsens with exertion. Is this a problem or should I be having something checked out on it?
Am I coming up with questions that are futuristic or should I just hope to be kidnapped by aliens from outer space and see what they can do? (just being funny)

I will wait to hear back from you on these questions. If you would rather call me than email my home number is
Thanks,
Jenny

As you can see with the aliens kidnapping statement my way to deal with disaster is joking, and lots of praying. It works for me.

January 19, 2009

Because we didn't have any instructions as to how to care for my eye except to continue the drops as directed, I felt I needed to request more detail. After not getting a response from Dr. Holland's office, I called Dr. Hohm in Sioux Falls. He had been kind enough to examine my eye in between trips to Cincinnati and agreed to see me again.

I made an appointment, and my friend, LaVonne took me to Sioux Falls. When Dr. Hohm saw me, he also asked, "What do you want me to do for you?"

I gave him the same list I had given Dr. Holland.

Dr. Hohm said, "I think you should go to Mayo Clinic in Rochester, Minnesota to see a Stevens-Johnson specialist." He asked his scheduler to set me up with Mayo Clinic. I overheard him tell her, "Tell them she is in danger of losing her only eye."

I was emotional and bowed my head to hide my frustration. Dr. Hohm put a comforting hand on my shoulder and said, "It gets tough at times, doesn't it?"

I nodded. I could not speak; tears choked my throat.

"I want you to see a corneal specialist, glaucoma specialist, and an oculoplastic surgeon."

I asked Dr. Hohm, "How great is the risk of me losing my eye?"

He said, "If we do nothing it is very possible. Mayo Clinic can't help stop the process that is already ongoing but perhaps they can do something to help."

I asked, "How long will I be at Mayo?"

He answered, "Depends on if they do surgery or not."

224

Ron didn't have school that day so he went with me Monday, January 19, 2009. My sister, Cathy, would be available if we needed her to come to Rochester so Ron could come home to go to school. Hopefully I could come home with Ron.

I sent this email message to one family member:

Sent: Wednesday, January 21, 2009
Subject: Re: Greetings
Thank you for the continued prayers, God is all we have left when the doctors say no more can be done but God is all we need so He is in control of this and we will see what He leads us to.
Stay warm,
Ron and Jenny

January 26, 2009
I saw Dr. Mac, the Stevens-Johnson specialist, I didn't see corneal, oculoplasty or glaucoma specialists. Most of Dr. Mac's patients had eye scarring and vascular scarring. He examined my eye and said, "I've never seen any of my patients with this much scarring on their eye, and your cornea looks to be breaking down. I don't think anyone should ever do surgery on your eye again. I think you are at the end of the road. As far as options, you don't have any left." Then he said, "You are a warrior, a very brave woman. You have been through a war."

Well, he had that right. I felt like it, too. "I don't actually know why I am here to see you," I said. "I'm not sure what to do for my eye anymore."

"Keep it protected, moist, and stay on the medications and drops that are prescribed. Follow-up with Dr. Hohm every month to six weeks to check the condition of your eye. No good surgeon will ever do surgery on your eye again. It will not improve anything, but it could cause even more problems."

Again, I was in tears because he was so kind. He thought I was a warrior, and I felt beaten down and tired of the fight. As Ron and I left Mayo Clinic, Ron asked me once again, "Are you going to be okay?"

"Yes, I am going to be just fine. God is on my side in this mess, and He knows what is best for all of us."

Dr. Hohm got a report from Mayo, and he wanted to see me every six weeks. The cornea was turning to skin, and there was not much else that could be done...again.

We got back into the routine of living. Ron stepped up even more and took on more of the household chores. He helped me with my computer, the cooking, and sorting clothes. Ron did the grocery shopping and on and on. In the evenings when we weren't finishing my computer work, Ron watched a program on TV or read. I sat in the living room on the couch and listened to books. I decided that my Bible on tapes was going to be an every-night read for me.

I sent this message to Dr. Holland after getting "back on my feet again" via his nurse:

From: Jenny Peterson
Sent: Tuesday, January 27, 2009
Subject: message for Dr. Holland
Stacy,
As you know Ron and I were both devastated by Dr. Holland's decision of not doing anymore with my eye so neither one of us could think of a single question we needed to ask but of course now I have a few, is that all right?
As far as keeping moisture in my eye now does it really matter as much? Do I need to do the humidifier, saran wrap, Systane and all of these moisturizers?
Can I now run water over my face, go swimming, and that type of thing or is that still not a good idea?
Will there ever be anything more to do with the cataract and cornea?

Can I go back to my normal exercising? This is my usual routine: I usually jump rope, use a rowing machine and work on an elliptical.

Am I remembering correctly that Dr. Holland or Dr. Kersten is going to find a plastic surgeon to do the work of getting the shell back in my eye? If nothing else we would go back to Denver and have Dr. Kersten do that too if he would agree to that.

Thank you Stacy for all that you did over the last 2 1/2 years to help us get through each step we do appreciate it and all that you have done.

Also if you could forward the following note to Dr. Holland I would appreciate it,

Jenny and Ron Peterson

Note to be forwarded to Dr. Holland:

Dear Dr. Holland,

Ron and I were both too devastated to even be able to talk while in your office on January 8th, 2009. We would have liked to have been able to tell you how much we admire all the good things you are doing for people. We thought when we started this process with you back in July 2006 that you were a "miracle worker" and we still feel that way, it just didn't work for us.

If nothing else we hope you have learned something from working on my eye to help someone else in the future. Thank you for giving this your best shot and trying to restore my sight.

Ron and Jenny Peterson

Sent: Tuesday, January 27, 2009
Subject: message for Dr. Holland
Stacy,
Sorry to bother you with this but could you forward this to Dr. Holland for me? Thanks.

Dr. Holland,

I am starting to think about how much of a risk there is to putting on another cornea and getting the cataract off my right eye. I truly have very little light perception through the little corner opening but I believe I could see through the cornea and scarring like I did before if the cataract was not in the way.

Can you tell me what risks I am running in trying to have you remove the cataract?

Would you be willing to try to remove the cataract?

Is it your opinion that my eyelid is going to seal down on my eye and I will eventually lose my eye, or is that not a possibility?

Is it still possible to do the corneal transplant to remove the cataract or has that window of opportunity passed me by?

I am struggling with this limited vision I have, so if you could reply to my email I would appreciate it Dr. Holland. Thank you.

Jenny Peterson

Weeks turned into months and I still hadn't heard back from Dr. Holland. I figured they had just written me off as a failure. In the meantime, I came up with my own plan and took my idea to God.

It was February, 2009. My great nephew had just been diagnosed with a brain tumor. He was only six years old, and I thought I knew just how to solve both our problems. I got down on my knees to have a little talk with God. I asked God to take the tumor from this little six year old and give it to me. Plain and simple. I was willing to die in his place. I knew what it was to die, and I was not afraid of it. I had already lived, and my kids were grown. Ron would be fine without me. I prayed, "Seriously, God, think about my idea, and if it be Your will, allow this little boy to live and take me in his place."

However, this was not God's plan. He had a plan for each of us, and sometimes they interacted, sometimes they didn't, and this particular idea was not a part of the plan that God had for me or my little six-year-old great-nephew. He passed away just before his seventh birthday, and I still lived, blind and unable to figure out what God had planned for me. All I knew for sure was that God had a plan for my life, and I was committed to serve Him with all my ability. I was not happy about my situation in life, but I would cling to God with everything I had.

Cathy and I had attended a church event in Sioux Falls when an ice storm hit and I became stranded at her home. Cathy had recently been diagnosed with heart disease, probably caused by a non-detected virus that damaged her heart muscle. I decided to be bold in my service to God.

I said, "We have prayed for me many times, but today I want to pray for Cathy. Dave, will you join me in this?"

Dave said, "Sure."

Cathy was sitting on a chair, and Dave and I both put a hand on her shoulder. I asked God very simply to heal her heart and make her well. I asked for His will in her life.

Later, I sent a message to my kids describing what happened:

Received: 03/05/2009
From: Jenny Peterson
Subject: A True Story
This is a true story, it happened just as I am telling it.
One day at home I realized that we had never prayed for my sister whose heart was weakened by a virus and was skipping beats. So after breakfast at her home I asked her husband and her if we could pray for her heart to be strengthened. They agreed. We prayed a very simple prayer, not long, not fancy asking God to heal her heart.
Today, she had an appointment for an echocardiogram, her heart beat did not skip once and even though her echo didn't show any improvement yet we believe God is working His miracle on her heart. Of course the doctor isn't saying it is better, he says it looks the same on the echo but God isn't done yet, I just know He isn't.

All praise and Glory be to Him: Father, Son and Holy Spirit. Amen.
Just in case you don't know who this was? It was Cathy, Dave and I.
God's blessing on each of you. He is alive and working yet in our lives.

Cathy's exam in 2011 showed her ejection fraction to have improved from an EF of low 30s to mid 40s. God heard and answered our prayers.

From: Heather
To: Jenny Peterson
Sent: Thursday, March 05, 2009
Subject: Re: A True Story
Awesome news and awesome story! Keep the faith.

From: Jenny Peterson
To: Heather
Sent: Thursday, March 05, 2009
Subject: Re: A True Story
I think so too. See you all tomorrow.
Mom

Two months after the end of the surgeries to restore my sight, family and friends could see I had returned to my faith and were relieved.

"How are you doing, are you okay?"

"I'm doing okay. I have stopped falling apart in the middle of everyday things, so I think I am going to make it. Thanks for asking."

I could actually speak about the failed attempt to restore my vision without breaking down. I talked to our minister about taking my name off the prayer list in our church.

He said, "I think we should leave it a little while. This is not finished yet."

"Okay," I said. "I will check with you later about it. I feel bad for everyone who has been disappointed by this outcome."

"Many churches and people still have you both on their prayer list," he said.

"We appreciate it, too."

April 2009

After not hearing from Dr. Holland or Dr. Kersten, for several weeks I found Dr. Kersten's cell phone number and called him myself. "Are you willing to do the surgery to open my eyelids and put the conformer back in so they won't scar down to the eyeball?"

His answer was not very professional, but maybe it was the callus way he said it that caught me off guard. "The next thing I would do for you is remove your eye."

"Remove my eye?"

"Yes, there is nothing more that can be done for it except removal."

If he was trying to get rid of me as a patient, it worked. I thanked him and hung up. I was shocked. I couldn't believe that a professional, even under a huge amount of stress, would suggest removing an eye when the optics was still intact. I would not contact or see him professionally ever again. If I did happen to come in contact with Dr. Kersten again, it would not be because I had instigated it. As far as I was concerned, this was an inappropriate and cruel thing to say after he had just seen me as a patient and sewn my eyelids shut due to a ruptured cornea, especially because he knew about the two-and-a-half years of failed surgeries I had undergone.

Chad felt horrible due to the fact that he was the one who had called me about the show and started the wheels in motion. I couldn't see as well as I had prior to the start of the surgeries. My eye was sewn shut, and I had only one little corner through which to look and put drops into. It was ridiculous to leave somebody in that condition.

231

I told Chad, "This is not your fault."

"If we hadn't seen *The Miracle Worker* show, you wouldn't have gone through fourteen surgeries and twenty-five trips."

He felt responsible, but this was no one's fault. Even Dr. Holland did his best to help me get my vision back. No one was at fault.

I continued to say, "God is not done with me, the doctors have quit but God has not. Watch what He does now."

But Chad still felt more responsibility than he should have for my failed surgeries.

"God has this plan, and it is going to all turn out well, better than we have been asking for in prayer. We just have to continue to believe and praise God for each step that is bringing us closer to His gift for us. Just wait. You'll see."

On April 25, 2009 Chad, Denise, and Connor Ray added a new little sister to their family, Jenna Elizabeth. She was named after me and two or three other grandmas. I was sure they were all as proud of that as I was. Chad put her in my arms and asked, "Can you see her at all, Mom?"

"Not really, but she smells like a newborn kitty," I replied.

That night, Chad and Denise stayed at the hospital, and Grandpa and I were going to take Connor Ray home and come back the next morning. When Chad walked us down to the vehicles to switch over the car seat, I gave him a hug and said, "God is going to let me see her someday, Chad, I just know He is."

Chad started to cry. "I hope so, Mom. I feel so responsible that you can't even see her face."

"It will be okay. Just wait and see."

Not only did I tell anyone and everyone that God wasn't done with me yet, I believed it.

I had thought all this time that it was God's plan for me to see again. Having the series of surgeries fail and leave me worse off than what I was before 2006 was heartbreaking. But I still believed that God was going to do something wonderful, something better than ever in my life. I didn't even know if that meant I was going to be able to see again. I just knew God's love was great and that He wanted for us tenfold what we wanted to give our own children. So how great was that!

May 9, 2009

I was asked to be the guest speaker at a Mother's Day luncheon. I thought I could get through what God had done in my life without crying. I was waiting to get up and speak. Cathy was with me and would help me up front. Suddenly, it was my turn. When Cathy helped me up to the front and behind the podium, she took my shoulders and turned me to face the women who were attending. She whispered, "Last time, you were a little crooked."

I smiled my thanks. I told how my hopes had been dashed during the fourteen surgeries and twenty-five trips, but not my faith in God and His plan for my life. I ended my testimony with this: "I know that these last three years have not gone well, but God has a plan for my life, just like for the blind man along the side of the road. Let's watch God's good works now."

As Cathy and I left the church and walked down the street to our car where Ron was waiting, a woman came running down the street behind us. She said, "I am a minister from a neighboring town and I wonder if you would be open to my praying for you and laying hands on you."

"Yes, by all means pray," I said.

She put her hand on my head and prayed to God. "Do not wait any longer, but heal this woman who is so faithful to you, and let her see."

I was so moved, and Ron said, "Wow."

Cathy, of course said, "Now all we have to do is wait."

She gave me a big hug, and we each went home.

Chad had been laid off from his job of sixteen years with Gateway, the computer company. He was now working as an office equipment salesman and sold office equipment and went into an eye clinic in Iowa. While visiting with the office manager, he began to talk about my eye condition and wondered if I might be seen by the doctor there. The office manager took Chad into the doctor's office where he told this doctor about my eye problems and all the surgeries I had been through. "Do you think you could take a look at my mom?"

The eye doctor asked, "Chad, is your mom just doctor seeking, trying to find someone who will tell her what she wants to hear? Is your Mom just looking for someone to say yes to whatever she wants done?"

Chad said, "She doesn't even know I am speaking to you about her. I am the one looking for someone to help her."

"I'll take a look at her," said the doctor, "but I'm making no promises."

"Fair enough," Chad replied.

He called and told us he had set up an appointment for me on May 15 in Sioux City.

I saw Dr. Hohm in Sioux Falls and told him, "I am going to see a doctor in Iowa."

He asked, "How did you get his name?"

I explained, and Dr. Hohm told me to come in and see him again after I got a report from the eye doctor in Iowa. The Iowa doctor did an exam and said, "I think you have been through a lot, and I don't think there is anything I can do to help you." One thing he told me that no other doctor had mentioned was this: "You don't necessarily have to have any pain to have your optic nerve blow. You could just simply wake up one morning and be in total darkness."

"Thanks for the encouragement," I thought. This was not very comforting, but I always wanted up-front and honest information, even though at times it was hard to take. I wanted to know what I was up against.

After the appointment, Ron and I met Chad in the parking lot. "There is nothing to be done. Thank you for checking this out for me. Something will come along some time. We just have to wait a little longer, have a little more patience, and let go and let God."

Chad couldn't speak. He just gave me a big hug.

The information about my optic nerve blowing without my being aware of a problem was very scary to me. However, I believed to the depths of my soul that God directed me to listen to that particular story in the Bible about the blind man. It was going to be okay. God still was not done with me.

When I went back to see Dr. Hohm in June 2009, he said, "I have a friend and colleague who practices at Johns Hopkins. She is a front-of-the-eye disease specialist, and I think it would be worth a trip to find out what she has to say about your eye condition."

My first reaction was no way, I'm done. My second thought was, "Here we go again." Both Ron and I were totally fed up with the travel. Cathy never even blinked an eye when I called and gave her my next appointment date, but she too had to be about wiped out with all the trips we had made over the last three years. Why was I still seeing doctors?

What I said was, "Can you find any place further away to send me?"

Dr. Hohm replied, "I do know this doctor in Florida."

We both smiled and I reminded him, "Every time a doctor touches me, I turn out worse than before. They love seeing my case. It is so interesting, but they can never help me. I would like to go home and pray and think about it first before deciding."

"The only thing is, I would hate for you to wait five years and wish you had gone to see them now. So keep that in mind while you are considering your options."

He was right. I hated it when I didn't want to do something and it just made sense to do it. It made perfect sense, but I was still reluctant.

I went home and prayed, and the answer I came up with was this. What if I could get my sight back now instead of five years from now? What would I miss seeing instead of just being present at events? I could see my grandchildren as babies instead of waiting until they are five and seven years old. The what-ifs always played a big role in my decisions.

I called Dr. Hohm and agreed to see his doctor friend. We were set up for a referral appointment in Baltimore at Johns Hopkins.

"I have been to some of the most prestigious medical facilities in the country," I said to Ron, "and no one has been able to help me."

I told my daughter-in-law, Denise, when we were visiting, "I just wish the doctors would quit on me so God would take over and do His will."

She expressed fear of my even thinking that way.

I truly felt that God would not desert me. I knew in my gut that God was working in my life, and every time some disaster befell us, I could see that God was working in the midst of the tragedy. It took time and patience and most of all faith. Clinging to faith when all hell was breaking loose was very difficult. But my question was, "Where does a person turn when no earthly being has the answer?" The answer for me, was, "to God." When I didn't know what to pray anymore because I wasn't sure which end was up, I prayed, "Thy will be done." This way I was assured that God was in control, and the best thing possible was going to take place out of the chaos. I still felt that God had something in the future that would blow us all away.

After all this time I finally got an answer from Dr. Holland:

From: Stacy
To: Jenny Peterson
Sent: Tuesday, July 14, 2009
Subject: RE: future
Jenny,
Dr. Holland said the problem with proceeding with any further surgery is your lack of lid function. Dr. Kersten

said that there is nothing that he can do at this point due to the scarring and lack of muscle function. Those issues are directly related to your underlying disease process. He said that your stem cells are still viable, it is simply a matter of exposure and severe dryness. The only way to keep the surface moist would be to sew your eye closed and that defeats the purpose entirely. He doesn't see any solution for you at this time. I am so sorry for you as you have gone through so much to be "stuck" at this point.
If I can be of any further assistance to you, please do not hesitate to call.
Take care~
Stacy

I had already moved on to follow God's lead to Baltimore so this message didn't matter anymore. Ron and I flew to Baltimore. Michael Jackson had just died and his music and photos were all over the city, celebrating the life and music of Jackson and his famous family.

We walked around the river fronts and enjoyed the outside markets. My mind was busy trying to figure out what God had in store for me. Would I have surgery at Johns Hopkins? Would there be anything at all that the doctors could do? The smells and loud voices of people on the streets were what I noticed most. Ron described what he could to me. We went for my appointment with Dr. Esen K. Akpek, who told me that they needed to scan my eyes. I agreed. The tech started to scan my left eye.

I said, "It's my right eye that needs to be scanned."

She replied, "It is routine for us to scan both eyes on every patient."

After having many more pictures taken of my left eye than my right, I asked, "What are you seeing in my left eye?"

"Has anyone ever told you that you have a freckle in your left eye?"

"No one has told me that because no one has scanned my left eye since the 1980s."

"Well, you have a freckle in your left eye."

Later, during the consultation, Dr. Akpek looked at the scan results and said, "I want you to get this freckle checked out and probably removed immediately. Do not wait. This can be done here, if you'd like. I can set it up right away."

"Why the urgency?" I asked.

Dr. Akpek sat down on her chair. "I believe you have a melanoma in your left eye. We don't know how long you have had it, but it is nothing to neglect. You need treatment immediately."

I knew that if this was melanoma, there would be checkups and many trips for follow-up appointments and possibly radiation or chemo treatment.

"I want to think about this," I said.

"Do not think too long, this is serious. Now, as for your right eye, the back of the eye is okay. The retina looks healthy, but the cornea is not good. The eyelids are not functioning. I don't feel that the eye will sustain a donor cornea. The area between the eye and the eyelid needs to have deeper pockets made surgically, but the lids will need to be reconstructed first. Then, after a three-month healing period, we can remove the cataract and implant a Boston K-Pro cornea. Let's have our plastic surgeon look at you and get his opinion about your eyelids. After you visit with him, I will see you again."

We saw the plastic surgeon at Wilmer Eye Institute in Baltimore, Maryland.

He told me, "I can do the surgeries Dr. Akpek wants. It will take several, however, to get your eyelids to close properly. Now, for the melanoma, we can also take care of that for you. Depending on what we find during surgery, we can then decide treatments."

"My husband and I need to discuss this, and we will get back to you."

"I understand. I'll just wait to hear from Dr. Akpek and you."

I said to Ron, "No way. I am not starting another three-year process that isn't any better than what we just went through. I do not want to start this entire process again. We have just traveled for over two years and made twenty-eight trips on planes, and I have already had my fill of trying to get flights through the cheapest airline, running through airports, having security dumping my bag every other flight, and trying to make connections. We are not going through that again. The early mornings to make flights and killing time in airports so we can connect with the next flight and getting home again after midnight is not for us." Just thinking about starting the whole process over was wearing on us. No, absolutely not. The surgeries, the restrictions of activity, the medications, I didn't think so.

Ron and I spoke to Dr. Akpek. She listened quietly and said, "You must do something about the melanoma in your left eye. This is cancer."

"I am sure you do wonderful work, but I think I need to be closer to home so we don't have to fly so much for appointments. I hope you understand."

"I would do the same if I were you," she said. "Being closer to home for this is a good idea."

"If possible I would like to be referred to the Mayo Clinic. That way we could drive to my appointments and not deal with the airport scene anymore."

Ron and I flew home with the expectations of Dr. Hohm referring us to Mayo Clinic to have this "freckle" checked out further.

August 15, 2009

I went to the follow-up appointment with Dr. Hohm in Sioux Falls. After my appointment with Dr. Akpek at Johns Hopkins and seeing the report, Dr. Hohm thought it was best to get rid of my left eye. He discussed it with me. "It seems this is melanoma, and since you have no light perception with this eye, it would be prudent to have it removed."

"I want proof that this is actually melanoma. How in the world did melanoma, which is caused from sun damage, get inside my eye? I don't want things just cut out of me, especially out of my head. It sounds like that might really hurt."

Dr. Hohm said, "I don't know if you understand the seriousness of melanoma. The sooner it is removed, the better. Getting you in to be seen as soon as possible at Mayo Clinic is also key. The problem, as I see it, is that if Dr. Akpek is the physician who found your melanoma, then possibly she has to be the referring doctor, or your insurance may not cover the charges. Dotting your I's and crossing your T's is all part of the process. You don't want your insurance not to cover this treatment, so let's take care of that first."

"Thank you for thinking of that. I am not thinking clearly and wouldn't have known that anyway."

The whole process began with a referral from Dr. Akpek and continued out of Dr. Hohm's office.

I called and requested to speak to Kathy in radiology at Johns Hopkins so films could be sent. She took my address and dropped the hard copy of photos in the mail, sending them directly to Dr. Jose Pulido at Mayo Clinic.

August 20, 2009

I had been walking around in a gold-brown haze from looking through a cataract and opacified cornea for eight months. Now I was on my knees most of my free time asking God to do something, anything.

"Okay, here's the thing. You know I am tired of not seeing, of bumping into things, of being blind. You know I mean what I say. I wanted so bad for You to let me take my little nephew's place, and that wasn't Your plan. Now I am asking You for one of two things: either take me home to Heaven, or let me see. Either one is fine with me. Thy will be done."

I sent this email message to friends and family:

August 22, 2009
I go to SF in two weeks to check my right eye pressure. In a month I go back to Mayo to check the right eye and see if the mass in my left eye has changed. No appointment dates are set up yet. One of the doctors called me Job from the Bible who struggled with Satan and won. That is where I am pointing my ship!!!
Jenny

August 27, 2009
Email from a secretary/scheduler at Mayo Clinic:

Good news, Jenny! Looks like we can actually schedule all the appointments you need in one day -- Monday, September 21.
We will have you starting at 7:45 a.m. with Dr. Keith Baratz, Corneal Specialist, then you will see Dr. Arthur Sit, Glaucoma Specialist, then have the ultrasound, then see Dr. Jose Pulido. You are scheduled to see Dr. Pulido at 11:30, if things go like clockwork (but don't hold your breath). There's a good chance that there will be waiting involved, as we are adding you on as an extra patient, so plan to spend the day with us just in case.
Hope 9/21 will work for you. The appointment is in the mail. Bonnie

I was set up at Mayo Clinic with Dr. Pulido, ophthalmologist oncologist. Ron had just started the new school year, so Cathy drove me to Rochester, Minnesota. Dr. Pulido said, "An MRI, globular ultrasound (vascular), and ocular ultrasound are ordered. Once the results are in, I will see you again. Next, I need you to see Dr. George Bartley, Plastic Surgeon." Cathy led me down the hallways following a nurse to my next appointment. Dr. Bartley examined me and looked with his light at my sealed closed eyelids.

"It will be challenging to remove the eye due to scarring," he said, "and we may not be able to get a prosthetic eye in the socket due to same scarring."

This really didn't surprise me. Everyone thought they could help until they saw me. I said, "The scarring goes crazy every time it is cut into or disturbed."

"You've already had a lot of surgeries. We will probably need to take tissue from inside your lower lip and use it in your socket."

"That has been done several times, and it hurts like crazy for about a week."

"I know, the stitches catch on everything and can cause discomfort."

I said, "Stitches? You put in stitches? Both times I had tissue removed from my lower lip in Ohio, they didn't put any stitches in, just raw, open tissue left to heal."

"You mean, your lip was left open to heal? This should be better with stitches in. Not so open and painful."

I heard something in his voice, but I wasn't sure if it was sympathy or disbelief that I had not had stitches during the procedure of harvesting tissue from my lower lip. "I will contact Dr. Pulido and let him know what I think, and if you decide on removal of your left orb, I think I can help you. We should probably set you up for removal of the eye as soon as possible. The problem is, I'm going to be out of the country for the next month, and then my schedule is full until October. We can get you in at the end of October for surgery if you so decide to go that route."

Cathy and I went back down the hallways of Mayo Clinic and into yet another waiting room. I needed to have photos of my left eye to compare to what had been taken in Baltimore. This ensured that the melanoma was not a fast-growing lesion. While they were taking these photos, I needed to look as far left as I could and hold my eye in place. I could not keep my eye turned the angle needed for a good picture to be taken, so I suggested, "Can I have a flashlight that I can look at with my right eye so I can keep

242

my left eye turned at the correct angle for the view needed?"

It worked.

"Dr. Pulido is ready to see you, Mrs. Peterson," the nurse said. I arose from my chair and stood in front of it until Cathy came in front of me, then I took her arm. We followed the nurse to an exam room. We settled into our chairs, Cathy on the side of the room and me in the big chair with equipment attached.

Dr. Pulido came in and said, "Mrs. Peterson, I believe the ultrasound is consistent with melanoma. We need to do a removal as soon as Dr. Bartley can fit you into his schedule."

"Can you do a fine-needle biopsy, or some kind of test to make sure this is a melanoma?" I asked.

"From the way the freckle looks, and from the growth pattern, I am 98.5% sure this is a melanoma."

"What about the 1.5%, if it isn't a melanoma? If I just let you take my eye, that's it! It'll be gone, and anything new that may come up in the future won't matter because I won't be a candidate for it anymore."

"Mrs. Peterson," said Dr. Pulido gently, "I'm trying to save your life here."

Looking in his direction, I said, "I've been dead before, and it ain't all that bad. I need to know for sure."

My wonderful sister Cathy spoke up. "She's been through a lot in the last two years. This is just more than she can think about right now."

Dr. Pulido said, "I can see you have been through a lot."

My tears were starting to form in my voice.

He said, "We have a little time here. Go home and think about what you want to do and let me know. You need to see Dr. Baratz, a Corneal Specialist, for your right eye today though. It is in tough shape."

To Cathy, I said, "I have good insurance, and they are going to run me through every doctor in this place before I get out of here. They all say they think they can help me, but only God knows how to help me."

243

Cathy quietly said, "It will be okay, Jen. This is a lot to think about. As long as we are here, just let them look at you. It won't take much longer, then we'll go home. What can it hurt?" I agreed, knowing that Cathy had my best interest at heart.

We trudged down more hallways and to another waiting room. I was called to see Dr. Baratz. He came into my exam room and said, "The pressure in your right eye is about forty tactilely, or maybe even more. Since Prednisone can elevate glaucoma pressure, I want you to taper the Prednisone to twice a day for one week, then stop it in two weeks. Check pressure at Dr. Hohm's office in Sioux Falls in September. He will let me know what he thinks it is. While you're here today, I want you to see our glaucoma specialist, Dr. Sit."

Just as I thought, they would run me through all the doctors they can while I was there and I'd get no help seeing anyway. I was tired of being a specimen that no one had seen before but still couldn't help. Dr. Sit could not measure the pressure in my eye. He could not see the optic nerve due to the cataract and opacity of the cornea.

He instructed, "Continue the medications, as they are appropriate for now. In my opinion, we need to do a surgery and place at least one stent, maybe two, in your eye to drain the fluid and keep the pressure from building and damaging your optic nerve. It may be low after surgery. The retina might swell, but that would be temporary."

"Do you have any idea how long my optic nerve will last?"

"No, let's increase the Diamox for the glaucoma pressure."

We went home, and I prayed for help with my decision. "What to do Lord, help me, what do I decide?" I had a few weeks before seeing all the doctors at Mayo again, so I would have to really pray about this.

244

September 20–21, 2009

Cathy and I went to my appointment at Mayo Clinic with Dr. Baratz, corneal specialist. He didn't think the pressure in my right eye was as serious as it was in August. We discussed some surgery options. "With the Boston K-Pro, there is a fifty percent chance it will last for five years. Most of them, however, need to be replaced in three years. It takes only one surgical procedure, and the lids are left open. This Boston K-Pro also has its down side. Scar tissue can grow on the back side of the prosthesis."

I felt like I had had all the surgeries I wanted. If I did have the Boston K-Pro, it would take only one procedure, and that sounded good to me.

We also discussed the option of using my eye tooth instead of the Boston K-Pro as a prosthetic. In this procedure, an eye tooth would be removed and the center drilled out. It would be placed under the skin, usually on the upper chest or upper shoulder/back area for three months, during which time skin and blood vessels would actually grow over the tooth. In a second procedure, the surgeon would remove the tooth from under the skin, and a lens would be placed in the center of the drilled-out tooth. The tooth would then be transplanted into the front of the eye between the eyelids, and the patient would see through the lens in the center of the tooth. This was a bigger procedure and took longer, but there was less chance of rejection because the tooth would be of my own body.

It didn't sound that great of an idea to me. Three months of waiting and removal of my tooth. Not what I wanted. Cathy and I got to the waiting room. We sat in chairs side by side. I started to chuckle. "What?" she said.

"My teeth are about the only thing in my head I have left that are good, and now they want to start pulling them and drilling holes in them to help me see. Can you see how ridiculous this sounds to me?"

By this time, we were both laughing. Sometimes, we just needed to laugh so we wouldn't cry. Photos were taken of my eye and sent to Miami and Boston for other doctors

245

to view and give their opinion on what procedure they thought would be best. They would get back to Dr. Baratz, as would I with my decision of what I would like to do.

After my Mayo appointment I sent this email:

A quick update on my Mayo Clinic visit. There is all bad news unless you have God in your corner!!! They are 98.5% sure I have cancer in my left eye. The right eye, which I have been having surgeries on, now has a very high pressure level. In a month's time if it is not better with decreasing some of the eyedrops that can cause elevated pressure I will be having a surgery to fix the glaucoma. Then the doctors might also remove the cataract and put in a prothesis as long as they are doing surgery on my eye. Overwhelming but I just need to stand strong in my faith and know that God is not done with me yet,
Jenny

By September 30, 2009, after praying about this, I thought, "What would I tell one of my siblings to do if they came to me and said, "I have a melanoma." I would tell them, "Get rid of it, it's cancer." So I had decided I was going to have the melanomatous eye removed. Rather than worrying about it spreading elsewhere, I would get rid of it. Once I had decided something, it would take a lot to change my mind, so I called Dr. Bartley's office at Mayo and set up the appointment.

Doctors and nurses came in to speak to us. One nurse said, "This is outpatient, so you will go back to your motel for the night."

"I don't think that is fair to Ron or me. What if I get uncontrollable pain and Tylenol doesn't cut it?"

"We normally do this outpatient."

"I've just spoken to a little boy's mom who said he was outpatient and was screaming in pain before they could get him any help. Unless you are planning to send a morphine pump with me, I'm not outpatient."

246

"I'll check on this for you with the doctor," replied the nurse. Consequently, I was admitted.

From Ron's journal:
PRAY
October 12, 2009
8:00 a.m. snow 1"/ streets wet/no ice
11:05 shuttle to St. Mary's Hospital.
12:10 hand IV, vitals
1:10 went to surgery
3:00 called me, were just getting ready to start surgery.
4:20 Dr. Bartley called me with an update. The eye is out. Brown stuff on outside of eye. He doesn't know if this is more melanoma or not. Will have to send to pathology. Putting pressure on eye now for 15 minutes. He had time, so he called me. Will now proceed to put in prosthesis. Will be another 1-2 hours. Will have to stay overnight as getting late in day. Will talk to me later.
Ate cafeteria.
5:30 moved all Jenny's belongings to floor 6 Rm 112A to stay overnight.
5:45 Nurse called
Took skin from inside of lip and put in eye socket. Will put in conformer. Another hour. Everything is going OK. Then another hour in recovery. Then eye socket will be ready for prosthesis later.
6:30 talked to Dr. Bartley
Jenny in recovery
Wants to see her in morning at 8:30 in his office on 7 west-Gonda. She has to stay overnight. He has seen nothing like this. Thinks it is melanoma. She can take radiation for this. Will know for sure by Wed (in 2 days) We can go home tomorrow after he sees her in his office. He gave me Rx we can fill at home for left eye. Need to call kids.
I found St. Mary's is 2 long blocks away from Gonda Bldg. Have to take shuttle.
Back in room: vitals good. We put in drops on schedule. Pain 2.

The next morning at my post-surgical checkup, I told Dr. Bartley, "No one had scanned my left eye for at least twenty-five years. I didn't have any changes in it. There was no pain from this eye. Once in a while, I would get a stabbing, knife-like pain, but it didn't last. When I mentioned it to doctors, they just chalked it up to normal pain from adhesions since there was so much obvious scarring under my right eyelid. They thought more than likely there would be scarring of the same degree or worse under the left eyelid."

Dr. Bartley had no reply.

On October 14, 2009, I sent out this email after getting home:

Hello,

I will keep this short, the pain is not bad, Tylenol is taking care of it, wonderful, prayers are answered. testing of lesion results hopefully today stitches from the corner of my mouth inside the lower lip to almost my eye tooth on the other side, eating pudding and ice cream, hate when that happens.

I have a conformer in my left eye, a clear shell to hold open the space. The doc told Ron a prosthesis later but my eyelid on the left is open after 25 or so years almost 30 I guess. My Dad says, "Maybe God will make it work and you'll see after all." Maybe He will.

Later,

Jenny

October 21, 2009

I went for my recheck with Dr. Bartley and he said, "Everything looks good after the surgery. The pathology report shows melanoma contained in the eye globe, no radiation treatment is needed. You are to check for metastasis every three months or as directed by Dr. Pulido." Praise God from whom all blessings flow. God had given me peace of mind about the possible radiation treatments because He didn't have that in my plan. Praise Him, Praise Him all ye little children. And are we not all children in His eyes?

I sent this email out after getting home:

Hello all,

Well another trip to Rochester, Minn. today. My sister, Cathy came up last night and stayed with us and Cathy and I left this morning and drove over, let the doc look at my eye and drove back. Crazy. I could have told him how it was doing over the phone but you know how these doctors are?

Here is what I have found out so far......

I actually had cancer, melanoma, in my left eye. It was contained in the eye, although I need to ask what the knuckles were that were outside the globe but this is what I was told, contained in the eyeball. The eyeball or globe was removed containing the melanoma so that is good. I will have to be checked, rechecked and checked again during my life to make sure no other areas come down with melanoma.

The oncologist, cancer doc is doing a genetic study on the melanoma to see where it originated and if I will need any treatment other than the removal and what the best treatment would be if needed should it spread. So I will go back in a week or two and let them look at me again.

One of these days God is going to surprise them and I am going to be looking back at them, looking at me. Or if not that then something else really exciting, I'm just sure of it. Thanks to all of you for the prayers, we so feel God's presence in our lives because of all of you praying for us.

Love,

Ron and Jenny

November 5-6, 2009

Ron and I returned to Mayo for a recheck on my left eye socket. Dr. Bartley removed stitches from my left eye and checked light perception in my right eye then instructed, "Continue ointment. Do not remove conformer from the left eye, only wipe the front off with a Q-tip. Switch to Erythromycin when TobraDex runs out."

I had been praying, as had many others, about whether to have the Boston K-Pro surgery done on my right eye. As God sometimes did when we were talking to Him, He placed a peace of mind on my heart that I could either stay as I was or grab a chance to see my little grandson and granddaughter, Connor Ray and Jenna Elizabeth. I had to take the chance and prayed God's hands were on these surgeons. My other option was to sit on the couch and wait for my optic nerve to blow.

As I sat down with my Bible to choose which book to read from, I thought, "God knows what He wants to tell me. Just put a tape in, and listen for His message."

I put a tape in, and the Book of John started. The story was about two disciples walking with Jesus. Jesus was teaching them as they walked. They came upon a blind man sitting at the side of the road, and the disciples asked Jesus, "Master, why was this man born blind? Whose sin caused him to be blind, his parents or his?"

Jesus answered, "It is not because of any sin that this man was born blind. It is so God's good works can be seen."

My heart jumped in my chest and I began to shake. I got up and felt my way down the hallway to our bedroom where Ron was watching TV. In a very shaky voice, I said, "Ron, God just told me it is going to be all right. He is going to let me see."

And Ron said in a rather pessimistic tone, "Oooo-kaaaay, if you say so."

I was filled with joy. I did not know when or where, but I knew in my heart that God didn't make promises He didn't keep. If the Bible said that the blind man was blind so that God's good works could be seen through him, then they could also be seen through me! I was back on track with God's plan. Even though God's "good works" didn't promise that I was going to see again, that was the way I took it. I claimed it as mine and clung to it as if to a life line. Ron, on the other hand, thought that I had lost my mind for sure. He felt all of this had been too much for me and I had finally snapped. He didn't say a word to me about how he really felt. He just quietly continued to take care of us.

I called and talked to Dr. Baratz to tell him I had decided to go ahead with the surgery. He said, "We can set up an appointment to discuss it."

"No need for an appointment. I have already decided to have the surgery, so let's just set up a surgery date."

"Okay. I'll have my scheduler get to work on it and send you an appointment for surgery." I was set up for January 6, 2010, for a pre-op at Mayo Clinic.

November 18, 2009
From: Jenny Peterson
Sent: Wednesday, November 18, 2009
Subject: scar Tissue
Hello,
I talked to Dr. Bartley, Ocular Plastic surgeon, yesterday evening. I told him my left eyelids are not really shutting at the edge of the eyelid, instead the skin of the eyelids is rolling over the top of the eyelid edge and coming together while the edges are still not together underneath that skin. Did I confuse everyone with that? Bottom line, I think and Dr. Bartley says of course he will have to see me to make sure what is going on BUT I told him this is what my right eyelid did when the scar tissue came back and was holding it up from closing.
He said it wouldn't make much sense to have an artificial eye put in if the scar tissue was eventually going to either 1) push the eye out or 2) have to be closed over it to try

and keep the eyelid stretched enough to close again someday.

No biggie, this has not been open for 25-30 years and it really is not anything we are going to lose sleep over. God has this plan for my life and when He puts that plan into action it is going to be amazing. I can't wait.

The other thing was a test on my melanoma. They did a monosomy 3 testing on it and I don't have it which is very, very good since having the monosomy 3 means the cancer most likely would kill me within a year. So what a blessing that is.

Just wanted to update you and keep you in the loop.

Have a great day. Wonderful weather and Happy Thanksgiving to each of you.

Jenny

December 1, 2009

My appointment was with Dr. Bruce, Dermatology at Mayo Clinic, as she would manage my anti-rejection medication and was a mucus membrane specialist. She did a full body scan because the medications could cause organ cancer or skin cancers or lymphatic cancer. She biopsied two spots, one on my upper chest and one on my back.

She would be working with Dr. Baratz to help manage the anti-rejection medications and check for skin cancer. They started me on one CellCept a day for a week, then increased it by one tablet each week until I was taking a total of four tablets a day.

I saw Dr. Bartley, and he thought the eye socket looked better than he expected. The lids were not closing well, so he suggested not spending money on an artificial eye until they saw how much curling the eyelids did, since the lids might not be able to hold the prothesis in place.

January 5, 2010

Cathy picked me up for my appointment with Dr. Baratz. Due to events at school, Ron couldn't go with me.

A snow storm was coming in, and we wanted to make it to my appointment on the 6th. We drove to Mayo Clinic. I thought I was supposed to be having an ultrasound, but it had been canceled, and the lab technicians knew nothing about it. I didn't need the blood work either, so we waited until my appointment with Dr. Baratz at 2:30. Everything was ready for surgery the next day.

Dr. Baratz said, "The surgery will probably last four to five hours. First, Dr. Sit will place one or two stents, depending on how he feels after he looks at your eye, to relieve pressure build up from fluid. Then I will remove the cataract and do an artificial Boston K-Pro, which will take maybe another hour. If all goes well and the surgery is a success, you should see in ten days to two weeks. Does that sound okay?"

"No." I said, "If the surgery is successful, I want to see tomorrow."

He chuckled but was serious when he said, "We would all like quick results like that, but it just doesn't happen that quickly. There is swelling and a healing process that needs to happen first."

"I understand."

We would be back in the morning, ready for surgery.

January 7, 2010

Ron called me before my appointment. "Do you know how many surgeries of this kind Dr. Baratz has done?"

"I don't know, but I will ask him." I did. "How many of these artificial corneal surgeries have you performed?"

He answered, "I have done thirty of this type surgery."

I told Ron this on our next phone conversation, and he said, "Do you think you should let him do this?" I told Ron honestly and directly, that I did. "Ron, I am going to do this. God is in control and has led us this far, and I am going to take this next step."

Ron agreed.

Cathy took notes while I was in surgery. She wrote in the journal the following:

The following morning, Cathy and I were tired. We had both sat up all night long, me in my hospital bed and Cathy in a chair by my side. We were to be in the Mayo Building by 7:30a.m. for my post op checkup with Dr. Baratz. The prep nurse was taking my tape off the bandage on my right eye. Did I see movement? I sat very still. I didn't want her to hurt my eye. It felt sticky and swollen. The door opened, and Dr. Baratz came in. "Good morning. How does your eye feel this morning?" he asked.

"Okay, if you don't touch it."

He was smiling in his voice. "Let's take a look. I'm going to touch your eyelid with a damp Q-tip to clean off some of the drainage from the surgery. I'm surprised there isn't as much swelling as I thought there would be."

"I've learned over the last two years that if I keep my head elevated or just sleep sitting up, my eye doesn't swell as much. So that's what I did last night."

He sat back and said, "There. How does that feel?"

I looked at him and said, "You have yellow stripes on your tie." I bowed my head, "Thank you, Lord, my heart is singing."

I raised my head, looked at Dr. Baratz and reached for his hand. With a shaky voice I said, "Thank you, thank you for giving me my life back."

As soon as my eye was clear, the drainage covered it again and I couldn't see. He finished his exam, and before Cathy and I left the exam room, I asked him, "Will you clear my vision once more so I can see my sister, Cathy?"

"Sure."

I looked into her beautiful green eyes filled with tears. She reached over the exam machine to give me a big hug. Dr. Baratz grabbed the equipment to save it from crashing to the floor. I said to Cathy, "You're beautiful, just beautiful." She had been my driver, my cheerleader, my guide, and my spiritual, uplifting force when times got tougher than I could deal with on my own. She was an angel walking this earth and had done more volunteer work than most of us put in for a full-time job. She was my sister and my friend.

Dr. Baratz said, "There is a healing process, and over the next week to ten days you won't have vision. Your eye will actually scab over first to heal, and then as the scab falls off we can tell better how good your sight is. I need you to know it will be frustrating. Underneath the scab is going to be sight, but you have to let it heal and fall off on its own."

I assured him, "I've been frustrated before. I can wait another week to see."

Dr. Baratz said, "You may let the water from your shower run over your face from the back side. Do not let it hit you in the face, however. That will be too much force on the new surgery site." I would obey each and every instruction.

Cathy and I got back to our motel and were stranded for the night. I-90 was closed due to the winter storm. I said, "Let's take a little Q-tip and wipe the surface clean so I can see you again tonight."

"Do you think so?"

"Yes."

She took the Q-tip and wiped but the healing tissue would not wipe off. Not wanting to do any damage, she said, "Jen, it just won't clear. I don't want to damage or hurt your eye. I think we should leave it alone."

We couldn't get the film that had formed over the front of my implant to wipe off and remembered that Dr. Baratz had to actually take a tweezers and pull that film off my eye for me to see Cathy in his office.

Cathy said, "I don't think he wants us to try that, and I'm not comfortable doing anymore to get that film off."

"Okay. I know you're right. I can wait to see when the time is right."

Then I would see Connor Ray and Jenna Elizabeth, Chad, Denise, Heather, my dad, the sky, the trees, the snow, and everything. For now, I was following orders and not lifting more than ten pounds and not touching my eye.

My dad said, "A knife and fork is all I think you should lift."

I sent out an email to thank everyone for praying all of these years and to spread the good news. I had an appointment January 15, 2010, at Mayo Clinic again. Ron was going this time so I would maybe get to see him, for a few minutes at least. I was at home in the shower getting ready to go. I let the water run over my face from the back side of my head as I had been doing the past week. I was blinking my eyes, and suddenly a ray of light beamed through the shower door. I was not sure whether this light was from the outside of my eye or the inside. I thought something was going wrong again. Then, as more water washed more of the scab off my eye, I could see, oh Lord, I could see!

I quickly rinsed the suds off and grabbed my towel. I called out the door. "Ron, come quick!" Ron appeared at the bathroom door, and I saw his face. He looked worried.

I said, "I can see."

He grabbed me around my shoulders and hugged me. Then he was gone. I looked down the hall, and here he came with pictures of our two little grand-babies. Connor was the spitting image of those Peterson boys, Grandpa Pete and Daddy. Miss Jenna had a little elastic flower stretched around her head and was the cutest little thing this side of the Rockies. I couldn't wait to see my kids and my dad next.

Ron said, "Are you almost ready? We need to get going."

I was not almost ready. I was standing there dripping all over the floor, but I could get ready in a short time, and we were off for my appointment with the Mayo doctors.

It was foggy as Ron drove to Rochester, Minnesota. We left our pickup at the EconoLodge and caught the shuttle to

256

the clinic. The nurse checked my vision. I saw fingers from three to four feet away. I saw the big E from twelve feet away and its legs pointing in different directions. Dr. Baratz said, "You are eight days out, so this is excellent." I told him that the moisture, or drops, in my eye caused cloudiness and less ability to see. He said, "Use the sterile saline solution two to three times a day. Let's leave the lift limit on for another three weeks. No exercise yet. Let's get an ultrasound to see how it looks in the back. I will see you in three weeks."

Because of the things I was able to see, I was in tears much of the time, although I still didn't produce tears. When I saw someone I hadn't expected to see or the beauty of nature as God created it, I just teared up.

January 23, 2010, 16 days after surgery.
I needed to send this letter to the surgeon who performed my miraculous surgery:

Dear Dr. Baratz,

I just had to send you a note to thank you so much for the procedure you did on my eye. I was not sold that this was the thing to do but followed along with your suggestion of the cataract removal and new lens, corneal transplant and implant. As well as the glaucoma valves that Dr. Sit put in.

I need to tell you how much this has changed my life already. I got to see my siblings. My Dad who is 80 years old is just amazed when I look at him and can actually see his face. We both have shed tears over this. My little grandson, Connor Ray is almost 3 years old now and for the first time ever I got to sit down on the floor and play Memory and Candyland with him. What a joy!!! My little daughter that grew up to be a beautiful woman, my son who resembles his Dad so much and his wife, Denise have all shed tears of great joy over the new vision you have given to me. My husband has held our little grand-daughter as I gazed into her blue, blue eyes and she hid her face against his shoulder. It is such a pleasure to just wake up in the morning and be able to see my hand in front of my face, God bless you many times over for this talent you have and for giving patients like me a new lease on life.

Sincerely,
Jenny Peterson

February 9, 2010

For a while, I was being seen at Mayo Clinic every two to three weeks after surgery. My sight just continued to improve with each visit. For my next appointment, Ron and I packed up and started driving even though the weather was not cooperating. We drove to Fairmont, Minnesota and stayed there overnight due to ice on the interstate. We drove the rest of the way into Rochester on the 10th and went to my appointment at noon. I could read the first two lines of the chart. On the third line, I could read the H and L, but the R in between was not clear. My vision was 20/100. On the fourth line I saw the T O and C: 20/80. I took a breath and tried to concentrate. This was very emotional and wonderful all rolled into one. Dr. Baratz put eye drops in my eye, did his tactile assessment of the glaucoma pressure in my eyeball, and said, "I think it is about 10, so that's good."

I thought, "Miracles abound."

He removed the stitches and okayed my use of Q-tips or the corners of a napkin, as long as they were clean, to wipe a film off my eye and clear my view of life again. He okayed lifting, which meant I could lift the grandbabies and exercise.

He suggested, "You probably should wear glasses, just to protect your eye from a hit of any kind. You might want to try different strengths of reading glasses just to see which one works best for you."

"Okay," I said as Ron took notes. I was still so consumed by people's eyes and hand gestures that I had trouble remembering what they were telling me. It was so amazing. I tried to convey that to each doctor as we left the exam rooms. I failed miserably, but they were each so caring and understanding of my loss for the right words to express what my heart was singing.

There were shuttles that ran constantly during the day, from 6:00 a.m. to 6:30 p.m., between the motels and the clinic. Our shuttle driver, Dave, was the best. He knew his returning passengers by name and what their medical problem was if they had shared that with him. From the first day he picked us up at our motel, we became friends. He was usually joking about men and women, and my mouth just wouldn't stay closed. We joked around each time we were on the shuttle. The day I got onto the shuttle with my eye still patched and Cathy leading me, I said to him, "I can see." I took a breath. Tears were choking me. "I got to see Cathy's face."

After we found our seats, Cathy whispered, "Dave is wiping tears from his eyes."

From then on he always told his shuttle riders that I was his "miracle lady."

He would start our shuttle rides by saying to me, "Are you ready to drive yet?"

I answered, "They haven't approved that yet, but I can take over if you're tired."

Dave then began to tell everyone about how God led us to Mayo Clinic after thirty-three years of being legally blind but now I could see. Many of the shuttle riders were amazed by how much sight I had: 20/25 to 20/30.

Dave then told his riders, "Never say never, she is proof of that."

I tried to answer questions and tell a little of how I lost my sight to start with. Cathy was my promoter. She said things about me that I wouldn't think of saying, how, like Job in the bible, I never cursed God but continued to praise His name and follow His lead. Mostly, I just prayed every day and thanked God for being there for me and my family. The rest was God's plan.

Dave would get out of the driver's seat to help people on and off the shuttle and greet them, but when I was getting on or off, he always got a hug. He was a very special shuttle driver and friend.

April 2010

After a wonderful Saturday of being able to see most of the family and friends, we had Jenna's birthday party on Sunday afternoon. Then Sunday evening, Cathy and I left for Rochester and my checkup, which started at 8:15 Monday morning. As I checked my updated list of medications, I noticed that my vision was not as good as at the last visit. I was working on a crossword puzzle in the newspaper one day, and the next day I couldn't see to finish it. The words were blurry, but I could still see well enough that I didn't worry about it. However, I did report it to the doctor at Mayo. He said, "The exam shows a film on the lens of the implant, which is common after cataract surgery."

I told the doctor, "I remember when my brother-in-law, Buddy, had his cataract removed. This very thing happened to his lens."

Dr. Baratz suggested lasering it off. Next I went for an ultrasound and pictures. They showed a swelling in the macula of my right eye. Dr. Baratz thought that the resolution to this problem was an injection of steroids into the eye or around it. I wasn't really sure about this because both meant sticking a needle into my eye. But we proceeded, and a numbing agent was needled into my lower eyelid, and then the steroids with a long, long needle after that. The resident doctor said, "You are tough. You didn't move during the injection at all."

"I didn't think it would help to jump around," I replied. They agreed with chuckles.

I could tell the difference in my reading vision immediately after the film was removed with the laser. Dr. Baratz said, "After a day or so, the steroids should improve the swelling, and that should also help the vision clear." I prayed it was so.

"You can have this shot every two months in your eye if needed," said Dr. Baratz.

I said, "If it is necessary, but I definitely will not look forward to coming to visit you as much as I do now." Again, we both chuckled. I would do whatever it took to keep this vision for as long as I could.

Next, we went to Dr. Bruce for dermatology and anti-rejection drug management. She said, "We should draw some blood and check on liver and kidney functions, and then you can go home."

Overall, the visit was a good one, nothing that was alarming to Dr. Baratz. I did ask him, "How are your other patients doing with their implants?"

He said, "Not as well as you. Some of them had retinal problems before the implant surgery and previous surgeries for that, so their vision isn't as good. Previous to this, I had two patients who were driving, one with my permission and one without."

I was not ready for driving. I just wanted to enjoy watching the beauty of God's creations come into view and not worry about other vehicles on the road. As far as the eyelid and my having to pull down on it to give myself a bigger area of viewing space, Dr. Baratz said, "I want to let it sag as much as it will on its own, instead of opening it and then having to go back and close it up some again. The less surgeries we do to this eye, the less trauma, the fewer problems. Do you agree?"

"Yes, oh yes, I agree."

I had always had fun at family events before, but seeing added new dimension to life. God was so wonderful to allow these surgeons the abilities to help people. So many at Mayo Clinic were not getting the kind of results we were enjoying. I believe our success was totally due to all of the prayers offered up on our behalf.

April 17, 2010

After a few months of steadily improving vision Chad said, "Maybe we should get everyone together so you can see them. We didn't want to do it right away but I think your vision is here to stay, don't you?"

"I think it will last a little while. Getting together is a great idea, but everyone is so busy. Do you really think many could make it?"

"Let's check it out with a few and see what they think," Chad offered.

After several family members started discussing an event, it was decided. We were going to have a potluck with our combined families, the Peterson's and the Martz's, at the Legion Hall in Centerville. Then an open house coffee afterwards would be held for anyone who might want to come and say 'hi'. There were so many who came, and it was really wonderful to see each and every face and add them to my memory bank. When a person walked up to me that I did not recognize immediately, I simply said, "Can you smile for me?" and then most of the time I knew who they were. Smiles very rarely changed. Wonderful, awesome, beautiful! Not even these words could describe how it felt for me to see the faces of family and friends once again. The emotion was more than words could express. I gave thanks to God for answering each one of our prayers. To God be the glory!

May, 2010

The phone rang one afternoon and I turned from the counter to answer it. I smiled as I saw it hanging on the wall in the sunshine.

"Hello?"

A woman introduced herself. "I'm a freelance journalist writing an article for *O Magazine*. Oprah's magazine."

"Okay," I said.

She continued. "I'm looking for Jenny Peterson. Is this she?"

262

"Yes, this is Jenny, but I think you have a wrong number. I'm just an ordinary South Dakota woman."

She continued, undaunted. "My article is about ordinary people who have had extraordinary things happen to them. Didn't you just get your sight back after thirty plus years?"

"Yes, I got my sight back in January after thirty-three years of being legally blind."

"I would like to include you in this article."

I tried to explain to her, "I didn't do anything extraordinary. I am the one who is blessed by this."

"Exactly," she agreed. "Would you be willing to do an interview now over the phone?"

"I really think you have the wrong person, but I do think this is a miracle, so I will allow the interview."

After a forty-minute interview, she said, "I will let you know if the article is going to be printed and when it will be coming out."

In a daze, I said, "Okay, thank you, have a nice day."

I called Cathy on my cell phone because I had to tell someone. "Cathy, I was just interviewed over the phone by a journalist writing an article for *O Magazine*."

"You mean the Oprah magazine?"

"Yes," I said. "Can you believe that?"

We were laughing and talking, changing the subject to other topics like we always did when my house phone rang and I said to Cathy, "Oh, I better get that. It might be Phil Donahue."

We both laughed and said good-bye. Then I answered the house phone. There was no way I believed I would be included in *O Magazine*, but I am. I was humbled by the fact that so many are interested my story.

January 2011

After having vision for a year, I realized that it may not last forever. The implant could stop working at any time, and if it could be redone, I might not get as good of vision. If the back of my eye was not healthy enough for a second surgery, then it would not be redone. It scared me, but I knew that I should be thankful for being able to see for however long a period of time and not dwell on the fact that it was not forever because God was in control and He had a plan for me. Any time a doctor left the decision up to me, I would pause and hesitate to go ahead with the procedure because if they didn't want to take responsibility for doing the procedure, then it might not be a good thing to do. Realistically, I had had more things that didn't work out by going ahead recklessly than I'd had work out, so I was starting to be more reserved when it came to risking my vision. Visual fields ordered by Dr. Sit were to see if the glaucoma had done any damage to my optic nerve. None was seen yet. Praise be to God! From now on, I would have visual fields each time I saw Dr. Sit to keep an eye on the glaucoma.

It has been such a thrill to see my little Jenna as a baby. She hides her eyes behind spread fingers to play peek-a-boo or tries to stand on her own leaning far back against the couch for support. I have played catcher for my Connor Ray while he bats and Grandpa Pete pitches. Connor Ray instructs me, "No, Grandma Pete, you need to stand like this," as he squats down in the grass with his little butt hanging over the backs of his shoes. I wasn't doing it quite like that, but we were having a great time.

I have been asked quite a few times, "Why didn't you just go to Mayo Clinic to start with?" My answer to that was just this, "God already knew that I had a melanoma in my left eye. He allowed the Cincinnati surgeries to be unsuccessful because His plan was that my life be spared from the cancer. No one had looked at my left eye with an ultrasound since it was closed over the nonworking implant back in the early 1980s. God knew that Johns Hopkins in Baltimore routinely scanned both eyes regardless of whether it was a working eye or not.

Ron said, "You had to wait thirty-three years for technology to catch up with your life."

I don't know why, but I know the One who does. For some reason, unknown to me or anyone else, God saved

264

my life once again, and I am anxiously waiting to do His will."

With each appointment, my vision continued to improve, 20/80 to 20/50 and even as good as 20/25. I was still blown away by the beauty of everyday things. The color of stop lights was so vibrant. The trees reaching up to the winter sky for warmth from the sun were beautiful, as were spring flowers, fall leaves, and snowflakes covering the earth. Most of all, I loved being able to see my family's faces, help others, and read the words from our hymnal to sing praises to God on Sunday morning, just to do the simple things of life. I saw beauty in each season. I could not repay this gift, but could only try to encourage someone else to not give up hope, to check out every avenue offered. We never know where God is leading. We can be assured, however, that if we follow Him, there will be great things awaiting us.

It is now 2014. At the writing of this book my vision is 20/30 and I am into my fourth year with sight. We are so thankful and amazed at what I can see. To the doctors who restored my sight, I say thank you and may God bless you as richly as He has blessed me. The ability to walk down the streets of my town, wave to people across a room, or just pick out my own food from a menu or smorgasbord is a pleasure.

Most of all, I enjoy sharing what God has done for me and encouraging people that He has a plan for each of us. When waiting for an answer to prayer that never seems to come, here is what I suggest. Find something positive in your life to focus on and stay close to your faith. For God can teach us all to "walk by faith not by sight".